The Science & Theology of Salt* in Scripture, Vol. I:

*Light, Water, Dust, and Stone too

By Stephen Michael Leininger

I0203641

The Science & Theology of Salt in Scripture

© 2008-2017, Stephen Michael Leininger

Licensed to STOSS Books, 2017

ISBN-13: 978-0692915516

ISBN-10: 0692915516

Except as provided by the Copyright Act of 1976, including amendments up to, and including, June 30, 2016. No part of this publication may be reproduced, stored in a retrieval system or transmitted in any form or by any means without the prior written permission of the copyright holder.

Cover design by: Ryan's Photography

I wish to acknowledge and thank those publishers who granted me permission to quote generously from their titles. These copyright holders are: Paulist Press, Inner Traditions – Bear & Company, Libreria Editrice Vaticana, Marian Press, Inter Mirifica, Servant Books, Random House, Ignatius Press, Letter & Spirit, Tan Books, Ave Maria Press, and Sophia Institute Press. I also want to include authors, Drs. Mark Armitage and Joseph Magee

Acknowledgements

I wish to acknowledge and thank my wife Donna for the many sacrifices she has endured and for the advice she has given me during the long years it took to research and write this book. Without her support, I could never have accomplished it. And for her support, I am most grateful.

I also wish to acknowledge and thank Fr. PJ Madden for all the help and advice that was given to me by him. His guidance and suggestions contributed greatly to the quality and success of this finished work.

Finally, I wish to thank Ryan Leininger of Ryan's Photography for contributing so much time and effort to produce the great photography and cover design for both Volumes of this book. I could tell you what a talented photographer and artist he is, but I'm sure you can see that for yourself.

Web address is: http://www.ryansphotographs.com/

Facebook page is:

https://www.facebook.com/ryansphotographyla/

Phone is: 951-840-575

Table of Contents

FORWARD -- 1

PROLOGUE -- 3

STYLE PROTOCOLS AND ABBREVIATIONS ------------------------------- 9

INTRODUCTION --- 11

CONTRASTING THE THEOLOGY OF THE BODY TO STOSS --------------- 15

PART I — SALT IN THE OLD TESTAMENT ------------------------ 17

CHAPTER 1 — LOT'S WIFE: THE KEY TO UNDERSTANDING SALT
AND SALT COVENANTS -------------------------------------- 17

1:A — SALT, DUST, STONE, AND ROCK ---------------------------- 26

CHAPTER 2 — TYPOLOGY: PREFIGURING AND FORESHADOWING
-- 34

CHAPTER 3 — OT SALT THEME #1: OUR POST-FALLEN STATE ----- 36

3:A — ROLE OF SALT OF DNA IN ORIGINAL SIN -------------------- 36

CHAPTER 4 — OT SALT THEME #2: GOD'S PLAN --------------- 42

4:A — STEP 1: CHOOSE A LINEAGE FROM WHICH JESUS WOULD COME ------ 42
4:B — STEP 2: MAKE A COVENANT TO PROTECT AND PRESERVE THE LINEAGE 45

4:C — STEP 3: PROVIDE THE LAW TO FULFILL THE COVENANT ------------------49
4:D — STEP 4: IN THE PLAN, ALLOW FOR THE FUNCTIONAL CHANGE OF OUR SALT OF DNA? --51
4:E — GARMENTS, ROBES, BODIES AND THE FLESH ----------------------------63

CHAPTER 5 — OT SALT THEME #3: PURIFICATION--------------------66

5:A — MOSES, ELIJAH, AND THE HOLY SPIRIT -----------------------------------67
5:B — EZEKIEL: WATER FLOWING FROM THE TEMPLE-----------------------------71

PART II — CREATED IN THE IMAGE AND LIKENESS OF GOD --------73

CHAPTER 6 — THE TRINITY: AN UNCEASING EXPRESSION IN LOVE
---73

6:A — THE "BODY": IS IT PART OF BEING IN THE IMAGE & LIKENESS OF GOD?
---79
6:B — THE HOLY SPIRIT: INEXPRESSIBLE, BUT PROMPTING EXPRESSION ------82
6:B:1 — TO SAY "I WILL EXPRESS MY LOVE" IS TO BE REDUNDANT ----------83
6. C — HOLY SPIRIT: THE LIFE OF GOD --86
6:C:1 — WHAT IS GRACE?---88
6:C:2 — TWO MAIN CATEGORIES OF GRACE: --------------------------------91
6:C:2:a — Gratiae Gratis Datae (Gratuitous Graces) ----------------92
6:C:2:b — Gratia Gratum Faciens (Sanctifying Grace)---------------93
6:C:2:b:(i) — Sanctifying/Habitual Grace--------------------------------93
6:C:2:b:(ii) — Actual Grace: --96
6:C:2:b:(ii):I — Internal Actual Grace------------------------------------97
6:C:2:b:(ii):II — External Actual Grace ---------------------------------98

CHAPTER 7 — THE MEANING OF "MOUTH" IN SCRIPTURE---------99

7:A — THE MOUTH OF GOD -- 100

7:B — The Breath From the Mouth Dwells in the Heart ------------ 100

7:C — The Meaning of "Sense-Able" and "Meta-Sense-Able" ------- 103

7:D — The Mouth Cannot Inaccurately Express the Spiritual Heart
-- 105

7:E — The Mouth of Man -- 108

7:F — The Heart and the Mouth of Man, Scripturally Speaking---- 110

7:G — The Language of the Body------------------------------------- 114

7:H — The Significance and Gravity of Fruitful Expression--------- 116

7:H:1 — Faith Without Works is Dead---------------------------------- 117

7:H:2 — I Will Spew You Out Of My Mouth-------------------------- 118

7:H:3 — Other Passages Regarding the Consequences of
Unfruitfulness--- 119

7:H:4 — For Each Tree is Known by its Own Fruit (Luke 6:44) ------ 121

7:H:5 — Multiplication: the "Modus Operandi" of the Holy Spirit 122

CHAPTER 8 — THE HOLY SPIRIT: POST-FALL TO REDEMPTION -- 126

8:A — Action of the Holy Spirit in Material Creation ---------------- 126

8:B — Power of the Holy Spirit on Fallen Man ----------------------- 129

8:B:1 — Scriptural Evidence that the Power of God Works Through
the Salt of DNA-- 131

8:B:1:a — Elisha's Bones --- 132

8:B:1:b — The Hemorrhagic Woman------------------------------- 132

8:B:1:c — The Burning Bush -- 133

8:B:1:d — The Transfiguration-- 134

8:B:1:e — Moses' Rod/Staff--- 135

8:B:1:f — Elijah and Elisha's Mantle--------------------------------- 137

PART III — SALT IN THE NEW TESTAMENT (NT) -------------------- 142

CHAPTER 9 — SYMBOLISM OF STONE/ROCK RELATIVE TO JESUS
-- 144

9:A — STONE: THE SYMBOL OF THE SON OF GOD INCARNATE ------------- 144

9:B — STONE: THE SYMBOL OF JESUS WHO IS TRUTH AND JUSTICE INCARNATE

-- 147

9:C — SYMBOLISM OF STONE RELATIVE TO MAN ------------------------- 149

CHAPTER 10 — THE WEDDING FEAST AT CANA -------------------- 151

10:A — ON THE THIRD DAY -- 154

10:B — FILL THE JARS WITH WATER -------------------------------- 156

10:C — CANA: FORESHADOWING THE PURIFICATION OF MAN ------------- 156

10:D — SIGNIFICANCE OF SIX STONE JARS -------------------------- 158

10:E — THE NUMBER 'SIX' -- 159

10:F — TASTED THE WATER NOW BECOME WINE ----------------------- 161

10:G — SIGNIFICANCE OF MARY AT CANA ---------------------------- 164

CHAPTER 11: — NOW IS THE NEW AND EVERLASTING COVENANT

OF SALT --- 166

11:A — THE SYNAGOGUE --- 166

11:B — THE OLD COVENANT TEMPLE -------------------------------- 167

11:C — WHAT IS A COVENANT OF SALT? --------------------------- 169

11:D — THE NEW COVENANT TEMPLE ------------------------------- 174

11:D:1 — THE STORY OF JACOB AND THE STONE PILLAR-------------------- 175

11:D:2 — CHURCH + TEMPLE = THE MYSTICAL BODY OF CHRIST----------- 178

11:D:3 — BILLIONS AND BILLIONS OF TEMPLES?? -------------------------- 181

11:D:4 — THE NC TEMPLE OFFERING ------------------------------------ 183

11:D:5 — ALL GRACE FLOWS THROUGH MYSTICAL BODY OF CHRIST ------- 189

11:D:5:a — Ezekiel's Rebuilt Temple ------------------------------------ 190

11:D:5:b — Role of Body/Flesh -- 193

CHAPTER 12: — REDEMPTION OF THE BODY VIA MYSTICAL BODY

OF CHRIST -- 195

12:A — REDEMPTION IS A PROCESS OF PURIFICATION, CULMINATING IN PURITY OF "HEART" --- 195

12:B — MEANS TO ATTAIN REDEMPTION OF THE HUMAN HEART ---------- 198

12:C — REDEMPTION IS FREEDOM FROM "BONDAGE TO DECAY" (ROM. 8:21) -- 200

12:D — THE INCORRUPTIBLES -- 202

APPENDIX A — IS JESUS PHYSICALLY PRESENT IN THE EUCHARIST -- 205

INTRODUCTION TO APPENDIX -- 205

EARLY EUCHARISTIC CONTROVERSY --- 208

SENSE-BASED ARGUMENTS FAVORING TRANSUBSTANTIATION AND A PHYSICAL PRESENCE OF JESUS IN THE EUCHARIST------------------------------------- 213

WRITINGS OF OTHERS RELATING TO TRANSUBSTANTIATION AND THE PHYSICAL PRESENCE OF JESUS IN THE EUCHARIST------------------------------------- 219

SPIRITUAL AND MATERIAL LIGHT AND THE SUBSTANCE OF MAN ------------- 228

EPILOGUE -- 232

ENDNOTES --- 235

FORWARD

I remember, in my distant youth, being told in a science class that "salt is the electrolyte of the body." Aside from using it at meals and hearing of it at Sunday Mass when Matthew's Gospel (5:13) was proclaimed, I never gave it much thought since then!

This book challenges our received wisdom on the use of salt through human history, and the deeper significance of Jesus using it to teach a message of spiritual union; salt is to the body what The Spirit is to the mystical Body of Christ.

Mr. Leininger takes us on a challenging examination of the significance of salt in the Old and New Testaments, with a view to opening our minds to the need to proclaim Christ's message. It is undertaken with a new urgency, in a material world where concern with salt as a possible contributing factor to heart disease actually misses the point of its positive use and symbolism.

Christ, in his short three years of public ministry, was very selective in his use of natural imagery and metaphor in proclaiming his message. That message was very clearly stated and summed up in all its theological beauty, in John's Gospel. In it Christ states bluntly that, even after three years of being partially understood by those who were his closest and chosen apostles, he and the Father are one! If we are to make his message our own, we must accept what flows from that: "The Father is in me and I am in you and you are in me"

He was teaching a community who were closely bonded by family and cultural ties, and who used salt daily as a preservative, a disinfectant, a healing of wounds, a cleansing agent, and a trading commodity! In a word, salt was VITAL for community wellbeing!

This book traces the "life" of salt through history, but with a spiritual application based on Scripture. It contains a most impressive bibliography which shows the author undertook serious study and, as a result, offers a challenging and informative theological insight to what St John Paul II described as "Theology of the Body". In our human condition, we are all parts of one body, the Church, one body, Christ, one faith, one godhead! As salt binds and sprinkles, so we are bound to Christ and yet sprinkled as missionary disciples to bring the taste of his healing grace and redeeming gift to all people.

I recommend this book as a challenge to fixed ways of seeing and understanding things. As an alternative narrative to explain our world's disharmony. As an invitation from Christ, renewed and made new each day at the Eucharistic sacrifice, to choose unity (not uniformity!) and to be an active part of a beautiful body, the Church; moving from mortality and imperfection to immortality and perfection. Next time you sprinkle that salt on a meal be aware you are also sprinkling grace on our world!

Fr. PJ Madden, MA, M div.
Pastor

PROLOGUE

When I was in my late teens or early twenty's I had a strong intuition that the degree to which a husband and wife had achieved, or conversely had failed to achieve, a state of true love (NOT to be confused with strictly biological "love" which is nothing more than organic reactions triggered by sensual input that produce feelings such as infatuation or lust) for each other would have a direct impact on any children they would conceive together. I'm not talking about the impact that nurturing would have as the child grows up, although that is also important. That to which I am referring takes place at the most fundamental biological level and at the very moment of conception — when the germ line DNA, i.e. the actual set of chromosomes passed from each parent to their child through the joining of the sperm with the egg.

At that time in my young life, proving or disproving this hypothesis was not high on my priority list. Caught up in the responsibilities of everyday living, my hypothesis, while never forgotten, took a back seat to pretty much everything else for the next twenty-some years. Then I became aware of two pieces of information within a relatively short span of time. The first came to my attention around the year 2000, when I read the book, *Scivias*, which is short for *Scito Vias Domini* (*Know the Ways of the Lord*), by St. Hildegard of Bingen. Her inspirations, as recorded in her writings, confirmed my intuition. The next challenge was to gather enough information to make a compelling case that could convince others as well.

Before proceeding, it has occurred to me that some readers may believe that there is nothing new to be found in Scripture; that all the big mysteries have already been uncovered and expanded upon. Consequently, there may be some resistance to embracing any new mysteries that may be uncovered as part of the unpacking of The Science & Theology of Salt in Scripture.

Let me address that belief by saying that St. Hildegard of Bingen, as part of prophecies she received from God, wrote that there are, indeed, "new secrets and mystical truths" hidden in Scripture,[1] which the Holy Spirit would reveal at a future time of great distress, both in the Church and in the world. Our God is an infinite God who could, and according to Hildegard did, hide layers (possibly many) of mystery in the words of Scripture.

I want to take a brief moment to discuss the importance with which I regard St. Hildegard. I will be citing her writings frequently in this book. Her book is what helped me to finally decide to write this book. It was with great joy that I learned that she would be *officially* canonized and named a Doctor of the Church in 2012. She is only one of four women who have been given that great honor in consideration of their enduring and ongoing contributions toward a greater understanding of the Truth of God. Other than Scripture (her book helped me to understand that better, as well), there is no other book that has more profoundly aided me in gaining a deeper understanding of God and His creation. I highly recommend it. Since then I have read some of her other books and been equally affected. I am naming St. Hildegard as the unofficial (and certainly unsanctioned by the Church as well) patron saint of STOSS.

Scivias is the written account of a series of exchanges/visions God granted to St. Hildegard. As she describes it, her writings do not come from her own mind, but from God himself.[2] That she caused the words of God to be written (others wrote as she dictated what she was seeing and hearing) was a result of God's command to her to do so[3] and threatened divine vengeance if any of the writings were altered in any way.[4] Let me be clear, I am not implying that St. Hildegard's writings are on the same level as Sacred Scripture. Of the written attempts to transmit the Truth of God, only Sacred Scripture is divinely inspired, i.e. guaranteed through the Holy Spirit to be free from error (Sacred Tradition would be an unwritten form of Divinely inspired Truth). However, as part of the process for canonization, her writings would have been thoroughly examined by the Church and found to be free from doctrinal error.

The second piece of information came my way very shortly after the World Trade Center attacks on 9-11. I was driving late one night and listening to a talk show program on the radio. The guest was talking about three experiments that had been performed in the field of quantum physics. While I will be discussing these experiments and many others in greater detail later in this book, suffice it, for now, to say these experiments dealt with the interactions between what is known in the scientific community as "subtle energy" or "ultra-weak EMR" and human DNA. Upon hearing of the results of these experiments, I came to believe I could make a compelling case for the validity of my hypothesis. I decided to write a book on the subject and came up with the title, *Sweet Seeds of Destruction — or of Hope.* Not exactly a happy sounding title!

For the next four years, I engaged in extensive research and each new discovery contributed to the "big picture" that was forming in my mind. At some point in my research, I received a flash of insight that changed the entire focus of the book. So profound, in my view, was this discovery, I remember letting out an audible groan when I suddenly realized that salt is the answer; understanding its meaning unlocks the door to many mysteries hidden in Scripture. Suddenly, the big picture had just gotten a lot bigger. At the time, I didn't even fully comprehend how dramatically "salt" would change the direction the book was taking. A fire was ignited in my heart and led me to eagerly seek new pieces of the puzzle. Slowly but surely, pieces of the puzzle began to fall into place. You've probably seen or maybe even put together one of those two thousand piece puzzles that are designed to severely test one's mastery of the virtue of perseverance. Looking at a single piece of the puzzle you may see what looks like a piece of the sky. Not particularly beautiful in and of itself, but it's a start. Next, you pick up a piece that contains a lot of green and looks like it could possibly be a portion of a green bush of some sort; again, not particularly beautiful, but you push on a piece at a time. It's only as the puzzle gets nearer and nearer to completion that you begin to see ever more clearly the big picture. Proceeding on, you can appreciate, maybe even be in awe of, the beauty of the entire landscape that is taking shape before your eyes.

This is what was happening as I began to see the beauty, intricacy, and wisdom of God's creation and His plans for those He loves infinitely. I began to realize that the Bible is like an ocean; one can stand on the shore looking out and see what seems to be a limitless expanse of water. What we are not seeing, however, is the great depths that exist beneath the surface. The words of Scripture are not two-dimensional; they are, in a sense, three-dimensional, containing great depths of Truth for us to explore. It is my fervent hope and prayer that this book will help each of us to see the bigger picture of God's creation; to see, as St. Paul tells us, "what is the breadth and length and height and depth, and to know the love of Christ that surpasses knowledge, so that you may be filled with all the fullness of God" (Eph. 3:18-19). During our lifetime in this world, we can never hope to see *the* "big picture" of God's creation, but we can continually strive to see an ever increasing portion of it. As a result of the discovery of a deeper meaning of salt in Scripture, the focus of the book greatly widened and a new and more appropriate title was chosen for the book. Thus, the title, *The Science and Theology of Salt in Scripture* came into being.

In the pages of this book we will examine more closely:

- Why Jesus tells us we are the salt of the earth and the light of the world;

- Why Lot's wife is a "map legend" for understanding salt in Scripture

- Why we hear so much about Jesus' Sacred Heart and not his Sacred _____ (fill in the body part of your choice);

- How the body contributes to our being created in the image and likeness of God;

- Why Jesus is often symbolized by a stone in Scripture;

- The deep mystery of the relationship between water and the Holy Spirit, and the implications of this relationship for the human person;

- Why and how many Catholic saints have incorruptible bodies;

- Why God has a 'mouth' and what that means for the "mouth" of man;

- What the NC Temple is, and why it is; and,

- The scriptural, molecular, and quantum basis for believing that we **literally** become one body, one flesh with Jesus Christ through Baptism and the Eucharist — and why God wills it so.

There is much more that will be covered in this book. After doing so, it is my hope that you will come to appreciate the salt and accept the challenge of being in Christ, who is the salt of the earth.

God has spoken to us through Scripture, the inspirations of the Holy Spirit, the writings of saints, the works of theologians, and material creation itself (explored more deeply through the sciences). I will be referencing all of them frequently in the pages of this book. In addition, I will be citing documents from the Church, to whom Jesus has given the promise of protection from doctrinal error (though not personal sin or error on the part of its members) through the guidance of the Holy Spirit. This book was written from a Catholic perspective. However, and I can't emphasize this enough, this book is not meant for Catholics alone. This book is <u>not</u> an attempt to convert anyone to Catholicism, though I believe all would benefit from it. Much of the material discussed in this book affect all of us, whether Catholics, Jews, Protestants, Muslims, atheists, agnostics, or _____ (fill in the blank). I have tried to support STOSS with evidence from three different avenues — Scripture, science, and religious writings from a variety of sources. That way, an atheist, for example, could examine the evidence solely from the scientific standpoint and reach his or her conclusions based on that alone. Jews and Muslims could examine the evidence coming from the scientific community and the Old Testament. Protestants could examine the evidence coming from the scientific community, the Old Testament, and the New Testament ... and so forth.

This book has been extensively researched using the most credible and reliable sources I could find. There are well over eight hundred endnotes listed in this book, not counting over one-thousand-five-hundred verses of Scripture referenced. I wrote this book in such a way that most people could read and understand its principles. However, I must admit that some of the topics, by their very nature, are very deep and complex. I tried to strike a balance between simplicity, clarity, and credibility. Only you can judge whether or not I was successful in achieving that goal.

Style Protocols and Abbreviations

• Italicized text within brackets, [*like this example*] indicates comments or explanations within a quote that are my thoughts alone, and do not necessarily reflect the thoughts of the original author of the quote.

• My italicized and underlined initials [*SML*] within brackets indicate that the emphasis placed on quoted text is my emphasis and not that of the original author.

• Unless otherwise noted, all Scripture quotes are taken from the Revised Standard Version Catholic Edition (RSVCE) translation.[5]

• Throughout this book, the terms "Living Water" and "bio-living water" are used frequently. To avoid confusion, let me clarify the meaning of these terms as they are used in STOSS. "Living Water" signifies the grace (especially Sanctifying grace) of the Holy Spirit that flows from the Sacred Heart of Jesus to man. "Bio-living water (aka Biological water)" refers to specifically structured molecules of biological water that exists within the body of man and is vital to living and functioning (on multiple levels) of the human body. Put another way, bio-living water is Living Water expressed into the visible world in the "language of the body" (a phrase coined by Pope Saint John Paul II).

• When I write the words, "See endnote," that means that there is additional information about the topic at hand that is written in the endnote followed by the source citation.

Abbreviations

- Catechism of the Catholic Church — (CCC)
- Pope Saint John Paul II — (JP II)
- Theology of the Body — (TOB)
- The Science & Theology of Salt in Scripture — (STOSS)
- Old Covenant/Old Testament — (OC/OT)
- New Covenant/New Testament — (NC/NT)
- Electromagnetic radiation/electromagnetic energy — (EMR/EME)

INTRODUCTION

Before beginning this Section, I want to offer you some advice on how to read this book. STOSS Volumes I and II were written and organized to create a sort of staircase of understanding. Each section of the book builds upon the previous sections. By failing to read each section in order, your personal STOSS knowledge-base, so to speak, would likely suffer. Your understanding of STOSS would likely be incomplete and, likely, inadequate. It has been said that we can more thoroughly know ourselves by knowing our prototype, i.e. the incarnate Son of God: Jesus Christ, True God and True Man. This book, when read step-by-step, will help you to gain a greater knowledge of Him, which will in turn lead you to a greater understanding of yourself. My advice is to read the book completely. After that, come back and re-read those sections that are of particular interest to you.

Between 1979 and 1984, JP II gave a series of Wednesday audiences in which he introduced us to the Theology of the Body (TOB). At some point after 1984, I distinctly remember hearing or reading, though I cannot specifically say where he was asking for others to build upon what he had already taught. I believe this great man was telling us that he believed TOB was not yet complete, there's more to be said. The subject of this book is the Science & Theology of Salt in Scripture. I believe it is appropriate to classify STOSS as a branch of TOB, though I am in no way presenting myself as fit to be in the same theological or saintly company as this great man of God.

Scripture scholars and theologians describe the Bible as being polyvalent, i.e. the words in Scripture contain multiple, maybe even infinite, layers of Truth. Each layer is complementary to the others and deepens our understanding of God and his creation. STOSS is my endeavor to glimpse some of the deeper meanings of God's words. A comprehensive treatment of this theology could easily fill several large books. The purpose of this book, however, is to present a broad overview — perhaps planting a seed that will grow and bear fruit. When I first conceived of writing this book, my second biggest fear (the first being my espousing a theology containing doctrinal error) was not finding enough things to say to fill up a book. Toward the end, my biggest problem became finding a spot in the book where I could feel comfortable shutting up without doing an injustice to the exposition of this theology.

I think it would be non-controversial to describe the Bible as a history book, a philosophy book, a theology book, and more. However, as I have become more familiar with its contents, I have come to realize that the Bible is also a very comprehensive and advanced science book. Not just a textbook on axiomatic science, but also an applied sciences book. The Bible is a collection of books that informs us of scientific truth as well as the application of that science in real world settings. It's so scientifically advanced, in fact, that so-called "modern" science is only now discovering some of the scientific mysteries God inconspicuously 'planted' in the words of Scripture. Often, but not always, these scientific truths are hidden in symbols and signs that point us to these amazing scientific truths. These truths, in turn, give us an even deeper understanding of what God is trying to teach us. We will talk about some of those scientific principles in this book. I identify thirty-four of these hidden gems of knowledge. I must admit that I find myself amused when I think about many, but not all, scientists who are so puffed up with Gnostic-orientated intellectual pride that they believe they can adequately explain creation without including God in the equation. How foolish they must feel — or at least should feel — at discovering the fact that thousands and thousands of years ago God revealed (in age-appropriate ways) cutting-edge scientific principles to shepherds, fishermen, and farmers. Incidentally, this should poke holes in the theory of some who say that the Bible is simply a book written by men unguided by divine Wisdom.

Before moving on from the subject of science, I want to briefly set the stage for understanding the certainty of the scientific principles set forth in this book. There are different terms used to describe the different certainty levels of scientific research. An *axiom* is a truth that is considered to be self-evident … not requiring proof. A *theorem* is a scientific principle/law that has been generally accepted as being proven. A *hypothesis* is an "intelligent guess" that something is likely to be true, but has not yet been proven to be so. Research and experimentation are performed to test hypotheses. When one has been sufficiently tested and the results have been found to support its acceptance, the hypothesis becomes a theorem. Every scientific discovery listed in this book is an axiom, a theorem, or a hypothesis that has undergone some degree of testing that tends to support the hypothesis. If I knew what God knew, then I could identify every scientific discovery talked about in this book as either an axiom or a falsehood. However, because of my limited knowledge, I am not able to make that judgment. There are one or two experiments talked about that can be classified as controversial. I will plainly label those.

It was Albert Einstein who said, "Science without religion is lame, and religion without science is blind."[6] I would modify Einstein's expression somewhat. I would say those who are adherents of Scientism, are willfully ignorant and disdainful of Scripture are doomed to fall far short of the full truth of creation. Likewise, theologians and Scripture scholars who are ignorant of science will also be unable to grasp a fuller understanding of Scripture and Tradition. There were times while writing this book that I shed tears. They were not tears of sorrow, but rather, tears of great joy combined with awe at how great and powerful is this God we worship (or, in all too many cases, should worship) who allows us to glimpse His majesty by penetrating the depths of his handy work, i.e. creation. It is my great hope that you, too, will find yourself shedding tears of joy and awe as you read the pages of this book.

Contrasting the Theology of the Body to STOSS

In the Theology of the Body, JP II examines how man's body should be understood in light of the Scripture passage that reads, "So God created man in his own image, in the image of God he created him; male and female he created them" (Gen. 1:27). He takes as the starting point of that examination a focus on the nuptial meaning of the body, i.e. on the unitive and procreative aspect of sacramental marriage and the fact of it being a sign of the Triune nature of God. He tells us that: 1) the body and it alone, is capable of bringing the invisible into the visible; 2) the body is absolutely essential for expressing love into the physical world; 3) the language of the spirit must be expressed through an adequate language of the body.

In the Theology of the Salt, we take a deeper look at the science of the body in order to help us better understand how a one-body relationship between the bridegroom (Jesus) and the bride (the Church) on one hand, and a one-flesh relationship between the individual members of the Church and Jesus in the Eucharist on the other, is possible. As it turns out, there is a multitude of Scripture passages (more than previously thought) that help us to gain a deeper understanding of the significance of the body relative to the union of persons; expressions of the heart; fruitfulness, i.e. judging a tree by its fruit; and, the body as a channel for certain types of grace. During the process of unpacking STOSS, we spend a good deal of time delving very deeply into a greater understanding of the language of the body, through which an accurate expression of the overflow of the heart is achieved. This language is both visible and invisible. It is also a language that must change in relation to the changes that occur to the inner heart of man as a result of choices made and graces accepted ... or rejected by each individual.

In short, JP II is much more theological and metaphysical in his approach to understanding the meaning of the body through TOB than I am with STOSS. I, on the other hand, take a more scientific approach which, I believe, also helps us to gain an increase of understanding as to what Scripture has to say about the body and its role in sanctification and redemption of ourselves and others. An analogy might be this: TOB looks at the theory behind the design and building of a car, while STOSS looks at the nuts and bolts of the car.

PART I — SALT IN THE OLD TESTAMENT

CHAPTER 1 — LOT'S WIFE: THE KEY TO UNDERSTANDING SALT AND SALT COVENANTS

God tells us of Lot's wife in the very first book of Sacred Scripture. Other than a single usage of the word "salt" to describe a geographical location, i.e. the Salt/Dead Sea (even this is significant, as we will discuss later), her story is the first time salt is mentioned in Scripture. I believe there is a very important reason why God wanted to tell her story almost immediately after making a covenant with Abraham (Gen. 17:4). The story of Lot's wife is significant. When we understand the deeper meaning of her becoming a salt pillar, a key is turned that unlocks a much deeper understanding of the very nature of man and all of God's covenants with him, up to and including the final and everlasting covenant ushered in through Jesus' passion, death, resurrection, and the establishment of his bride, i.e. the Church.

I'm sure most people are familiar with map legends. For those who aren't, a map legend is sort of glossary that defines the meaning of symbols instead of words. The symbols enable one to read a map and interpret the information it contains. For example, a typical road map might contain a picture of an airplane or a green colored road. If one looks at the map legend, next to those symbols will be the word "airport" and the words "toll road", respectively. When map readers see an airplane on the map, they know it means there is an airport at that location. Likewise, when map readers see a green line, they know it represents a toll road. What does this have to do with Scripture? I believe God is including Lot's wife as a type of scriptural "map legend," so to speak. He is telling us that 'salt' in Scripture should be interpreted as directly referring to a very particular aspect of the human person, the entirety of which is in the image and likeness of God.

Scripture tells us, "Then the Lord rained on Sodom and Gomor'rah brimstone and fire from the Lord out of heaven; and he overthrew those cities, and all the valley, and all the inhabitants of the cities, and what grew on the ground. But Lot's wife behind him looked back, and she became a pillar of salt" (Gen. 19: 24-26). I'm convinced that God did not turn Lot's wife into a "different" material than she was already, i.e. geological salt. Consider this: *every single one of us is a pillar of salt*. The difference between each of us and Lot's wife is this: the former is a living and moving pillar of salt, while the latter, because of her disobedience and hesitation, became a dead pillar of salt.

Let me explain what I believe God means when He uses "salt" in Scripture. In 1953 James Watson, Francis Crick, and Maurice Wilkins published a paper titled, "A Structure for Deoxyribose Nucleic Acid [DNA]." The first sentence in the article is significant. It informs us that DNA is a biological salt.[7] The article, published in Nature magazine, includes commentary by Tom Zinnen. Through his commentary, we are able to gain a better understanding of the chemistry by which this is so. According to Zinnen, after losing positively charged hydrogen ions (an ion is any particle, e.g. atom, molecule, etc., that has a net negative or positive electrical charge), the DNA phosphates (phosphate and sugar comprise the backbone of the DNA double helix — the "handrails" of the spiral staircase of the double helix which is the structure of DNA) become negatively charged. Consequently, they bind to a cation (a positively charged ion) to achieve electrical neutrality–usually, but not limited to, Na+ (sodium) or K+ (potassium). That makes the DNA polymer a "salt" of [Na+] x [DNA-] (sodium phosphate) or [K+] x [DNA-] (potassium phosphate).[8,9] Physicists Perepelytsya and Volkov describe DNA as a salt of alkali.[10] Russian scientist Maxim D. Frank-Kamenetskii in his book, Unraveling DNA: The Most Important Molecule of Life, tells us that DNA, despite being called an acid, is actually a salt. He further states that calling it an acid is an error of the highest magnitude, comparing it to the error that would occur if one referred to ordinary table salt as hydrochloric acid.[11] In all honesty, it's not really critical to understand the chemical underpinnings for the validity of the fact that DNA is a salt. What is important, is to recognize it as a scientific fact. The role of salt is critical to our understanding of DNA and life. It is hypothesized that life began in a high-salt environment. A research team at Florida State University College of Medicine headed by structural biologist Michael Blaber is championing the hypothesis that the emergence of life (known as abiogenesis) began through the presence of 10 pre-biotic amino acids (amino acids are the "building blocks" of DNA-produced proteins) existing in a high-salt environment. As of this writing, they were 80% of the way towards proving their hypothesis. Their findings were published in the journal Proceedings of the National Academy of Sciences in 2013 (see endnote for Journal Source).[12]

Excluding matter we consume (water and food), we are, from the top of our head to the tip of our toes, nothing but cells (I have seen estimates ranging anywhere from 10 to 100 trillion cells in the human body). In every one of those cells, we have a complete copy of our salt of DNA. We have so much <u>salt</u> of DNA in our body, if we were to place every strand end to end, it would extend 10 billion miles; enough to go to the planet Pluto and back.[13] Yeah, I'd say we're all pillars of salt.

Let's return to our discussion of Lot's wife. We know from Genesis that fire and brimstone were raining down from the sky. We also know that more than just the cities of Sodom and Gomorrah were affected. My contention is this: when Lot's wife looked back, whatever destructive force or energy God used to accomplish His will, overtook her — likely encasing her body (much like the residents of Pompeii) and/or dehydrating every ounce of liquid that was present in her body. As I see it, there are four main possibilities for interpreting the events of Lot's wife's death. As you may recall, there was fire and brimstone raining down from heaven and she became a pillar of salt. The options are the following: A). She was encased by raining brimstone (sulfur liquefied by extreme heat), causing her to become a pillar of the salt of DNA, and the DNA was the only salt present; B). She was miraculously transformed into a chemical salt, replacing her salt of DNA. I don't view this as likely. I give my reasons a little later; C). A chemical reaction occurred within the falling sulfur, causing it to become a salt. Sulfur could, for example, become a sulfide salt through a change in the number of electrons in the ion. This option is not likely considering that which is written in Deuteronomy 29:22-23. These passages specifically separate the presence of the chemical salt from the elemental brimstone in its description of a burnt-out wasteland (i.e. Sodom and Gomorrah, among others); and finally, D). The molten sulfur in which she was encased could have been mixed with the geological salt that was abundant in the region.

Ignoring option 'B', the remaining three options leave us with a critical question that needs to be answered. All three of the remaining options involve scenarios in which multiple materials are involved. With option 'A', there's sulfur and salt of DNA. With option 'C', there's sulfur that has become a possible sulfide, and the salt of DNA. With option 'D', there's the salt of DNA, sulfur, and geological salt. So the question is this: if multiple materials were involved, why did God only mention the salt in the demise of Lot's wife? Why focus on the salt? I believe it was God's intention to use Lot's wife's DNA as a map legend; whenever salt is mentioned in Scripture, we are to interpret it as meaning the salt of DNA

Of the four options, I believe that option 'D' is the most probable. The science of DNA ... the knowledge that we are made of it, and that it is an organic salt, wouldn't become available until very recently, historically speaking. So God gave

Abraham's people a sign within a sign. The geological salt part of the sign would give them something they could understand while the thousands of years passed until the discovery of the salt of DNA was made. Any other options you choose for interpreting the scriptural meaning of becoming a pillar of salt will not negate the scientific fact that, in addition to any alternate exegesis, she also *became* a pillar of the salt of DNA.

Only the element 'brimstone' (aka sulfur) is specifically mentioned as falling from the heavens. Sulfur is an element in the Periodic Table. It is not a chemical salt. This is confirmed by science and Scripture. If we assume that sulfur was somehow involved in the "encasing" process, it would be germane to note that science has discovered the existence of a proportional relationship between the amounts of sulfur in the cell and the degree of water loss in the cell; the higher the sulfur content, the greater is the loss of water — potentially leading to cell death.[14] The importance of this fact will be clearer when we discuss water's role in the process of the redemption of the body (cf. Rom. 8:23). I believe the symbolism relating to brimstone/sulfur is profound. It is also profound that this event occurred right next to the Dead/Salt Sea, but much more on that later.

Most of us are likely familiar with time capsules. For those who aren't, a time capsule is a container filled with items from the present that, when opened, will help a future generation/civilization to understand a civilization from the past. The capsule is buried in the ground with the hope that it will be uncovered at some point in the distant future. As it turns out, God planted a time capsule in Sacred Scripture. In this capsule, He simply put "salt". He knew it would take thousands upon thousands of years for man to gain enough scientific knowledge to decipher the deeper meaning of the word "salt", then use that knowledge to gain a deeper understanding of God and his greatest creation, man.[15] Having read the title of this book, you may have thought to yourself: SALT! How in the world can salt be a theology? Excluding the use of salt in proper names, such as the Salt Sea, Scripture makes reference to salt approximately thirty times. After reading this book, you will gain a deeper understanding of those passages and many others that are connected to salt in ways that will be made clear later in the book. First, I want to bring up a few points that will help to demonstrate why the reference to a pillar of salt does *not* refer to geological salt. I'm not expecting to present an open-and-shut case through this reasoning alone, but I think a convincing case will be made when combined with discussion of other Scripture texts relating to salt. In this book, I will make reference to over 1,500 Bible verses. The vast majority of these passages will either directly or indirectly support the correctness of my interpretation of the meaning of salt in Scripture. In turn, the verses themselves will be understood more deeply through this interpretation.

In this book, we will be discussing the belief that the 'body' is an *integral part* of what makes the human person be in the image and likeness of God. Expounding on JP II's TOB, Christopher West tells us man is the perfect integration of body and soul, through which is expressed the nuptial meaning of the body.[16] According to JP II, the body is *required* in order for man to manifest (i.e. make known, communicate) love.[17] The necessity of a body-soul as a prerequisite for man to be in the image and likeness of God can also be seen in the words of St. Seraphim of Sarov. We read, "All these parts [*body*] of our nature were created from the dust of the ground, and Adam was not created dead."[18] Consequently, if God had turned Lot's wife into a pillar of inorganic geological salt, He would have taken away from her the very thing that was given her in order to manifest love — to be in His image and likeness, i.e. body and spirit.[19]

We *are* dust. We will discuss this statement in greater detail shortly, but for now, let me just say that our salt of DNA **IS** also dust of the earth. So when we die, we simply revert to that from which we were made. In fact, in Scripture, we are repeatedly told that we <u>all</u> will return to the dust from which we were formed. In Genesis we read, "In the sweat of your face you shall eat bread till you return to the ground, for out of it you were taken; you are dust, and to dust you shall return" (Gen. 3:19). God did not tell our first parents that they were made of dust and to some *different material* they will return. In Ecclesiastes, we read, "All go to one place; all are from the dust, and all turn to dust again" (Eccl. 3:20). The transition from organic biological dust to inorganic geological dust (an important distinction, as we will learn through the course of this book) occurs after death and is a consequence of death. Lot's wife was <u>not</u> formed of the inorganic geological rock-salt of the earth. By turning her into a pillar of <u>geological</u> salt, God would have actively killed her, which is certainly within His power and prerogative to do — but did He? Would he change her human <u>nature</u>, killing her in the process?

When we read in Scripture about the Lord killing people, the wording is very blunt, direct, and action oriented — even though He may employ something or someone else as the acting agent of His judgment. Here are a few examples: 1) "At midnight the Lord smote [*'smote' means to inflict a heavy blow*] all the first-born in the land of Egypt" (Ex. 12:29); 2) "And about ten days later the Lord smote Nabal; and he died" (1 Sam. 25:38); 3) "'You have not lied to men but to God.' When Anani'as heard these words, he fell down and died" (Acts 5:4-5); and 4) "Jerobo'am did not recover his power in the days of Abi'jah; and the Lord smote him, and he died" (2 Chron. 13:20). I could go on, but we can see a common theme. In these passages, it is clear that it is the Lord who actively smites and kills, even if the secondary agent is used to do the actual killing. In stark contrast, let's look again at the passage regarding Lot's wife. It reads, "But Lot's wife behind him looked back, and she became a pillar of salt" (Gen. 19:26). By comparison, this passage seems much more passive than the previous passages

23

and is much more indicative of a narrative describing a naturally occurring event rather than a direct lethal intervention by God. There's no mention of the Lord striking, killing, or smiting Lot's wife; it only states that she "became" a pillar of salt.

Scripture is not silent about a direct link between organic substances (e.g. humans, food, juice, etc.) and the word 'salt'. Let's take a look at some very interesting wording that Luke used. Discussing the resurrected Jesus' appearance to the Apostles prior to his ascension, Luke writes, "And eating together with them, he commanded them, that they should not depart from Jerusalem, but should wait for the promise of the Father" (Acts 1:4: Douay-Rheims 1899 American Edition). Pope Benedict places great significance on the wording that Luke chose when talking about Jesus' eating with them. According to Benedict, the word that Luke used is "synalizômenos". Benedict tells us this wording is very important to Luke; he must have deliberately chosen to employ it. The literal translation of the phrase in question is "eating *salt [SML]* with them."[20] What Jesus ate with his Apostles was food. What does food consist of? The answer: primarily, the salt of DNA together with biological water. If I'm not mistaken, Lot's wife was organic and, therefore (according to Luke), organic salt. Of course, the meaning of this phrase goes much deeper (Benedict links it to the Eucharist), but we will wait until we discuss covenants before taking it up again.

As Benedict inadvertently pointed out, all living creatures are composed of organic salt. If Lot's wife were turned into geological salt, the philosophical substance of her nature would have changed. She would no longer belong to the family of man. I'm not aware of any other passages in Scripture where it tells us of God turning something from a higher nature into a lower nature. He doesn't turn an angel into a man. He doesn't turn a man into a frog. He doesn't turn a frog into a stone and so on. When Adam and Eve fell through a far greater sin than Lot's wife's sin, did God take away their human nature? No! He only took away that which was supernatural, i.e. above human nature.[21] When Satan, the father of all lies and a murderer from the beginning, and his followers fell, their angelic nature was not taken from them. If God did not alter the angelic nature of the personification of pure evil, why would he alter the human nature of Lot's wife by changing her into inorganic geological salt? What is written, however, about philosophical substance in Scripture is this: on multiple occasions, God turned something from a lower nature into a higher nature. Here are a few examples: reminiscent of man's creation, He turns dust into gnats (Ex. 8:16); He turns inorganic water into organic blood (Ex. 4:9); He is tempted by Satan to turn stone into bread (Mt. 4:3); and we are told that God can turn stones into children of Abraham (Mt. 3:9). Hmm; based on the above passages, it seems as though there is a connection between salt and dust. Let's examine that further.

1:A — Salt, Dust, Stone, and Rock

Knowing the meaning of salt in Scripture, what conclusions can be drawn concerning the deeper meaning of dust, stone, and rock in Scripture? According to St. Hildegard, of the three qualities of a stone, the one that denotes the Son is the solidity of touch, because it signifies the ability of man to see, touch, and know him.[22] Let's examine why, in physical creation, it is proper to refer to the Son of God as a stone or rock.

All rocks and, therefore, stones (which come from rocks) are formed from two or more minerals (minerals are generally defined as inorganic solids that have a crystalline structure).[23] Some minerals are composed of only one element listed in the Periodic Table, and some are mixed with other elements, such as aluminum, silicon, sodium, and magnesium.[24] Some elemental minerals are classified as metallic, e.g. gold, silver, and copper. The minerals of sodium[25] and potassium[26] are both elemental alkali metals that combine with the phosphate minerals of the DNA backbone (the two "sides" of the double helix "ladder") to make it a salt — *a salt that is also a stone*. Furthermore, and this cannot be overemphasized, the *DNA itself has a crystalline structure,*[27] as do all minerals. In fact, it was x-ray crystallography that allowed James Watson, Francis Crick, Maurice Wilkins, and Rosalind Franklin to discover that the "B" form of DNA was in the shape of a double helix.[28] Our DNA is a bonded collection of very, very small stones — dare I say DUST — held together by electrically charged ions and surrounded by dynamically structured molecules of water (more on the importance of that fact later in the book). William Whitman, a microbiology professor in the Franklin College of Arts and Sciences, tells us that DNA by itself, absent any of the other biological systems that make for a living cell, is nothing more than a "rock" (see endnote for Journal Source).[29] That's right — dust! Let's recall the words of God to Adam: "In the sweat of your face you shall eat bread till you return to the ground, for out of it you were taken; you are dust, and to dust you shall return" (Gen. 3:19). Unbeknownst to Prof. Whitman, it would not be correct to equate the word "rock" with DNA relative to both Scripture and geological circles, because 'rock' generally refers to the original mineral formation from which stones come.[30] Dust/stone is nothing more than pieces of rock that have been separated and gradually worn down to very, very, small mineral crystals, i.e. stones that are the size of dust.[31] More specific to man in Scripture is the use of the word "clay". God revealed to Hildegard, "Out of clay God so shaped humanity that through this tiny spark of the soul we become flesh and blood out of clay."[32] The use of clay in Scripture is significant. Clay is composed of two primary substances: 1) dust that is even *finer than silt*, i.e. 2 microns (aka micrometer; two-thousandths of a millimeter) or less;[33] and, 2) water. Considering the size of our DNA (the nuclear volume of an entire sperm cell, containing an entire molecule of DNA, is only about 30 microns[34]). Thus the symbolism of clay is most appropriate — how could it not be, it's the Word of God. In order for clay to be mold-able (technical term is "plastic"), which is scripturally symbolic of a biologically and spiritually alive human person (e.g. Num. 5:17; Job 10:9, 27:16; Is. 64:8; Rom. 9:21), it must contain water within its mix. The significance of this fact will become much clearer as we progress through those parts of the book that discuss bio-living water, fresh water, salt water, and more. If you examine Scripture references to clay, I am confident that you will begin to see in each passage a much deeper meaning relating to grace, the Holy Spirit, the redemption of the body, and Truth incarnate — especially after reading this book. Our bodies — including Jesus' body — are made up entirely of cells which contain within their nucleus, the biological (*not* geological) salt of DNA — the "stone/dust/clay" of DNA.

Note to adherents of Scientism (aka, Scientific Materialism), it looks like God beat you to the scientific punch, so to speak. Scientism, by the way, is the belief that all truth about the material world comes through scientific research and discovery … .and only through science. They believe religion has no part in determining the truth.[35] Many adherents are atheists or agnostics. If there is a conflict between scientific theory and Scripture, they believe Scripture is de facto wrong. In a sense, their intellect has become self-imprisoned within a box labeled, "Big Bang and By-Products Only: God NOT Allowed." This self-imposed imprisonment does not allow them to even consider God's intervention into, and supremacy over, all that exists. The outcome of which is exemplified by studies and conclusions concerning the so-called Mitochondrial Eve. I will talk a little bit about that later. The vast majority of scientists are good people, doing good work (including many of the adherents of Scientism). We owe a great gratitude for much of what they have accomplished.

The most sought after prize in science is to discover something new and, as a result, having your research published in a respected journal. So, let's keep a running tally of who beat the other in publishing (in God's case: published in Scripture; in adherents of Scientism's case: published in any scientific journal) the discovery of some previously unknown scientific mystery concerning the body.

TALLY UPDATE:

Let's start with what we have already discussed:

1) Man is made from dust;

2) DNA is dust;

3) DNA is an organic salt;

4) The particles of dust that make up our DNA are roughly the size of the dust present in clay; a term used frequently in Scripture;

5) DNA, when present along with biological water, is "moldable" like clay; and,

6) Understanding the biological ramifications of the element sulfur, God uses sulfur to demonstrate to us, via Lot's wife, the consequences for disobeying his commands.

I could come up with more, but I can see the beginnings of a need to invoke the slaughter rule. Some of the above will be discussed in even greater detail throughout the book. Let's look at the tally so far. By my count we have:

Cumulative Score:

God: 6

Adherents of Scientism: 0

Judging by the initial results, I think we can characterize God as the speeding bullet in this race so far and the unbelieving scientists as ... well, I was going to say as a tortoise, but I just saw a tortoise pass them by. I have more bad news — the tally is only just beginning.

Think about the following very carefully. I know of no one who believes or writes that God is speaking symbolically when we are told we are made of dust of the earth — that ALL of us are made of dust! If one interprets Genesis quite literalistically, one would have to admit that only Adam could have been made from actual geological dust — dust of the earth. For **all** the rest of us, there are at least two people (our mother and father) who can vouch for the fact that we were not made from geological dust. For all the rest of us (we will talk about Eve later), our body was made through one event, and one event only — the union of a sperm cell (with the exception of Jesus) and an egg cell, both of which contain the biological salt of DNA. Everything we are, from the physical body perspective, came from the sperm and egg — and only the sperm and egg. The only material in either of those two cells that could be called dust, is the salt of DNA. If you're wondering about the cell material in which the DNA resides ... nope, not salt, not dust! The structural material of the cell is composed of complex chemicals called proteins. Therefore, only the DNA can be identified as dust. Recall that Scripture tells us we are made from the dust of the earth (cf. Gen. 2:7, 3:19, 18:27; Tobit 3:6; Job 10:9; Eccl. 3:20; and many others) and we will return to dust. Ergo, Scripture verifies the fact that our salt of DNA *is also dust, i.e. very small stones*, but stones nonetheless. To my way of thinking, the above argument constitutes an open-and-shut case. I cannot conceive of how Scripture passages equating man with dust can refer to anything else but the salt/dust of DNA. Let's look at some passages that link inorganic salt/dust/stone with organic salt/dust/stone: 1) Satan tempted Jesus to turn stones into bread. Satan would not tempt him this way unless he knew Jesus could do it (Lk. 4:3, Mt. 4:3); 2) God turned dust into gnats (Ex. 8:16-17); 3) God could turn stones into children of Abraham, i.e. members of the Chosen nation (Mt. 3:9, Lk. 3:8); the rebuilt Temple (Jesus' body, per John 2:19-21) is referred to as the 'cornerstone' (same material, but a much larger version of dust) of the Temple (1 Pt. 2:6), and; 4) multiple linkages made between man and mud/clay (e.g. Is. 64:8; Job 10:9, 33:6; Rom 9:21; Jn 9:11; and many more).

One last example: In Rev. 2:12-17, we read about the church at Pergamum. The people of this church are told, "To him who conquers I will give some of the hidden manna, and I will give him a white stone, with a new name written on the stone which no one knows except him who receives it." So, what was it that the Spirit wanted this particular church to conquer?

Interestingly, none of the other churches were promised a white stone if they conquered their sinfulness. The sin of the church at Pergamum was fornication, both of the flesh and of the spirit. We know this because of the reference to the "teaching of Balaam, who taught Balak." In order to make God angry with the Israelites, Balaam taught Balak to place stumbling blocks (I am assuming the symbolic stumbling blocks were also stone) before them. So Balak employed some of the most beautiful women in his kingdom to lure the men into unclean fleshly and spiritual acts, i.e. sexual intercourse and idolatry.[36] The stumbling blocks were the DNA/salt/dust/stone bodies of beautiful and desirous women. This is why the Spirit informs them of the white stone. He is telling them, if the men conquer their lust of the flesh, then, at the resurrection, their bodies will be raised from the dead, be glorified, and become as pure as snow (as clean as a white stone).[37] The deeper meaning of this passage will become even clearer as we progress through the book.

Over, and over, and over again throughout Scripture, the embodied soul, i.e. man, is referred to as some sort of stone. Whenever we encounter salt, dust, clay/mud, and stone in Scripture, I believe it would be wise to include in our consideration of each passage's meaning, the knowledge we have gained in this section.

Before proceeding forward, I want to provide another reason (there will be even more throughout the book) that my interpretation of salt in Scripture is the best for explaining all of the different connotations of salt in Scripture. There are several passages in the OT that deal with these seemingly contradictory scriptural usages of salt. In Psalms, we read, "He turns rivers into a desert, springs of water into thirsty ground, a fruitful land [*a metaphor for our pre-fallen bodies*] into a salty waste [*a metaphor for our salt of DNA after original sin, and the subsequent loss of the indwelling of the Holy Spirit*], because of the wickedness of its inhabitants" (Ps.107:33-34). In

Deuteronomy, it is written, "... see the afflictions of that land and the sicknesses with which the Lord has made it sick — the whole land brimstone and salt, and a burnt-out waste, unsown, and growing nothing, where no grass can sprout ..." (Deut. 29:22-23). In Jeremiah, we read, "'Cursed is the man who trusts in man and makes flesh his arm, whose heart turns away from the Lord. He is like a shrub in the desert, and shall not see any good come. He shall dwell in the parched places of the wilderness, in an uninhabited salt land'" (Jer. 17:5-6). There are other passages, but the common message contained in all of the passages is this: as a result of sin, i.e. our disordered nature, our bodies' (salt of DNA) have become a wasteland where (pre-Redemption) there is no life, no living water, a place where nothing grows, where no good fruits can be found.

This is where some of the more "traditional" interpretations of salt run into trouble. Here are a few of those interpretations:

- Salt is used as a preservative. Therefore, it is a sign of an eternal covenant with God. It is a sign of eternal life;

- Salt is a spice that adds flavor to our food. Therefore, it is a sign that our works must be joyful and filled with truth, not dull and boring, and;

- Since salt was a valuable commodity in OC days, it was a sign that the Messiah does not want to pay a high price for salt that has no flavor, i.e. is tepid/lukewarm.

All of these bear some truth, but all of them lack a unifying context which unites the good connotations of salt with the bad. Examples of this shortcoming are: 1) Salt certainly didn't preserve the life of Lot's wife. In fact, it killed her; 2) salt certainly wasn't a sign of life for the Salt Sea (aka the Dead Sea). To drink from it was to die. It was completely absent of all life and fruitfulness; 3) Again in Scripture, salt is a sign of death and barrenness. When Abimelech conquered Shechem and all its inhabitants, he sowed the city with salt (Jdg. 9:45) so that it would be a wasteland, as was the land of brimstone and salt described in Deuteronomy (Deut. 29:22-23). As I said, the traditional interpretations of salt in Scripture lack a unifying context through which all connotations of salt in Scripture can be understood. I believe I provide that context. As I said earlier, the story of Lot's wife contains a sign within a sign. The first sign is purely symbolic (see the reasons in the previous paragraph). The sign that was hidden within, is the one modern science has helped us to uncover. What we now know is that salt/dust is also a concrete reality. We are ALL pillars of salt/dust/stone ... literally. This is the context that unifies all the other connotations of salt in Scripture.

CHAPTER 2 — TYPOLOGY: PREFIGURING AND FORESHADOWING

Before delving into our treatment of salt in Scripture, it is important to note the OT's critical role in arriving at a correct and, therefore, a deeper understanding of the NT. Understanding the meaning of salt in the OT will aid us greatly in also understanding the meaning of stone, clay, and mud in the NT. The Church teaches that God intended the full meaning of the NT to be hidden within the OT which, in turn, manifests and sheds light on the NT.[38] Going all the way back to the early Church Fathers, Augustine shows this understanding of typology was present very early in Church teaching.[39] In the OT, foreshadowing, fore-announcing, or pre-figuring always ultimately points to the final fulfillment of the covenant made with Abraham, i.e. the coming of the Messiah, the establishment of the eternal Temple, and the establishment of the Church in the new (fulfilled) and everlasting covenant. The word "type" in Scripture refers to a person or event that foreshadows a future person, happening, or event.[40] A likeness exists between type and antitype. The antitype (some people use the term archetype) is always greater than the type. For example, Moses was a type of Christ, but Christ is the antitype of Moses.[41]

Using, for example, St. Cyprian's treatment of Melchizedek, it would be accurate to say that Melchizedek's bread and wine offering did not foreshadow the eating of the first Passover in Moses time, but was the same "type" that were all Passovers. It was a "type" of the Last Supper during which Jesus instituted the Sacrament of the Eucharist; the Passover that prompted him to say, "I have earnestly desired to eat this passover with you before I suffer" (Lk. 22:15). The Eucharist is the antitype to Melchizedek's offering of bread and wine.[42]

Since DNA is both salt and stone, typology can help us to

gain a deeper understanding of those passages in Scripture that employ them. As we progress through this book, we will learn that salt, when used to denote death, unfruitfulness, disobedience, etc., is a type and sign of *fallen* man's body. This is also true if salt is used in connection with water. Both salt and stone, when used in a positive context, are almost always a type and sign of Jesus' pre- and post-resurrected body. Armed with this understanding, Scripture may become clearer and start to provide us with a better view of the "big picture" of God's plan for our redemption and salvation. In all of the passages that we cite, you can correctly substitute the word "salt" with the phrase, "salt of DNA." In the OT, the usage of salt reflects three main themes. By examining salt in the first theme, we learn of the deeper consequences of original sin and the absolute need for our purification. By examining salt in the second theme, we learn of God's plans to prepare us and enable us to be purified in the "fullness of time" (Eph. 1:10). Incidentally, the very use of the phrase "fullness of time" indicates: 1) that God intended the plan of our redemption and salvation to unfold gradually; 2) that He had no intention of just snapping His fingers, so to speak, to accomplish this redemption and salvation, and; 3) that He intended to use what was created (including the Messiah's human body and soul) in order to redeem what was created. By examining salt in the third theme we learn: 1) there is a purification coming; 2) the means by which purification will happen, and: 3) what would be purified. Let's begin our examination of the three themes by examining the Scripture usage of salt relative to describing fallen man.

CHAPTER 3 — OT SALT THEME #1: OUR POST-FALLEN STATE

Keeping in mind the bad connotations of salt in Scripture we discussed earlier, let's proceed. Now we'll look at some scientific aspects of the salt of DNA's role in original sin and our fallen nature.

3:A — Role of Salt of DNA in Original Sin

Before we can understand original sin, we must first understand original perfection. JP II dealt with this subject extensively in his treatment of the TOB. I, however, will be looking at original sin and its consequences from the standpoint of STOSS.

St. Thomas Aquinas wrote, "Now we have it on the authority of Scripture that 'God made man right' (Eccles. 7:30), which rightness, as Augustine says (De Civ. Dei xiv, 11), consists in the perfect subjection of the body [*i.e. salt of DNA*] to the soul."[43] Aquinas goes on to show the role that supernatural grace played in our original perfection. He writes, "Subjection of the body to the soul and of the lower powers to reason, was not from nature; otherwise it would have remained after sin ... Hence it is clear that also the primitive subjection by virtue of which reason was subject to God, was not a merely natural gift, but a supernatural endowment of grace."[44] The body is, in fact, meant to be fully subject to the soul. St. Catherine of Siena tells us that at our resurrection on Judgment Day, our bodies will be "imprinted" with the fruits of the sufferings and labors endured by the body in "partnership" with the inner heart in the practice of virtue. This "imprinted ornamentation," so to speak, will not occur through the power of the body, but through the power of the soul, as it was prior to the fall.[45] This makes sense in light of the philosophical understanding that the soul is the form of the body.[46] To help us understand the soul, body, and form concept, think of a hand and glove. The hand represents the soul and the leather glove represents the body. Without the hand inside of it, the glove has no form.

When Adam and Eve sinned they lost supernatural grace, forfeiting perfect subjection of the body to the soul. Consequently, human DNA started to function in the same way that it does in any other animal — sensual appetites and all. The bodies of sensual animals function under the same guiding principle, i.e. what pleases the senses is good and what displeases the senses is bad. No longer subject to the dominion of the soul, the salt of DNA functions in such a way as to reward and encourage behavior/experiences that *feel* good, and to punish behavior/experiences that *feel* bad. Were it not for this fact of nature, all animals would die out. This is a perfect design — for animals, but not for man. The sensual appetites of animals and the actions that proceed from them are morally neutral. A lion that kills his offspring is not 'bad,' he is just following his animal nature. Man, however, is not simply an animal (contrary to what modern society tries to foist upon us).

In response to stimuli from the five senses of the body, the salt of DNA produces hormones (hormones are only one of very many types of proteins produced by DNA). Some proteins initiate a sensual appetite ... then reward the behavior that satisfies the appetite. The hormone dopamine, for example, not only increases the sex drive in both sexes, but it also consolidates the neuronal connections responsible for the behavior. For example, giving in to lust causes physical changes to our brains,[47] changes that will create a very strong sensual appetite that is extremely difficult to resist. Dying to oneself is a good description of successfully resisting the sinful temptation. The incentives can range all the way from mild cravings to physical discomfort to out-and-out withdrawal symptoms if the appetite is not fed.

The body seeks a type of happiness that translates into that which is pleasing to the senses; when satisfied, our salt produces sensual rewards so powerful they can be described as addictive. The body tries to bring the soul over to its way of thinking, so to speak, by offering hormonal rewards that can be *very* persuasive. Let's take a closer look at the role of hormones in concupiscence. Can we show a direct link between original sin and hormones? I believe we can. The biological sciences tell us, unlike most other proteins, hormones are carried to their target cells primarily, but not exclusively, *via the bloodstream.* Hildegard informs us that after Adam's sin, blood carried within itself: 1) sweet, but deadly, poison;[48] 2) shameful and turbulent acts, thus increasing the body's appetite for those very crimes carried in the blood;[49] and, 3) impure filth which changed Adam's blood into a liquid of pollution.[50]

Immediately after Adam and Eve's disobedience, Scripture tells us of the first two outward signs of concupiscence: "Then the eyes of both were opened, and they knew that they were naked ... the man and his wife hid themselves from the presence of the Lord God among the trees of the garden" (Gen. 3:7-8). The phrase, "the eyes of both were opened" is meant to convey that something sensually-related is going to start happening that wasn't happening before. In *Crossing the Threshold of Hope*, JP II tells us, everything in the intellect came to us first through the five senses.[51] The opening of their eyes really means receiving input from the five senses, i.e. sight, touch, hearing, taste, and smell, but without the supernatural grace to modulate the responses to said 'knowledge' from the sense-based input. In other words, our salt of DNA was now going to start responding to that sensual input in a manner in which the weakened soul could no longer control (cf. Rom. 7:14-25, Jn. 8:34).

TALLY UPDATE:

7. Role of hormones in addictions and concupiscence

Cumulative Score:

God: 7

Adherents of Scientism: 0

We know that Adam and Eve experienced shame as a result of their nakedness[52] (arguably, lust and stress were probably at play at the same time) and that they were afraid.[53] All of the physical aspects of concupiscence described above are attributable to the production of hormones which would have been secreted into the bloodstream in response to sensual stimuli resulting from their "eyes being opened." Both shame and stress are associated with, among others, the production of the hormone cortisol.[54,55] Lust of the flesh or, what I call biological (so-called) 'love', which is completely different from spiritual love (a distinction greatly misunderstood in today's culture), is associated with multiple hormones, e.g. dopamine,[56] testosterone,[57] oxytocin,[58] and vasopressin.[59] Fear is associated with the "fight or flight" hormone, adrenalin. I could elaborate further on the hormones associated with other physical consequences of concupiscence such as pain in childbirth, hunger,[60] greed, avarice, etc., but I think the point has been adequately made. Just a quick note regarding hunger and original sin: some might be confused by the fact that Jesus suffered hunger in the desert (Mt. 4:2, Lk. 4:2) and yet, at the same time, we know that he was not born with original sin. Aquinas explains the apparent contradiction thusly, "the penalties, such as hunger, thirst, death, and the like, which we suffer sensibly in this life flow from original sin. And hence Christ, in order to satisfy fully for original sin, wished to suffer sensible pain, that He might consume death and the like in Himself."[61] Put another way, because Jesus' body was completely subject to his human soul (he did not inherit original sin) and, therefore, his soul possessed the power to will and allow his body to experience some of the consequences of original sin; this without having sinned himself. St. Paul writes, "For our sake he made him to be sin who knew no sin, so that in him we might become the righteousness of God" (2 Cor. 5:21).

Without supernatural grace, and the strength which the soul receives from it, our salt of DNA will enslave us to the sensual appetites created through the production of hormones and will lead us to equate happiness with the satisfying of those appetites and the avoidance of pain. How strong is the power of hormones to enslave us? Remember the hunger hormone, ghrelin? Is your willpower strong enough to overpower the urges created by ghrelin by not eating anything for a day, a week, a month, or forty days? How about those hormones leading to addictions? How hard is it for a smoker to stop smoking? How hard is it for an alcoholic to stop drinking? How hard is it for a drug addict to stop taking drugs? All of the aforementioned addictions (normally, I wouldn't classify food as an addiction, but it can be for certain people) are the result of hormones.

What necessarily follows from the repeated satisfaction of hormonal appetites is self-centeredness instead of other-centeredness.[62] This was, and is, the sad state of fallen man. We seek hormonal happiness at the expense of spiritual happiness. We are even confused about which is true happiness (if we are even remotely aware there is a difference). For example, there is a huge difference between "biological compassion" and "spiritual compassion." Fallen man's intellect is easily fooled by the compassion that originates from the flesh. Biological compassion originates from the body and is fed by the release of hormones, primarily oxytocin,[63] that cause a person to *feel* good. This hormonally induced **feeling** fools the person into thinking that a *real good* has just been accomplished when, in fact, it was only an *apparent good* (i.e. a perceived good that is <u>not</u> a *real good*).[64]

The Holy Spirit — and only the Holy Spirit — dwelling within the inner heart motivates spiritual compassion. He leads man to acts focused on obtaining ultimate and eternal happiness for others. Here is a litmus test to help judge which type of compassion is behind any particular act of *helpfulness*: If the particular act being enabled is of a sinful nature, then biological compassion is at the root. PERIOD! The Holy Spirit <u>will not</u> prompt anyone to be an accomplice to another person's sin!

CHAPTER 4 — OT SALT THEME #2: GOD'S PLAN

God's plan for fallen man from the very beginning was to send us a purifier, someone to redeem us, to save us. By understanding the deeper scriptural meaning of salt, we can begin to understand the process through which we get from OT point "A" (the fall of Adam and Eve) to OT point "Z" (the birth of Jesus; the fulfillment of God's covenants; and, the beginning of the new, final, and everlasting covenant)? This process would consist of: 1) choosing a lineage from which Jesus' salt of DNA would come; 2) making a covenant of salt with that lineage in order to preserve Abraham's seed from corruption and decay, and; 3) provide the laws and commandments to accomplish the purpose of said covenant. In detail, these steps are:

4:A — Step 1: Choose a Lineage From Which Jesus Would Come

In order to redeem man, the Son of God chose to join the human family by taking upon Himself the burden of the salt of DNA that originated from Adam (cf. 1 Cor. 15:45, Lk. 3:23-38) and has been passed along to ALL succeeding generations of man. The reason it was essential for Jesus to take on Adam's DNA will become clearer as we proceed through the book. Since God ordained to use matter to redeem matter, His plan had to take into account and rectify the problem of fallen Adam's corrupted seed. God planned to "find" a just and righteous man. Then, through a covenant of salt (of DNA) with him, protect the succeeding generations of his seed from irreparable corruption until such time as the intended mother of Jesus, i.e. Mary, through the overshadowing of the Holy Spirit, could provide the Son of God with an unblemished and perfect copy of the salt of DNA. Later in the book we will talk much more about what I am about to say, but suffice it to say, the Holy Spirit works through multiplication of what is judged by God to be good (as was man in his pre-fallen state). Ergo, in order for Mary's DNA to have been multiplied, thus bringing forth the body of Jesus, God must have judged it to be perfectly good.

God chose to make the aforementioned salt covenant with Abraham. Why Abraham? Scripture tells us, "And he believed the LORD; and he reckoned it to him as righteousness" (Gen. 15:6) and, "I have chosen him, that he may charge his children and his household after him to keep the way of the LORD by doing righteousness and justice; so that the LORD may bring to Abraham what he has promised him." (Genesis 18:19). God chose Abraham because he was a righteous and just man whose seed was worthy of preserving and multiplying. Key to understanding this passage is the direct link between, 1) **do**ing righteousness and justice by succeeding generations of Abraham's seed, on the one hand, with, 2) **so that** the promise made to Abraham could be fulfilled. What was the promise? To build a great nation through which all nations would obtain blessing (Gen. 18:18), and bring forth from his seed the Messiah (cf. Mt 1:1-2, 1:17).

I used to wonder why an eternally loving God could be so *seemingly* cruel as to test the righteousness of Abraham by commanding him to kill his only son (born of his wife, Sara, that is). One day I received an insight that answered my question. Essentially, God was saying this: *if you love me so much that you would not deny me anything — even to the extent of offering to me your son, Isaac, who you love greatly and is your own flesh and blood, then I will withhold nothing from you and your seed. From your seed I will give to man my Only-Begotten Son, whom I love infinitely, to sacrifice Himself on a tree for man and raise him up.*

The significance of Abraham's obedience to God should not be underestimated. Obedience speaks volumes about a person's righteousness and love for God. In a homily, Pope Benedict XVI on April 23, 2009, said that obedience to the will of God is an unmistakable sign of an intimate union with him.[65] After passing the test and proving himself with heroic virtue, God entered into a covenant with Abraham, and the first step in God's plan was completed.

4:B — Step 2: Make a Covenant to Protect and Preserve the Lineage

What is a covenant? In the non-Biblical sense, a covenant is a binding agreement, a contract, between two or more persons. In the Biblical sense, a covenant is <u>much</u> more: it is a solemn oath ('sacratemtum' in Latin) and a gift of persons.[66] To help us appreciate the wide gap in the relative gravity of a civil covenant versus a Divine/Sacramental covenant, Dr. Scott Hahn tells us that the Trinity is a covenant relationship of three Persons in one God.[67] A covenant is, therefore, a "family" oath, as can be seen by the very names given to the Persons of the Trinity, i.e. Father, Son, and Spirit. A covenant forms a sacred kinship with God.[68] Being in a covenantal relationship with God is the very means by which we are able to become sons and daughters of God. A type of this covenant is matrimony. A Sacramental marriage (as opposed to a civil marriage) is a covenant through which a man and a woman become *one-flesh* (Mt. 19:5-6, Mk. 10:8). Subsequent sections of this book will show how, through a Sacramental marriage, the one-flesh relationship between a man and woman is more literal than previously thought.

So why a covenant? Why a chosen people? Why circumcision as the sign of that covenant? Without a covenant, mankind had been and would continue to be, virtually incapable of resisting Satan's power. In fact, God told Hildegard that <u>*virtually all*</u> of Adam's seed, up until the time of the first covenants with Abraham and Moses (and the giving of the Law), had been devoured by Satan. Without a covenant, Abraham's seed could not be preserved from corruption, decay, and death until the fullness of time had been reached.[69]

The purpose and goal of the covenant with Abraham can be ascertained by examining the very sign that God chose to sacramentally (small "s") initiate someone into that covenant. It is interesting that immediately upon making a covenant with Abraham directly relating to his seed, God establishes as the sign of that covenant the permanent alteration of the very instrument through which his seed is given. When I was younger, I remember thinking to myself — why circumcision? That is a dramatic sign for God to choose! I can imagine what went through the minds of Abraham's kin — *You want me to do WHAT! Thanks for the offer Abe, but I'm not so sure I want to be "chosen" after all. How about if I just carve 'God's chosen' on my forehead or cut off one of my fingers instead?*

Instituted at the command of God himself, circumcision possessed a sacramental nature for the Israelite nation.[70] Circumcision was replaced by the NC sacrament of Baptism. Thus, it follows that circumcision, a 'type' of Baptism, was also sacramental in nature. Aquinas tells us that a sacrament is an outward sign of an inward effect.[71] What does the visible and outward sign of circumcision tell us about its inward effect? The inner effects revealed by water in Baptism are purification and a mystical one-body union with Jesus, thus becoming a member of the Bride of Christ, his Church. This is what circumcision represents; the salt (of DNA) covenant with Abraham is ordained by God to preserve the body, heart, and seed of man from impurity (cf. Rom. 2:25, 28-29; Col. 2:11). That circumcision was performed on the only organ capable of making a *fruitful* one-flesh union with a spouse possible makes its symbolism even clearer. St. Paul writes, "Real circumcision is a matter of the heart, spiritual and not literal" (Rom. 2:29). Real circumcision is purity of heart. However, as we will learn later, the physical body changes so that it *accurately* expresses the overflow of the heart. As the heart is purified, the body is purified; as the body is purified, the seed of man is purified (a fact of science that will be discussed at a later time).

Medical literature regarding circumcision gives us some insight into the sacramental nature of this Law. Dr. Brian J. Morris from the School of Medical Sciences and Bosch Institute at the University of Sydney describes the uncircumcised male sex organ as an environment that favors the growth of harmful micro-organisms and the build-up of dead cells, excretions, and urine. Furthermore, the harmful effects of this environment are passed along to any sexual partners.[72] He goes on to say that circumcision virtually eliminates cases of invasive penile cancer and significantly reduces the incidence of inflammation of the penile head, urinary tract infections, sexually transmitted infections, and general urological problems, to name a few out of many possible examples.[73]

It is extremely significant for God to choose an outward sign that physically alters and affects the male organ. After all, it is through this sex organ that man's seed is given to the woman. Recall that the covenant with Abraham only involved the seed, not the egg. Women do not carry seeds within them, so God did not deem it necessary for them to receive the sign of the covenant, i.e. circumcision. So what does all of this mean? We know that an uncircumcised man is much more likely than is a circumcised man to transmit sickness via impurity and contamination to his partner during the act of procreation. Jesus likened sin to a physical sickness that requires the attention of a physician (Lk. 5:30-32). By choosing circumcision as the outward sign of the covenant, God is telling the Israelites that when they are sick (with sin), their seed is also sick. Thus the child conceived will inherit that "sickness".[74] Luke warns us about this, "For no good tree bears bad fruit, nor again does a bad tree bear good fruit; for each tree is known by its own fruit" (Lk. 6:43). We will talk about this in much greater depth later in this book. Through the covenant and the Law, God preserved His people — as long as they obeyed His commandments and Laws — from contracting deadly spiritual and physical sickness which would have spread to Abraham's seed, and to succeeding generations.

According to St. Catherine of Siena, the inner heart is constantly changing; it is always moving closer to, or away from, God; towards virtue or towards vice.[75] A basic tenet of STOSS is this: as the degree of purity of the inner heart changes, the function of the salt of DNA changes in order to accurately express the overflow of that heart. Further, this change in DNA function will lead to a biological impact on the germ-line DNA (the actual copy of the salt of DNA contained in the sperm and egg), which will then be 'given' to the newly conceived child. Scripture, science, and other credible writings provide us with enough evidence supporting this statement that we could characterize it as summarizing a theorem. We will be referencing many sources later in the book.

Once God chose the lineage from which the Son of God would become a man, the final steps in the process towards the "fullness of time" were comprised of those necessary to preserve Jesus' future seed from irreparable corruption during the time spanning from Abraham to Mary. To accomplish this He gave the chosen people the Law and the Commandments.

4:C — Step 3: Provide the Law to Fulfill the Covenant

As we learned from Pope Benedict's earlier quote, obedience was critical for the Israelites. Aquinas tells us the Law given to the Jews in the OT repressed concupiscence.[76] Concupiscence is a state whereby the appetites of the flesh are in conflict with the desires of the spirit (the inner heart and intellect).[77] Thus, obedience to the Law would repress the rebelliousness of the flesh (salt of DNA) against the soul.

The use of salt in Old Testament offerings to God, such as sin offerings and grain offerings, are part of the sacraments of the Mosaic Law.[78] According to one rabbi, the use of salt in sin offerings, and all other offerings of the Israelites was indicative of its preserving power along with the spiritual implications of which it foretold.[79] Later, it will be shown how the use of salt in Jewish offerings is intended as a sign conspicuously pointing out that we must intimately unite our own sacrifices with the physical (salt of DNA) and spiritual sufferings of Jesus on the cross (cf. Gal. 2:20). Thus by dying with him, we will rise with him — one in body.

God preserved the Israelite's salt of DNA from decay and corruption by giving them a strict code of behavior and by severely punishing disobedience ... even unto death. As we progress through this book it will become more apparent why, in order to preserve Abraham's seed from corruption, sin was dealt with swiftly, necessarily, and severely. Furthermore, we will learn why enemies of Israel and those not of the covenant were judged seemingly more harshly than those in the covenant, and why separation from the "unclean" or the evil was also commanded. Scripture tells us, "Beware lest there be among you a man or woman or family or tribe, whose heart [*the body changes in order to accurately reflect the overflow of the heart*] turns away this day from the Lord our God to go and serve the gods of those nations; lest there be among you a root bearing poisonous and bitter fruit, one who, when he hears the words of this sworn covenant, blesses himself in his heart, saying, 'I shall be safe, though I walk in the stubbornness of my heart.' This would lead to the sweeping away of moist and dry alike" (Deut. 29:18-19). What does the "moist" and "dry" in the above passage mean? According to Rabbis Moshe Shamah and Ronald Barry, these two terms serve as a symbol for the righteous and the wicked respectively (cf. Isa. 58:11; Jer. 17:6-8; Ez. 19:12-13; Ps. 1:3-4), thus indicating the sinners discussed in this passage would bring destruction to all — both the evil and the good of the nation of Israel — alike.[80]

In Part III & IV of STOSS, you will see just how profoundly salt of DNA and created (aka material) light (cf. Mt. 5:13-14) affects not only us, but also our 'neighbors' as well. Arguably, we could state the following: if God had not been so harsh (cruel, as some foolish people might say) on OT man, the seed of Abraham could not have been preserved from irreparable damage. Thus, the Son of God — our Redeemer — would not (could not??) have come into the world **as a member of the family of man**, the entirety of which was in need of redemption.

4:D — Step 4: In the Plan, Allow for the Functional Change of Our Salt of DNA?

The very fact that God formulated a plan to preserve the seed of Abraham from *irreparable* corruption indicates that salt of DNA is subject to change in structure or function. Can it change? With scientific certainty, the short answer to this question is yes. As it turns out, God is an infinitely intelligent designer. The instruction manual (aka DNA) written for building and maintaining bodies is, metaphorically speaking, written in pencil. Furthermore, he gave us an eraser! We have already touched on the fact of the body changing to accurately reflect and express the inner heart of man. We will go into greater detail in subsequent sections of the book. Let us look at some other reasons God would design a body with the inherent ability to change.

Following his command to be fruitful and multiply (which was never revoked in any subsequent covenant, including the NC), God knew we would eventually populate many different geographical areas of the planet. He knew that we would encounter a multitude of environments and have to cope with different environmental challenges. He designed our salt of DNA to change and adapt in order to survive and thrive, despite environmental changes/challenges. For example, the genes of people living in high altitude environments would have to function differently than the genes of those living in a low altitude environment. The air in high altitudes contains less oxygen than in lower elevations. Consequently, hypoxia would develop if genes had not altered their function in order to compensate for living in a low oxygen environment. Indigenous dwellers in three different high altitude environments (Andeans, Tibetans, and Ethiopians) have experienced three unique genetic adaptations that allow them to function in their respective severe climates.[81]

God went one-step further. In addition to environment, He

51

also designed our DNA to react and adapt to our behavior —
even to what we think about. The acronym I use to describe this
phenomenon is BEIRBO, an acronym of Behavioral and
Environmental Input w/Reactive Biological Output. Is there
any scriptural evidence to support this belief? In Genesis
30:25-36 we read of Jacob's colored rods or, as I like to call
them, his BEIRBO rods. After working for Laban (the father of
his future bride, Rachel) and greatly multiplying his flocks of
sheep, Jacob agreed to take as his wages the spotted, striped,
speckled, and black sheep of Laban's flocks. Unbeknownst to
Jacob, however, Laban instructed his sons to sequester all of
those types of sheep far away from all the others so that only
white sheep remained. Let's pick up the story from there. We
read:

> Then Jacob took fresh rods of poplar and almond and
> plane, and peeled white streaks in them, exposing the
> white of the rods. He set the rods which he had peeled
> in front of the flocks in the runnels, that is, the watering
> troughs, where the flocks came to drink. And since they
> bred when they came to drink, the flocks bred in front of
> the rods and so the flocks brought forth striped,
> speckled, and spotted. And Jacob separated the lambs,
> and set the faces of the flocks toward the striped and all
> the black in the flock of Laban; and he put his own
> droves apart, and did not put them with Laban's
> flock. Whenever the stronger of the flock were breeding
> Jacob laid the rods in the runnels before the eyes of the
> flock, that they might breed among the rods, but for the
> feebler of the flock he did not lay them there; so the
> feebler were Laban's, and the stronger Jacob's. (Gen.
> 30:37-42).

TALLY UPDATE:

8. DNA "software" (detailed later) is altered, thus altering function through what is known as epigenetic plasticity. Scripture references to clay also refer to this phenomenon (e.g. Job 33:6, Sir. 33:13, Jer. 18:16, Is. 45:9, and many others);
9. epigenetic change can be altered by both environment and individual behavior;
10. Genes whose function has been altered by epigenetic methylation can be passed on to succeeding generations — up to the third or fourth generation (Ex 20:5, 34:7; Num. 14:18; Deut. 5:9).

Cumulative Score:

God: 10

Adherents of Scientism: 0

Without question, Scripture is pointing to the fact that environment affects the germline DNA (the copy of DNA in the sperm and egg cells) that goes to a sheep's offspring. Scripture is describing a process we now know as epigenetic modification, which affects a gene's function, but not its architecture. Epigenetic modification and inheritance by succeeding generations of offspring are not speculative science. Very many experiments have proven its validity. Researchers at the University of California — Santa Cruz, using fluorescent labels, were actually able to watch the process occur. Details of this experiment were published in the Sept. 19, 2014, issue of *Science* (see endnote for Journal Source).[82] It's important to note that the basic function of DNA is the same across all species. The differences are the genes contained within the DNA of each species. Using automobiles as an analogy, we could say that all cars function about the same. They all have engines to propel them, tires that allow for locomotion, a steering wheel to guide them, etc. What varies from one make of car to another are the types, styles, and functions of the various engines, tires, and steering wheels incorporated into each design. The story of Jacob's colored BEIRBO rods (as I like to refer to them) is equally applicable to man.

It is worth noting that BEIRBO can — both biologically and spiritually — work either 'for' or 'against' our benefit. Through holy desire and receptivity to God's abundant graces received in the Sacraments, we can overcome temptation and our body's sinful appetites. These sensual appetites are controlled by genetic "thermostats" (aka genetic and epigenetic switches). Grace purifies both our inner hearts and our outer bodies (the two are inextricably linked). Consequently, our genetic thermostats are "lowered" and our sensual appetites become gradually weaker. If, however, we give in to temptation, the functioning of our salt of DNA will change such that the truth of Jesus' words will ring true. He tells us, "Truly, truly, I say to you, every one who commits sin is a slave to sin" (Jn. 8:34). God revealed to St. Hildegard, when we engage in vice, we actually nourish our flesh, i.e. make it stronger, but not in a good way.[83] Whatever we nourish/feed grows and becomes stronger. Whatever we starve becomes weaker. Jesus is telling us: when we feed sinful appetites, those appetites become stronger and enslave us. Another aspect of BEIRBO is this: changes can occur as a result of an environment that includes both our personal behavior and also the behavior of others in our environment. Let's look at just four (two involving our own behavior and two involving the behavior of others) of many available examples of the principal of BEIRBO in action:

1) Researchers at Wake Forest University Baptist Medical Center wanted to find out the effects of cocaine use on the genome. They chose monkeys as the subjects because the genetic and behavioral similarities with humans are

significant. They used a state-of-the-art "proteomic" technology that allows researchers to compare the proteome (all proteins produced by genes at a given time) between two groups of monkeys, one that self-administered cocaine and the other that did not. By way of background, proteins are what genes produce. Proteins are the "chemical language" of our DNA. A protein is a "messenger" delivering instructions that tell cells or the genes within cells, to start or stop a particular action — to build or destroy something. According to lead researcher Nilesh Tannu, M.D., as a consequence of the cocaine usage, the changes to the structure, functioning, and communications of neurons (types of cells) within the brain of the subjects were very significant and were not prone to reversal.[84] Changing the structure, metabolism, and signaling of the neuron could only be accomplished by altering the very function of our salt of DNA — all the way down to the molecular and quantum level. As can be seen through our next study, the conclusions reached from this research are applicable to other types of addictions such as pornography, alcoholism, gambling, smoking etc.

2) Researchers at the University of Texas demonstrated how addictions change the functioning of our DNA and do so permanently. Starting with a single dose of an addictive drug, a protein identified as ΔFosB (delta Fos B) begins to be produced by our salt of DNA and is accumulated in the neurons. Every time the drug(s) are used it causes more ΔFosB to be stored in the cells. When a sufficient quantity is present, a genetic switch is flipped that, more or less, permanently alters which genes are expressed (turned on) and which ones are not (turned off). As a consequence of this functional change, the brain's system for handling dopamine (the "reward" hormone associated with addictions) is irreversibly damaged. This process is not limited to drug addictions. Repeated activities such as

jogging and consumption of sugared drinks also lead to accumulation of ΔFosB and permanent changes to the dopamine system.[85]

3) Scientists from the Max Planck Institute of Psychiatry in Munich studied the effects of repeated and/or severe abuse on both children and adults victims. Of the approximately 2,000 subjects tested, approximately one-third of them had been found to have experienced an epigenetic change to the FKBP5 gene as a direct result of the abuse (other illnesses were ruled out as a potential cause). The FKBP5 gene regulates the stress hormone system within the body. Interestingly, researchers believe that these abuse-responsive changes to the function of the FKBP5 gene and the resultant stress hormone system dysfunction would likely last for the rest of the victim's life (see endnote for Journal Source).[86] While this particular study did not ascertain whether or not the malfunction was passed on to succeeding generations, a great number of other studies have shown that epigenetic changes to DNA are frequently inherited by succeeding generations of each subject's offspring.

4) In our previously cited study, we talked about the effects of severe abuse of children within the family unit. The question arises: does mild to moderate family problems (e.g. argumentative environment, some emotional abuse, lack of affection, etc.) encountered on a chronic basis also lead to genetic-based developmental changes? A study was conducted by the University of Cambridge and the Medical Research Council Cognition and Brain Sciences Unit. Researchers found that children between birth and 11 years old who were exposed to this challenging environment developed a smaller cerebellum (area of the brain associated with sensory-motor control, stress regulation, and skill learning). According to the study's leader, Dr.

Nicholas Walsh, this finding is significant because childhood adversities are the biggest risk indicator for the development of psychiatric illness in later life. Interesting to note is this: adolescents whose exposure to similar environments did not begin until around the age of 14 actually developed larger cerebellums than normal, as seen when they were scanned 3-4 years after onset. This seems to indicate a possible inoculating effect that helps these teenagers to better cope with stress in their later life (see endnote for Journal Source).[87]

Scripture is not silent about the negative physical consequences of sin or the positive physical consequences of virtue. Examples of negative consequences are:

- "For any one who eats and drinks without discerning the body eats and drinks judgment upon himself. That is why many of you are weak and ill, and some have died" (1 Cor. 11:29-30). Sounds like some serious physical consequences for the sin of receiving our Lord in the Eucharist unworthily.

- "For thy arrows have sunk into me, and thy hand has come down on me. There is no soundness in my flesh because of thy indignation; there is no health in my bones because of my sin" (Ps. 38:2-3).

Now let's look at some passages that indicate positive physical effects of following God's laws. We read:

- "My son, do not forget my teaching, but let your heart keep my commandments; for length of days and years of life and abundant welfare will they give you" (Prov. 3:1-2);

- "Be not wise [*prideful*] in your own eyes; fear the Lord, and turn away from evil. It will be healing to your flesh and refreshment to your bones" (Prov. 3:7-8).

TALLY UPDATE (again):

11. Following God's laws will affect us spiritually AND physically ... right down to the molecular level; not following God's laws will have the opposite effects (see below for a small sampling of these types of studies).

Cumulative Score:

God: 11

Adherents of Scientism: 0

Let's look at some examples from existing science of the positive consequences indirectly referred to in the last two Scripture passages:

• According to Dr. Herbert Benson, many physical ailments are linked to stress; heart attacks, severe headaches, back problems, and depression to name a few. Methods employed that induce relaxation are helpful in counteracting stress and its resultant physical dysfunction. He cites the recitation of the rosary as a perfect way to accomplish this goal.[88]

• Forgiveness is a virtue that, according to recent research, leads to very positive physical consequences. For example, being a forgiving person can lead to: A) a drop in the production of the stress hormone, cortisol; B) a strengthening of the immune system; C) reduction of back and stomach problems; and D) reduction in the hormones that contribute to anger, depression, and many other negative emotions.[89]

• Fasting is a recommended practice in Scripture (e.g. Judges 20:26, 1 Sam. 7:6, 2 Sam. 1:12, Is. 58:6). According to the American Heart Association, approximately 33% of adult Americans suffer from some sort of heart-related disease. In a study conducted by Benjamin Horne at the Intermountain Medical Center in Utah, it was discovered that people who fasted (abstain from all food for around 24 hours) on a regular basis were 39% less likely to suffer from heart-related health problems. Researchers looked at the health records of approximately 5,000 patients who had undergone x-ray examinations to detect the presence or absence of coronary artery disease. They found that those who fasted regularly, whether for religious reasons (e.g. Mormons) or not (e.g. for health-conscious reasons), seemed to receive some sort of heart-protective benefit.[90]

Let's look at the phenomenon of BEIRBO in real life. First, we must ask: what is the epigenome? Literally translated, the word means "above the genome". To help visualize the role of the epigenome, think in terms of our DNA as being a computer. DNA and the genes within it are the hardware of the computer; the epigenome is the software that tells the hardware what to do. It's the epigenome that tells the cells to divide and what types of cells they are to become (heart cells, muscle cells, etc.). It's the epigenome that turns on the genes needed for a heart cell, for example, to function as a heart cell should. Conversely, it silences the genes (tells them to stop making proteins) that aren't necessary to a properly functioning heart cell (see: https://www.genome.gov/27532724/). According to Drs. Carlo

Ventura and Rollin McCraty, organic chemistry is an integral part of the epigenetic phenomenon but so also is physical energy, e.g. light, magnetic fields and sound vibrations. This process is controlled by a complex interaction between cell signaling, environment, and a non-stop remodeling of (what used to be thought of as junk) DNA into a seemingly endless array of loops and domains. In experiments performed by Dr. Ventura and his team, they were able to change cell chemistry and program stem cells to become beating cardiac cells using extremely low-frequency magnetic fields (magnetic waves run perpendicular to electron waves as part of electromagnetic energy).[91]

TALLY UPDATE:

12. Electromagnetic energy (light) and sound waves (e.g. voice) significantly impact cell function (the visitation of Mary to her cousin Elizabeth is just one of many examples in Scripture);

Cumulative Score:

God: 12

Adherents of Scientism: 0

Manel Estellar of the Spanish National Cancer Center in Madrid wanted to find out how much epigenetic change occurred because of life experiences. He and his team gathered DNA samples from forty pairs of identical twins ranging in age from 3 to 74. In a study of this nature, subjects that are identical twins are very important for gaining an accurate understanding of the role of environment on epigenetic plasticity. Identical twins share the exact same DNA with each other. You could say that identical twins are genetic clones of each other. Consequently, if the identical twins develop different outer appearances, e.g. one is fat while the other is skinny, then it is most likely the result of epigenetic modification of gene function, <u>not</u> structural changes to the genes themselves. Falling back on our previous analogy, the two twins have the same computer hardware, but the software running the computers has somehow changed, producing different effects.

After a detailed process that rendered genes that were turned off to be seen as a particular color, researchers performed a side-by-side analysis of the DNA from each of the two twins. They repeated this process for each set of twins. The results were far from subtle. When twins are still very young, the proteins made by their genes are virtually identical. By the age of three, as a direct result of behavior and environment, small changes in the functioning of their genes started to occur. As they aged, however, life-experiences caused their epigenome to change so dramatically that by time the twins reached an older age, hardly any of the genes turned "on" in one twin were also "on" in the other.[92] This is Jacob's colored BEIRBO rods in action. Other than the example of Jacob's rods, does Scripture support the concept of BEIRBO? I believe that it does. By examining the usage of garments, robes, etc. in Scripture, we can see a very particular reason the Holy Spirit uses these metaphors to describe man's salt of DNA, i.e. our flesh.

4:E — Garments, Robes, Bodies and the Flesh

Let's continue our biblical analysis of STOSS by examining the case for the belief that Scripture references to flesh, robes, and garments are usually referring to the body ("clothes" of the spirit, so to speak) i.e. the salt of DNA. As we tackle this subject, and throughout our continuing exploration of STOSS, we will begin to realize just how important is the fact that we are an embodied spirit that is in the image and likeness of a Triune God. He gave us a body for a much deeper reason than meets the finite eye.[93] Another theme that will begin to emerge from our examination of references to garments, robes, bodies, and flesh is this: the endeavor to achieve perfection of the human person is a joint endeavor of the body and soul — one cannot be perfected separately from, or to a different degree than the other. In OT times, all garments were made of organic material, i.e. the cells of organisms containing the salt of DNA of whatever animal from which the clothes came. There were no synthetic materials in those days.

In the parable of the marriage feast (a *type* of the Eucharistic celebration), Jesus says, "But when the king came in to look at the guests, he saw there a man who had no wedding garment; and he said to him, 'Friend, how did you get in here without a wedding garment?' And he was speechless. Then the king said to the attendants, 'Bind him hand and foot, and cast him into the outer darkness; there men will weep and gnash their teeth'" (Mt. 22:11-13). The wedding garment that is referred to in this parable is a body washed clean of the guilt of sin (cf. Is. 61:10-11) via Baptism and, thereafter, Reconciliation. Relating the words of God, St. Catherine writes, "[the soul] will re-clothe herself on the Last Day of Judgment, in the *garments of her own flesh* ... [SML]. Wherefore, know that the glorified body can pass through a wall, and that neither water nor fire can injure it, not by virtue of itself, but by virtue of the soul."[94] And also, "Do you [believe you can] be admitted to the marriage feast in foul and disordered garments ... you must leave mortal sin by a holy confession [*aka reconciliation*], contrition of heart, satisfaction, and purpose of amendment. Then you will throw off that hideous and defiled garment."[95]

There are passages in Scripture that seem to apply directly to DNA, but without actually using the word "salt." For example, St. Paul writes, "But God gives it a body as he has chosen, and to each kind of seed its own body. For not all flesh is alike, but there is one kind for men, another for animals, another for birds, and another for fish" (1 Cor. 15:38-39). I think it is reasonable to assume that when St. Paul uses the word "flesh", he is really talking about the salt of DNA that builds, maintains, and directs the functioning of the different types of cells that comprise the varieties of flesh he describes.

The overriding scriptural theme associated with the words "garment" and "robe" is this: if you want to come into the presence of God, your garment, i.e. your body (in unison with the *inner* heart) must be clean (e.g. Num. 8:7, 21). Our flesh/garment/robe was made by God to be changeable or washable so that it can accurately reflect the increasing or decreasing purity of our inner heart. Contrast this with the many Scripture references to a hard heart or a heart of stone, which indicates a heart that the possessor stubbornly refuses to change. Let's look at a couple examples of the contextual use of garments and robes, relative to the presence of the Lord, in Scripture. It is written:

1) "And the Lord said to Moses, 'Go to the people and consecrate them today and tomorrow, and let them wash their garments, and be ready by the third day; for on the third day the Lord will come down upon Mount Sinai in the sight of all the people'" (Exodus 19:10-11);

2) "So Jacob said to his household and to all who were with him, 'Put away the foreign gods that are among you, and purify yourselves, and change your garments; then let us

arise and go up to Bethel, that I may make there an altar to the God who answered me in the day of my distress and has been with me wherever I have gone'" (Genesis 35:2-3).

The parallels between this last passage and the NC are striking. The word "Bethel" means house of God;[96] the NC house of God is the rebuilt Temple, i.e. the resurrected and glorified body of Jesus (Jn. 2:19-21). Furthermore, we become one body with the Temple through Baptism, through which we are purified and our garments are changed (cf. Eph. 2:15, 4:24). In his lectures on the mystery of Baptism, St. Cyril of Jerusalem (a Doctor of the Church) writes, "For since the adverse powers made their lair in your members [*body*], you may no longer wear that old garment."[97] God, Himself, describes the body as being a garment. These are His words to St. Catherine of Siena: "I sent My Word, My own Son, _clothed_ [*SML*] in your own very nature, the corrupted clay of Adam."[98] The word "clay" is particularly germane to our current topic. The fact that clay can be changed, i.e. molded (just like clothes can be corrupted, washed, or changed) seems to indicate that our salt of DNA, together with biological water (biological water will be discussed in greater detail later in STOSS), has something to do with our garment's changeability.

Another example of clothing used to describe the salt of DNA is in Apocalypse. John writes, "These are they who have come out of the great tribulation; they have washed their robes and made them white in the blood of the Lamb" (Rev. 7:14). A verse similar to the one above is, "Blessed are those who wash their robes, that they may have the right to the tree of life and that they may enter the city by the gates" (Rev. 22:14). Foregoing any further discussion at this point, these two passages are directly referring to the New and eternal Covenant of salt between the Father, his only begotten and incarnate Son, and the Father's adopted children ... mankind.

CHAPTER 5 — OT SALT THEME #3: PURIFICATION

Absent the understanding that salt in Scripture refers to the salt of DNA, the very use of the word salt by Scripture writers would seem to be contradictory. In several passages (e.g. Dt. 29:23, Job 39:6, Ps. 107:34, Jer. 17:6) salt is used to describe a barren and lifeless wasteland. Scripture tells us how enemies, after capturing a land, would sow salt so that nothing would grow (e.g. Judges 9:45). In other passages, it is used to describe the source of goodness and purification (e.g. 2 Kgs. 2:20-21, Ez. 47:9, Mt. 5:13, and Mk. 9:50). How could this be? Every explanation I have ever read regarding salt in Scripture seems to be appropriate to only one of the two different contexts. The only way I am aware of to resolve this *seeming* contradiction is to realize that Scripture authors are writing about two different "states" of the same salt. The barren, death-producing salt is the corrupted salt of DNA of Adam and his seed. The purifying and life-giving salt is a foreshadowing of the salt that is to come — the salt of Jesus' DNA, which has never fallen. Even before understanding the deeper meaning of salt in Scripture, we knew that we needed purification. We knew that Jesus is the Redeemer. What is God trying to tell us by the contents of the time capsule containing salt?

5:A — Moses, Elijah, and the Holy Spirit

Beginning with this section and going forward, we will more earnestly begin assembling the building blocks that will provide us with a deeper understanding of that to which all of the OT points. All OT typology, either directly or indirectly, points to the final and eternal Covenant of Salt, aka the New Covenant. Both the salt of DNA of the incarnate Son of God and the salt of man play a vital and intimate role in this Covenant. Through this salt covenant with God, all mankind is capable of ...: 1) receiving an indwelling of the Holy Spirit and a gradual purification of body and soul; 2) becoming a body/soul that can send and receive grace;[99] 3) redemption of the body (Rom. 8:23); and, 4) becoming **true** sons and daughters (via adoption) of the Father, through the Son, and in the Holy Spirit. The integration of Scripture with science will enable us to vastly increase our understanding of this covenant. To further develop our understanding of #2 above, it will be essential to differentiate the types of graces God grants and whether or not there is an indwelling of the Holy Spirit. These distinctions will be explained later in the book.

When the Word of God took on the salt of DNA (a body), it necessarily followed that the Trinity (which includes the Holy Spirit) entered into physical creation in a very special way (cf. Col. 2:9). The Holy Spirit is the sanctifier/purifier of the heart of man. I believe the OT use of salt both directly and indirectly reveals to us the important role the salt of DNA plays in the expression and reception of grace and the indwelling of the Holy Spirit. Jesus himself tells us this is so. He says, "Truly, truly, I say to you, unless you eat the flesh of the Son of man and drink his blood, you have no life in you" (Jn. 6:53). The Holy Spirit is the life of the Trinity (cf. Rom. 4:17, 7:6, 8:2, 8:6-8).[100] It is only through the union of our salt of DNA with Jesus' salt of DNA in Baptism and the Eucharist that we receive the life of God, i.e. the Holy Spirit.

In the Transfiguration of Jesus (Mt. 17:3; Mk. 9:4), two prophets appeared with him in his glory. They were Moses and Elijah. Of all the OT prophets, why only these two? It seems to me that a special presence of the Holy Spirit, perhaps through a mysterious encounter with the Son of God, is the common thread that helps us to understand the link between Moses and Elijah. Scripture tells us that each of them gave some of "their" (possessive case) Holy Spirit to others, with some very dramatic results. In the case of Moses, we read, "Hear my words: If there is a prophet among you, I the Lord make myself known to him in a vision, I speak with him in a dream. Not so with my servant Moses; he is entrusted with all my house. With him I speak mouth to mouth, clearly, and not in dark speech; and he beholds the form of the Lord" (Num. 12:6-8). This intimate relationship was manifested through the exercise of great power by means of the staff of God, e.g. the parting of the Red Sea (Ex. 14:21). Elijah manifested the power of the Holy Spirit in equally powerful ways, such as parting the waters of the Jordan River with his sheepskin mantle (2 Kgs 2:8) and the resurrecting of a dead child (1 Kgs 17:21-22). John the Baptist, who was prominently linked to Elijah by Jesus, was one of the first persons to receive the Holy Spirit directly from the Word of God incarnate, i.e. Jesus (Lk. 1:41-44). It was John the Baptist who proclaimed the coming of the kingdom of God — the coming of the Holy Spirit through union with the Messiah.[101]

I am in good company in my belief that the common link between Moses, Elijah, and John the Baptist is the Holy Spirit. St. Augustine writes, "Whence it is also written of John [the Baptist], that he 'came in the spirit and power of Elias;' and by the spirit of Elias is meant the Holy Spirit, whom Elias received. And the same thing is to be understood of Moses when the Lord says to him, 'And I will take of thy spirit, and will put it upon them;' that is, I will give to them of the Holy Spirit, which I have already given to thee."[102] For the time being, we will divert our discussion on the topic of salt and purification to the story of Elijah's successor (Elisha) and to Ezekiel's prophetic dream of the New Covenant Temple.

In 2 Kgs 2:1-8, Scripture relates how Elisha faithfully followed his master, Elijah. Before Elijah is taken up in a chariot of fire, Elisha said, "I pray you, let me inherit a double share of your spirit" (2 Kgs. 2:9). Elijah is taken up and his mantle falls to the earth to be taken possession of by Elisha, who "took up the mantle of Eli′jah that had fallen from him, and went back and stood on the bank of the Jordan. Then he took the mantle of Eli′jah that had fallen from him, and struck the water, saying, 'Where is the Lord, the God of Eli′jah?' And when he had struck the water, the water was parted to the one side and to the other; and Eli′sha went over. Now when the sons of the prophets who were at Jericho saw him over against them, they said, 'The spirit of Eli′jah rests on Eli′sha'" (2 Kgs. 2:14-15). We again take up the story almost immediately after this event. We read,

> Now the men of the city said to Eli′sha, "Behold, the situation of this city is pleasant, as my lord sees; but the water is bad, and the land is unfruitful." He said, "Bring me a new bowl, and put salt in it." So they brought it to him. Then he went to the spring of water and threw salt in it, and said, "Thus says the Lord, I have made this water wholesome; henceforth neither death nor miscarriage shall come from it." So the water has been wholesome to this day, according to the word which Eli′sha spoke (2 Kgs. 2:19-22).

The new bowl symbolizes Jesus' body. The fact that it is a *new bowl* signifies that it is not Jesus' mortal body, but his glorified body, the body that has been resurrected from the dead. This body has been Divinized/Spiritualized through the Holy Spirit. This glorified body is transcendent — neither confined nor affected by material creation, space, or time. Contained in that "new bowl" is Jesus' salt of DNA.

When the men of the city complained to Elisha that the water was bad and it was causing the land to be unfruitful, Elisha pours the salt from the new bowl into the spring. Doing so, the water from the spring was made wholesome, life-giving, and fruitful. Pay attention to the similarities between the passages we just read, and our next passages, which are about Ezekiel's dream of the restored Temple. In Scripture, water is quite often linked somehow to the Holy Spirit and his life-giving, purifying actions within creation. What this act symbolizes is how the "old water" from the "old earth" will be purified in the "new earth", giving us Baptism of water and the Spirit. This gift comes through the new bowl containing salt, i.e. the resurrected salt of DNA of Jesus, from which we receive "Living Water".

How can salt purify water, especially in light of the next passages we will be discussing in which salt water is described as producing only death? How do we reconcile these passages? The answer is, as was stated previously, the salt which produces death represents <u>man's</u> salt of DNA, while the salt that Elisha used represents <u>Jesus'</u> salt of DNA through which the Holy Spirit, purifies and is fruitful.

5:B — Ezekiel: Water Flowing From the Temple

Rev. Mitch Pacwa is a well-known and well-respected Scripture scholar. On March 20th, 2007 he gave a homily that was broadcast on EWTN radio. His focus for the homily was a discussion of Ezekiel's prophetic dream (Ez. 47:1-12) of the restoration of the Temple that was destroyed by the Babylonians in the year 587 BC. In the narrative of the dream, Ezekiel describes an interesting feature of the restored Temple: he describes a fresh water river that flows out from the altar within the Temple and down through the desert, transforming everything in its path into a paradise rich in vegetation and life. It continues to flow onward to the Dead Sea which, as Pacwa describes it, is nine times saltier than the oceans. It is so salty that if you drink its water you will die. The high concentration of salt prevents life from surviving in or around it. It is utterly fruitless. Other rivers, such as the Jordan, flow into the Dead Sea but their waters immediately become salty. In Ezekiel's vision, however, the waters that flow from the restored Temple turn the salty water of the Dead Sea (aka Salt Sea) into sweet/pure/fresh water. As a result, its waters become fruitful and full of life, as does the land surrounding it. The Gospel reading for that same day was about a man paralyzed for thirty-eight years who couldn't make it to the healing waters of Bethesda, or Beth-zatha, as it is written in some manuscripts (Jn. 5:1-16). By explaining how the two readings complement each other, Pacwa made the case that the Temple in Ezekiel's vision was Jesus and that from Him would flow Living Water that heals the sick and transforms death into fruit-bearing life.[103]

I would like to take Pacwa's conclusions a step further. I believe the salt of the Dead Sea in Ezekiel's vision is really a representation of our fallen and disordered salt of DNA working together with our biological water, which Jesus will purify and return to life and fruitfulness when we become living stones built into that Temple (cf. 1 Pt. 2:4-5). The key to unlocking a better understanding of this vision is the Temple itself. It is the outer structure that houses God within. Jesus is clearly making the connection between the Temple and Himself. In Scripture, we read, "Jesus answered them, 'Destroy this temple, and in three days I will raise it up.' The Jews then said, 'It has taken forty-six years to build this temple, and will you raise it up in three days?' But *he spoke of the temple of his body* [*SML*]" (Jn. 2:19-21). It is through a one-flesh union with the Temple of his resurrected body and blood, fully united to His divinity, that our salt of DNA will be healed, purified, and given a new and fruitful life in the final Covenant of Salt (we will expand on covenants of salt in Part III). Ezekiel received a vision that shows us God's plan for the redemption of the soul *and* the body (cf. Rom. 8:23). Jesus' body is the Temple from which Living Water flows to purify our bodies. This is the reason He took upon himself our human nature. Through his resurrected salt of DNA he "lifts" us up to union with his crucified and glorified body. As we will see as we progress through this book, this union of our fallen salt with His resurrected and glorified salt *physically affects* our salt of DNA (redemption of the body) and sanctifies our inner heart.

While this ends our current discussion of the OT treatment of salt, we will be returning to these and other OT passages when we delve deeper into STOSS. Next, we will lay the foundations for a more in-depth understanding of the ramifications of STOSS. In Part II we will explore what it means to be in the image and likeness of God and how the salt of DNA is a necessary component of being thus created.

PART II — CREATED IN THE IMAGE AND LIKENESS OF GOD

To gain a fuller and deeper understanding of the implications of STOSS, it is necessary to first talk about two foundation stones upon which a greater understanding must rest. The first and most important foundation stone, the cornerstone of STOSS, is the Trinity in whose image and likeness man is created. The second foundation stone has to do with the scriptural meaning of the "mouth" of God, the "mouth" of man, and the role of expression in the one Divine Essence of God.

CHAPTER 6 — THE TRINITY: AN UNCEASING EXPRESSION IN LOVE

Being created in the image and likeness of the Trinity, we cannot know and understand ourselves and the reason we have been given a body without first gaining a deeper understanding of the Trinity. Nowhere in Scripture does it say we were created in the image and likeness of God ... *except for our bodies*. In fact, the opposite is true. In Genesis it is written, "So God created man in his own image, in the image of God he created him; male and female he created them (Gen. 1:27). It is absolutely impossible for us to gain anywhere near a comprehensive understanding of the Trinity. Entire books have been written on _each_ Person of the Trinity. Saints and scholars have endeavored to understand and communicate their understanding of God. All have fallen immeasurably short. Even the angels, with all of their knowledge, cannot fully understand the Trinity.[104] Nonetheless, God wants us to desire to know Him and to follow through on that desire, but to do so prayerfully and with humility. In this book, we will not be attempting to achieve anything approaching a comprehensive understanding of the Trinity. However, we will endeavor to gain sufficient knowledge upon which we can understand how it is that we, as embodied spirits, are in the image and likeness of God. We will focus our study on the eternal expressiveness and fruitfulness of a Trinitarian God's essence.

God is a Trinity of three Persons in an eternal and unceasing relationship. In other words, it is essentially a relationship that is alive. Better yet, it is a relationship that IS life.

Aquinas writes, "The very nature of God is goodness, as is clear from Dionysius (Div. Nom. i). Hence, what belongs to the essence of goodness befits God. But it belongs to the essence of goodness to communicate itself to others."[105] To restate: **God is goodness**, and it is the **nature of goodness to communicate itself** to others. Fr. Martin von Cochem writes:

> From all eternity, before anything was made, God magnified Himself, and the three divine Persons rejoiced in Their majesty and grandeur. God the Father magnified the unsearchable wisdom of His Son; God the Son magnified the bounteous goodness of the Holy [Spirit]; and God the Holy [Spirit] magnified the infinite power of the Eternal Father. This is shown in the revelations of St. Mechtilde, to whom Christ said: "If thou desirest to honor Me, praise and magnify Me in union with that most excellent glory wherewith the Father in His almighty power and the Holy Spirit in His loving-kindness have glorified Me from all eternity, in union with that supreme glory wherewith I in My unsearchable wisdom have glorified the Father and the Holy Spirit from all eternity, and wherewith the Holy Spirit in His ineffable goodness has magnified the Father and Me from all eternity."[106]

Notice that Christ, through St. Mechtilde, is copiously employing verbs to describe the Trinity. God is eternally expressing, doing, and communicating. St. Bonaventure of Bagnoregio (circa 1274) develops an understanding of the Trinity that re-volves around four themes. They are: 1) the theme of beatitude, goodness, charity, and joy. He tells us that these cannot be achieved in a God who does not pour himself out completely, indicating communication and plurality; 2) the theme of per-fection which entails the begetting of a Person of the same na-ture' i.e. Divine fruitfulness [Bonaventure, 1 *Sent*. D. 7, a.1, q. 2, concl.,;d. 27, 1, a. 1,q. 2, ad 3 (*Opera Omnia*, vol. 1, 139, 470)];[107] 3) the theme of simplicity, and; 4) the theme of primacy. From a metaphysical standpoint, primacy indicates the fullness of the source. This primacy designates the fruitfulness and the *"wellspringness"* of primordial reality.[108] God is pure act. There is nothing of Him that is potential. God *is* perfect and eternal.[109] He concludes, "In God, this fecundity [*fruitfulness, SML*] relative to God **can only exist in act [SML]** [Bonaventure, 1 *Sent*. d. 2, a. 1, q. 2, fund. 4 (*Opera Omnia*, vol. 1, 53]."[110]

'Magnifying', 'praising', and 'glorifying' are all expressions, acts of the will, and "do"ings. They are all expression, in the Holy Spirit, that constitute a relationship that is 'life'. Referring to John 1:18, Benedict XVI tells us, "Only the one who is God sees God — Jesus. He truly speaks from his vision of the Father, from unceasing dialogue with the Father [SML], a *dialogue that is his life* [SML]."[111] This is echoed in the great Amen at Mass. The priest raises the consecrated species and pronounces the doxology, "Through him, with him, and in him, in the unity of the Holy Spirit, all glory and honor is yours, almighty Father, for ever and ever." St. Hildegard writes, "For this life is *God, who is always in motion and constantly in action [SML]*."[112]

Is creation itself an expression of God? Scripture itself gives us the quick and short answer. In Genesis, we read, "Let us make man in our image, after our likeness" (Gen. 1:26, cf. 3:22-23). There is much that can be gleaned from these eleven words. This is not simply an idle conversation between the Three Persons of the Trinity. Firstly, they are in dialogue about creating, and the design of that creation. They are 'talking' about how we are to be created. Secondly, they are telling us that all three, Father, Son, and Holy Spirit, are involved in the creation event. The unity of the Trinity is such that, absolutely everything God does, is accomplished through the actions of all Three Persons.[113] Lastly, because all Three are involved, we can conclude that all creation is an expression of God in the Trinity.[114] Simply put, God speaks creation into existence.[115] The psalmist wrote, "For he spoke, and it came to be; he commanded, and it stood forth" (Ps. 33:9; cf. Ps. 33:6, 104:30). Also, "When I look at thy heavens, the work of thy fingers, the moon and the stars which thou hast established; what is man that thou art mindful of him … Thou hast given him dominion over the works of thy hands; thou hast put all things under his feet" (Ps. 8: 3-4, 6). All 'work' is an expression, whether it be God or man doing it. In the previous passages, the heavens are the work of God's fingers and all God's works are under the power of man. Since all creation is an expression of a Good God, it follows that creation reflects the intellect of God. In other words, creation was made ordered, reflecting all the perfections of that same God (cf. Ps. 19:1).[116]

Hildegard writes, "And why is he called the Word? Because he has awakened all creation by the resonance of God's voice and because he has called creation to himself! For whatever God expressed in a verbal way was ordered by the Word with his resonance, and whatever the Word ordered [*not as in commanded, but as in making harmonious, coherent, etc.*] was spoken by God once again in the Word."[117] The book of Wisdom tells us, "But thou hast arranged all things by measure and number and weight. For it is always in thy power to show great strength, and who can withstand the might of thy arm? Because the whole world before thee is like a speck that tips the scales, and like a drop of morning dew that falls upon the ground" (Wis. 11:20-22). Since the Son is begotten from all eternity (see Scripture passage below), then creation would, necessarily, have been expressed, through the Word, by God continually and unceasingly throughout all of created time. After all, it would be impossible for there to be a point in history that is not within the eternal 'now'. Also, take special note of the phrase, "whatever God expressed in a verbal way" in direct relation to creation. Let us look at a couple of examples in Scripture that help us to understand God as eternally expressing.

1) "He said to me, 'You are my son, today I have begotten you'" (Ps. 2:7). In the eternal 'now' of God, the Father is eternally and fruitfully begetting the Son, which would encompass all of creation ... in 'time';

2) "And this was why the Jews persecuted Jesus, because he did this on the sabbath. But Jesus answered them, 'My Father is working still, and I am working'" (Jn. 5:16-17). As I said earlier, *working* is also '<u>Do</u>ing' and all doings are expressions;

3) "Jesus said to them, 'Truly, truly, I say to you, the Son can do nothing of his own accord, but only what he sees the Father doing; for whatever he does, that the Son does likewise. For the Father loves the Son, and shows him all that he himself is doing'" (Jn. 5:19-20). Hmm. There's a lot of doing/expressing going on in this verse;

4) "I can do nothing on my own authority; as I hear, I judge; and my judgment is just, because I seek not my own will but the will of him who sent me" (Jn. 5:30), and;

5) "No longer do I call you servants, for the servant does not know what his master is doing; but I have called you friends, for all that I have heard from my Father I have made known to you" (Jn. 15:15). Doing, hearing, and befriending are all ways of expressing.

If God is an eternal dialogue among the three Persons of the Trinity, then we can ask the question: are all three Persons necessary for God to be God and for God to be Love? God tells St. Hildegard that if any one of the three Persons were missing, then God would not be God.[118] Ergo, God could not be Love. This is because the three Persons of the Trinity are one indivisible unity that CANNOT be separated. She writes, "In the Father is the Son, in both the Holy Spirit, and They are one, and work inseparably with each other ... They are undivided unity."[119] They are ... *together* ... Love! How does the body fit into our understanding of the whole image and likeness passage in Scripture? God is an eternal expression of Truth and Light in the Holy Spirit. So let's address the question of whether or not the human body is an essential part of that image and likeness.

6:A — The "Body": Is It Part of Being in the Image & Likeness of God?

Let's take a moment to reflect on the meaning of image and likeness. According to JPII, man's being in the image and likeness of God is due, not only, to the fact of our humanity (body and soul), but also to our being created as a communion of persons, i.e. male and female. From the very beginning, man consisted of this union of persons. As JP II so aptly points out, the very function of an image is to reproduce that which is being imaged. We are an image of a Living Triune God ... not a God of Three isolated Persons, each "keeping to themselves", so to speak, but of Three Persons in an active relationship, eternally expressing, eternally glorifying the other, eternally "do"ing together.[120]

JP II is telling us the purpose of 'image' is to reproduce its own prototype. To be in the likeness of God is for us to be fruitful, just as God is fruitful by means of communion and expression. I once wrote that men and women, through the conjugal union, co-create a person who is in the image and likeness of God. I received a response from someone who is knowledgeable in theological matters. Paraphrasing, he wrote that parents only provide a body. Into this body, God infuses a soul which, exclusively (having intellect and free will), is in the image and likeness of God. This is a widely held belief, but is it right? Both recent and past theology indicate this view falls short of the mark.

The belief that the whole man — body and soul — is necessary for man to be in the image and likeness of God extends all the way back to the time of the early Church Fathers. St. Irenaeus (circa 125-202), in defending against the errors of the Gnostics, took on the subject of whether or not the body was part of being in the image and likeness of God. The Gnostics believed that the entire image and likeness of God was in the *nous* (intellect) of man, and the body is merely a transitory vessel of little or no importance.[121] To the contrary, Irenaeus' interpretation of Genesis chapter one is this: the entire body and soul are intended as a necessary part of being in the image and likeness of God.[122] St. Irenaeus' writings concerning the importance of the body as part of man's creation in the image and likeness of God is still relevant today given the fact that most modern theologies based on the writings of Thomas Aquinas still locate the image and likeness of God solely in the faculties of intellect and will. As we will see later, this understanding is not accurate.[123] Another saint who believed the whole man is necessary to be in the image and likeness of God is St. Paschasius Radbertus. He is largely responsible for writings that later led to the formulation of the doctrine of Transubstantiation. There is much more information on this saint in Appendix A.

Before moving on, I want to give you a little background on the International Theological Commission (ITC). This commission produced the work titled, COMMUNION AND STEWARDSHIP: *Human Persons Created in the Image of God.* The ITC is a Vatican commission which consists of 30 theologians who are appointed by the pope to serve renewable five-year terms. Its function is to study doctrinal issues, write reports on those studies, and advise the Magisterium of the Church, especially the Congregation of the Doctrine of the Faith. The ITC is a theological heavyweight at the Vatican. The ITC cannot claim infallibility, but when the ITC speaks ... the Church listens and seriously considers. The ITC, after numerous meetings of its sub-commissions and plenary sessions taking place between the years 2000 and 2002, approved the aforementioned text *in forma specifica.* It was submitted it to Joseph Cardinal Ratzinger (later elected Pope Benedict XVI) who approved it for publication and distribution.[124]

The ITC acknowledged that man's creation in the image of God is central to biblical revelation (cf. Gen. 1:26f; 5:1-3; 9:6) and that man cannot be understood apart from an understanding of the mystery of God.[125] According to the ITC, It is the entirety of man (both body and rational soul) that constitutes a person in the image and likeness of God. Locating the image in a particular aspect of man, e.g. his intellect or sexual nature, would be wrong. Further, both dualism and monism are to be avoided when considering man's nature. The physical, social, and spiritual aspects of man are to be considered as one single dimension of a man created in the image and likeness of God.[126] Further, "Present day theology is striving to overcome the influence of dualistic anthropologies that locate the *imago Dei* exclusively with reference to the spiritual aspect of human nature."[127] When we couple this with our understanding of God as three persons in an eternal living relationship of fruitful expression, we can understand a little better how the body is important to that *imago Dei*. Scripture makes it quite clear that, like the Trinity itself, man is a relational being. The ITC writes, "According to this conception, man is not an isolated individual but a person — an essentially relational being [*cf. Gen. 2:18*]."[128]

Jesus Christ incarnate is the perfect image of God (2 Cor. 4:4; Col. 1:15; Heb. 1:3).[129] Adam was not the prototype of man, it was Jesus who was the prototype. Adam was made in Jesus' image and likeness. Fallen man's transformation back to the image of the Son occurs through the sacraments which strengthen and confirm us in this radical transformation.[130] According to the ITC, "Jesus redeems us through every act he performs in his body."[131]

6:B — The Holy Spirit: Inexpressible, but Prompting Expression

Since the body is an inseparable part of man's being in the image and likeness of God, it can be surmised that its function as the temple of the Holy Spirit (1 Cor. 6:19) is no small matter. I offer this brief reflection on the third Person of the Trinity. This will better equip us to tackle our next two main sections, i.e. the body's role in the work of the Holy Spirit and the meaning of "mouth" in Scripture as it relates to both God and man.

In addition to the Son, did the Father also beget the Holy Spirit? According to Durrwell, the answer is no.[132] He says the Holy Spirit is inexpressible. If the Spirit were able to be expressed, He would have been another *begotten Word*, just as is the Son. The Holy Spirit is, among other appropriations, the fire from within the Father and the Son to express what is known and good, but is not Himself expressed. When one sees pictures of the Sacred Heart of Jesus, they may notice flames coming from his heart; those flames are a symbol of the Holy Spirit — Holy Desire. Recall Pentecost when the Holy Spirit descended upon the Apostles (Acts 2:1-4). He took the form of fiery tongues, inflaming the hearts of the Apostles. The fire represents the radiating Love of the Holy Spirit 'bringing' all truth and recalling to their minds all that Jesus had taught them (Jn. 14:25-26). The tongues represented the fact that all true Love (not to be confused with biological/chemical "love") MUST be radiated outward — must be expressed. In fact, the person in whom the Spirit dwells is on fire to do so (cf. Lk. 24:32, 3:16). Expressing God's words, Hildegard wrote, "The watery air indicates the holy works of exemplary and just individuals. Their works are as pure as water and cause every impure work to become pure, just as water washes away filth. Because of this condition such a work can achieve in its perfection whatever God's *grace enkindles in this way by the fire of the Holy Spirit [SML]*."[133] Too many people put the emphasis on "speaking in tongues" and entirely miss the much greater meaning of the sacramental sign employed by God during Pentecost. For the person filled with the Holy Spirit, it is a greater suffering to not express what is known, than is the worldly suffering that would occur as a consequence of expressing the Truths received (cf. Jer. 20:7-9). At Pentecost when the Holy Spirit descended upon the Apostles in the form of fiery tongues, they were practically falling all over themselves to go out and express/preach the Word of God.[134] The Spirit of God is not the Light, but he is the principle of action whereby the Light and Truth of God is enkindled within and on fire to be radiated out.[135] I don't believe that the symbolism of fire and breath as related to the Holy Spirit are pure coincidence and completely unrelated. After all, without oxygen, which is an integral part of a breath, there can be no life and there can be no fire.

While the Holy Spirit does not himself express,[136] nor can He be expressed, it is nevertheless true that it is the action of the Spirit that is behind all expressions within Love (note that I didn't say "of" Love — the distinction will be made clear later). It is for this reason that Pope Leo XIII tells us the Holy Spirit, who is Divine Goodness, is the <u>ultimate cause</u> of all things, including the completion of man's salvation.[137] Just as the Holy Spirit is not able to express, so, too, it is with our souls. They, too, are a spirit. Hildegard writes, "Our body is the concealing garment of our soul ... and our soul could do nothing without the body."[138] The scriptural significance of that fact will be discussed in Chapter 7.

6:B:1 — To Say "I Will Express My Love" is to be Redundant

In Scripture, the word "love" is mentioned approximately 700 times (exact number may vary depending on Scripture translation). How many times are the words "express" and "love" used in conjunction with, or in close proximity to, one another? After checking hundreds of them, the answer was — zero! Why is that? It is because love, i.e. Triune Love, *includes* expression of Truth and Light which is always fruitful. If this were not true, then the Holy Spirit, who is the Divine force behind the breathing in and out of God — the life of God (cf. Ez. 37:14; Jn. 6:63; Rom. 7:6, 8:2, 8:6-8) would not be a part of God — i.e. God would not be Triune and the statement that God IS Love would not be correct. No fruitful expression of Truth ... no love.

As I said, there is no mention of expression in conjunction with love in Scripture, but in the NIV translation, there are approximately 13 times when the word "show" is used in conjunction with the word "love." One might be tempted to think that to "show love" means the same thing as to "express love". That would be an incorrect interpretation. 'Showing', and 'expressing' (as a necessary component for there to be Love) denote two completely different meanings in Scripture. Here's an example. Jesus tells his dinner hosts, "You did not give me any water for my feet, but she wet my feet with her tears and wiped them with her hair. You did not give me a kiss, but this woman, from the time I entered, has not stopped kissing my feet. You did not put oil on my head, but she has poured perfume on my feet. Therefore, I tell you, her many sins have been forgiven — as her great love has shown" (Lk. 7:44-47 NIV). As we can see in this verse, the fruitful expression, within love, is quite distinct from her showing love. Mary loved Jesus by perfuming his feet, washing his feet with her tears of sorrow, and by kissing his feet continuously. Because other people *saw her acts*, her love was also shown. Another example is: "they hear what you [Ezekiel] say but they will not do it; for with their lips they show much love, but their heart is set on their gain" (Ez. 33:31). In this passage, we clearly see the distinction between "showing" and whether or not there is true love. The people _showed much love_, but it was only the sensual appearance of love; it wasn't spiritual love at all.

Saying something like, "I want to express my love for you," is actually redundant. If this were not so, then it would be glaringly inconsistent and odd, indeed, that Scripture fails to mention fruitful expression in conjunction with love. Scripture is very clear that 'trees' that fail to express fruitfully will be cut down and thrown into the unquenchable fire (e.g. Mt. 3:10, 7:19; Mk. 11:12). Trees, as well as other wooden organisms, such as vines, branches, and doors (made from the DNA of trees), are often used by God as a symbol for the body of a man.[139] See also: Jn. 1, 4-5; Ex. 15:25; Judges 9:7-15; Neh. 10:35-37; Mt. 7:18; Mk. 8:23-25).

6. C — Holy Spirit: the Life of God

The Holy Spirit is described as the eternal ebb-and-flow of God.[140] However, a descriptive word that is more in line with Scripture usage and is also more indicative of the actions of the Holy Spirit, is his description as the Breath of God which is eternally inhaled and exhaled.[141] Pertinent to this topic are the words of God to St. Catherine of Siena regarding Elisha's resurrecting of a dead child. He tells Catherine: after the Holy Spirit entered the dead child, the soul of the child *breathes* as a sign that it has life. Notice that God didn't say the body breathed; He said the soul breathed as a sign it has life.[142] When the <u>soul</u> breathes, it is taking in and sending out the Breath, i.e. the Holy Spirit. If we were to keep our breath inside of us, we would die — there would be no life in us. Try doing that, or try inhaling but not exhaling and see how long you have life in you. Our bodies will not allow that. Mechanisms within the body will *force* us to breathe. Force is a strong word, but an appropriate one when using the body as an analogy. With the soul, however, this "force" does not violate our free will. This is why the Holy Spirit is divinely described as the life and the Breath of God. Love is dynamic. It exists in the will as a force — a principle of movement, a weight or force of attraction.[143] The Holy Spirit is the personification of action, the "working" Person of the Trinity, so to speak.[144] The Holy Spirit does not speak the Word, but He is the force, the breath, by which the Word is expressed by the Father.[145] Quoting St. John Damascene, Durrwell writes, "'The Spirit is the breath from the mouth [*the word <u>mouth</u> will take on special significance a little further on*] of God, the one who announces the Word.' By reason of the Spirit who lives in him, our God is a God who speaks. He comes out of himself and enters into an intimate relationship with mankind."[146] Put simply, the Holy Spirit is the power that urges God to come outside of Himself.[147] This is what is meant by breathing out — being the force behind the expression. <u>*All*</u>

expressions — within Love — are (and it cannot be otherwise)
fruitful[148] (cf. Is. 55:10-11). The Father fruitfully expresses
Himself by expressing/begetting the Son. The Son eternally
glorifies the Father and fruitfully expresses by doing the will of
the Father when he said "Let it be done,"[149] thus creating all
things visible and invisible. The Holy Spirit cannot be
expressed,[150] but the Holy Spirit prompts all expressions
within Love[151], and when the Word is expressed (sent), the
Breath goes with it (is also sent).

To help us understand the concept of the Trinity as
breathing in and breathing out, and how this is applicable to all
of us who are created in that Trinitarian image and likeness, we
can examine what St. Faustina wrote about her visit, in the
Spirit, to heaven. She tells us of how the happiness of God is
breathed out to all the inhabitants of heaven and how it returns
to its source, only to be breathed out again. While the essence
of the source of this happiness is unchanging, it is always new
to the saints because it is always being newly expressed (she
uses the term, "gushing forth").[152]

Another image is that of two musical composers, may also
help. Each one conceives a symphony in their mind. Each one
evaluates the symphony to be a very beautiful piece of music.
Each one believes that it will bring great joy to all who hear it.
The first composer is very proud of the music that he has
conceived and decides to keep the music to himself so that he
can control its dissemination and make a lot of money doing so.
The second composer wants to share his symphony and
multiply the joy that listening to his symphony provides.
Consequently, he expresses his music through sheet music,
concerts, and recordings — distributing them freely to all who
desire to hear it. Ask yourself, who more closely epitomizes
love; the proud and selfish composer or the generous and
gifting composer? This would be analogous to breathing out the
Breath of God. Through penetration of the Divine Light, the
Holy Spirit prompts fruitful and multiplicative expression of

that Light. According to Durrwell, the Spirit is the source of all being and life (cf. Rom 4:17, 25).[153]

The loving composer in our analogy has produced much fruit. His symphony is played everywhere, and everywhere people experience great joy when they hear it. All those who hear it think to themselves, if this composer's music makes me feel so happy, then the one who produced it must be the source of this happiness (goodness). Because of the nature of the soul, it wants to be close to the source of that happiness. The soul experiences a "call/attraction" to be close to the music's creator. This phenomenon can be seen very clearly in the cult of celebrity that exists in our current culture. I am incredulous when I think about auctions that occur during which people can bid on something that belongs to and/or has been touched by a celebrity. Obviously, this attraction would fall under the "apparent good" category and is indicative of a society that has lost its spiritual compass.

6:C:1 — What is Grace?

The scriptural meaning of the word "mouth" will be discussed in Chapter 7. We will further develop the reasons for, and the consequences of, our body being a part of the nature of man, i.e. the whole man; a man, which is in the image and likeness of a God that eternally expresses. First, we must answer the question: what is grace? When I was younger, I could never quite grasp the concept of grace. What exactly is it? Is it a sort of pixie dust that would come down from Heaven? Let's try to answer that question now. First, we'll discuss graces relationship to 'good' and 'attraction,' then follow up with a more specific discussion of types of graces.

According to Leen, there are two types of *good*: 1) *real good* (when the object perceived as good helps to complete and perfect the person's state of being in the image and likeness of God), and 2) *apparent good,* which is a perceived good that is not a real good. An example of the latter would be an interpretation of the biological ecstasy of sex outside of marriage as a *good*. True goodness is always attractive and results in a call to all men from God. The grace of the Holy Spirit is: 1) the interior illumination of Truth; 2) the recognition that this Truth is infinitely good; 3) the fire in the inner spiritual heart for union with the source of that Truth; and 4) the desire to express (share) that Truth — thus being fruitful and creative. Apparent good is also attractive and provides man with a call, but it is the flesh or the world that is producing the call, not the Spirit dwelling within the inner heart.[154]

Interpreting the words of St. Paul, Durrwell writes that this "call," this "attraction" is the grace of the Holy Spirit (cf. Eph. 4:4; Gal. 1:6, 15, 5:13; 1 Cor. 7:15; Col. 3:15; 1 Th. 2:12) that is beckoning us to become one with the source of that goodness.[155] Pope Leo wrote, "… nothing is more lovable than love."[156] It is grace itself that brings us into the interior life of God[157] and, ergo, into Love itself. When we say that someone is full of grace, we are saying they are full of the Holy Spirit.[158] It is only through cooperating with God's grace that we can gradually arrive at the purity of heart that is necessary to be freed from the slavery of sin and to obtain true union with the Son of God (cf. Mt. 19:25-26).

It is a tenet of STOSS that an individual man can communicate to others the grace he or she has received from God. I base the credibility of this tenet on several factors that will be discussed in greater detail elsewhere in the book. For now, however, I will simply cite four sources. They are: 1) the words of Jesus as relayed by St. Faustina; 2) the words of Scripture, 3) the words of Archbishop Fulton Sheen, and; 4) JP II.

1) Jesus tells St. Faustina that "I am Love and Mercy itself. When a soul approaches Me with trust, I fill it with such an abundance of graces that it cannot contain them within itself, but radiates them to other souls;"[159]

2) In the Gospel of John, Jesus tells us, "If any one thirst, let him come to me and drink. He who believes in me, as the scripture has said, 'Out of his heart *["believers heart" in this passage would correspond to Jesus saying "approaches with trust" in his conversation with Faustina]* shall flow rivers of living water'" (Jn. 7:37-38). This living water is the grace of the Holy Spirit and it is a river *flowing out from the believer's heart.* Additionally, St. Paul writes, "Let no evil talk come out of your mouths, but only such as is good for edifying, as fits the occasion, that it may impart grace to those who hear." (Eph. 4:29-30); and,

3) St. Paul wrote, "For it is the God who said, 'Let light shine out of darkness,' who has shone in our hearts to give the light of the knowledge of the glory of God in the face of Christ. But we have this treasure in earthen vessels, to show that the transcendent power belongs to God and not to us" (2 Cor. 4:6-7). Fulton Sheen so completely viewed himself as an earthen vessel that he titled his autobiography, "Treasure in Clay." In Sheen's book, *The Mystical Body of Christ*, he wrote, "The graces of God are communicated through 'frail vessels [SML].'"[160] It is the body that is the frail vessel, not the soul. Remember the phrase: *The spirit is willing but the flesh is weak.* Did Sheen really equate the frailty of the earthen vessel with the human body? Later in the book he wrote, "The Mystical Christ of Pentecost, like the physical Christ of Bethlehem, was small, and delicate, and frail like any new-born thing [*the newly breathed soul is sinless and, therefore, not weak — SML*]. Its members were small; its organs were in the process of formation."[161] This is why the Church is considered to be the "Prolongation of the Incarnation through space and time."[162] This understanding will take on even greater significance when we talk about the meaning of the 'mouth' in scripture (Chapter 7 of this book).

4) According to JPII, just as a sacrament is an outward sign of an inward (and unseen) reality of grace, the body, itself, enters into the "definition of a sacrament" (loosely speaking). This is so because it is a visible sign of an invisible reality. Not only is the body a sign of grace received, but it also visibly expresses that which it has received, and does so efficaciously for self and others. Furthermore, the body not only expresses grace but, as we shall see later, "produces" it. The body contributes to grace becoming "part of man."[163]

This logically leads us to ask two fundamental questions. First, how or by what means do these graces radiate/flow from one soul to other souls? Second, of the many different types of grace, which ones are capable of being radiated from one soul to another soul? The first question will be answered in subsequent sections, so I will not dwell much on that subject here. As to the second question, it would be cumbersome and counterproductive to attempt to list and classify every possible grace into a yes or no category. Consequently, we will confine ourselves to some broad generalities.

6:C:2 — Two Main Categories of Grace:

1) *Gratiae Gratis Datae:* These are charismatic graces which are meant for the building up of the Church and for the spiritual aid of those other than the person who receives them.[164] Hereafter, we will refer to this category as "Gratuitous grace".

2) *Gratia Gratum Faciens:*[165] These are graces that are meant for the sanctification of the person who is the recipient of these graces. There are two main categories of this type of grace. They are ...:

(A) Sanctifying grace

(B) Actual grace. Hardon divides this category further into:

(i) Internal Actual Grace

(ii) External Actual Grace

Let's discuss each category a little further.

6:C:2:a — Gratiae Gratis Datae (Gratuitous Graces)

What is Gratuitous Grace? While all grace is ultimately gratuitous (freely given, not earned), graces falling within the classification known as "Gratuitous," are given for the benefit of others and are independent of the moral character of the person being used as the instrument of said graces. Included in this category are such graces as charismata (gifts of prophecy, miracles, speaking in tongues, etc.) and the priestly power of consecration and absolution.[166] As an example of the fact that some gifts of the Holy Spirit are independent of moral character, we have to look no further than the high priest Caiaphas who was given the gift of prophecy strictly because he sat on the chair of Moses (Jn. 11:49-52). Having said this, we also must not overlook this fact: when God wishes to express/communicate his graces to souls, he <u>usually</u> uses human instruments that possess the same kind of sanctity that he wishes to give.[167] Ignatius writes: "In like manner, to transmit the form of humility, patience, charity, and so forth, to others, God wills that the immediate cause which He uses as instrument, such as the preacher or confessor, be humble, charitable, patient."[168] While the presence of sanctity is not necessary for that which is being used by God as a human instrument, it is usually God's desire that it be present to some degree. Aquinas writes,

> As the Apostle says (Rom. 13:1), "those things that are of God are well ordered." Now the order of things consists

in this, that things are led to God by other things, as Dionysius says (Coel. Hier. iv). And hence since grace is ordained to lead men to God, this takes place in a certain order, so that some are led to God by others. And thus there is a twofold grace: one whereby man himself is united to God, and this is called 'sanctifying grace'; the other is that whereby one man cooperates with another in leading him to God, and this gift is called 'gratuitous grace,' since it is bestowed on a man beyond the capability of nature, and beyond the merit of the person. But whereas it is bestowed on a man, not to justify him, but rather that he may cooperate in the justification of another, it is not called sanctifying grace.[169]

More charisms of the Holy Spirt can be found in 1 Cor. 12:4-11 and Rom. 12:6-8.

6:C:2:b — Gratia Gratum Faciens (Sanctifying Grace)

6:C:2:b:(i) — Sanctifying/Habitual Grace

• Sanctifying grace elevates the natural life of man so that he is able to (and does) participate in the supernatural life of God, i.e. sanctifying grace gives man a participation in the divine life of God.[170] As St. Athaneus wrote, "For the Son of God became man so that we might become God. [St. Athanasius, *De inc.* 54, 3: PG 25, 192B]."[171] Hardon tells us, "If we are regenerated, this implies we have received a new principle of life, for as generation means the communication of nature from one person to another, so rebirth, by definition, signifies that a new *principium vitae* has been received, whose nature is in the same order of reality as the generator, who in this case is God."[172]

• Sanctifying grace is a direct communication of God in which supernatural life is permanently (as opposed to transiently) infused into, and inheres in, the soul of man.[173] 'Permanent' does NOT mean that Sanctifying grace cannot be increased, decreased, or lost through either our meritorious or despicable actions.

• Sanctifying grace is communicated to man through the Sacraments of the Church, starting with Baptism. Not only Sanctifying, but also Actual grace is given to us in each of the Sacraments.[174]

"According to St. John, grace is the life of Christ."[175] Grace is "constantly and perennially" given to us through the communication of His Holy Spirit.[176] This leads us to one final point which is important for understanding the nature of a Triune God in which we become partakers through Sanctifying grace. That point is this: Sanctifying grace and charity cannot be separated. They are either both present or both absent.[177] Very briefly, charity can be described as the holy desire and the act of gifting oneself completely (without any regard for cost or harboring any expectation of recompense) to others for the purpose of gaining for them true and eternal happiness (not the happiness which I like to call, 'hormonally-induced false/bodily happiness'). Our understanding of the grace-charity link will become more appreciated when we talk about the meaning of "mouth" in Scripture.

Absent further evidence, I do not believe that Sanctifying/Sacramental/Habitual grace is the grace that Jesus is referring to when he tells St. Faustina that His grace will overflow from our souls and into other souls. As was said earlier, Sanctifying grace is the result of the direct communication between Jesus' Holy Spirit and our soul. There are three exceptions to my first statement of this paragraph. They are: 1) Jesus, whose humanity is the instrument through which all of God's grace enters into the world. His humanity does not cause grace, but because his human nature is hypostatically united with his divine nature, his humanity (body and soul) is the instrument by which we receive all grace, Sanctifying or otherwise;[178] 2) bishops/priests who, through Holy Orders, receive an indelible mark on the soul which enables them to confect the Sacraments "in persona Christi." In other words, it is actually Jesus who is confecting the Sacraments using the priest's humanity. Here's something to ponder, if the soul is indelibly marked, wouldn't the body also be so marked? After all, the soul is the form of the body. Didn't St. Catherine tell us (in Chapter 3:A) that, through the power of the soul, our body will be "imprinted" with the fruits of the sufferings and labors endured by the body in "partnership" with the inner heart?[179], and; 3) Mary, whose union with her son is unique among all creation, and who is doctrinally defined as the Mediatrix of all grace (see: https://www.catholic.com/magazine/print-edition/making-peace-with-the-mediatrix).[180] In Chapter 14 (located in Volume Two of STOSS), results from scientific discoveries will reveal how the depth of the union of Mary with Jesus goes far beyond what we previously imagined.

What I believe regarding the channeling of grace by ordinary man is this: a heart purified by Sanctifying grace and inhabited by the Holy Spirit (who always brings with him the infused virtue of charity) cannot help but overflow (express) in love, i.e. in charity. Were this not so, then Hardon[181] and Aquinas [St. Thomas Aquinas, *De Veritate*, XXVII, 2 (corpus)][182] would be wrong about Sanctifying grace and infused charity being inseparable. According to Archbishop Luis Martinez, the virtue of infused charity is the image of God[183] and also the perfect image of the Holy Spirit, who is uncreated Charity.[184] Archbishop Martinez writes, "The

Christian spirit is a spirit of charity, and charity requires communication [*i.e. the expression of actual grace*] — and not only charity, but justice and many other virtues as well."[185]

Before going on to a discussion about Actual Grace, I want to make one thing very clear about Sanctifying Grace. It is true that the body does not radiate sacramental Sanctifying Grace. However, it is also true that, without a human body, it would be impossible for fallen man to receive Sanctifying Grace. Jesus tells us, "Truly, truly, I say to you, unless you eat the flesh of the Son of man and drink his blood, you have no life in you" (Jn. 6:53). Notice that Jesus didn't say: *unless you become one with my human soul, you have no life*. Jesus also said, "He who eats my flesh and drinks my blood abides in me, and I in him" (Jn. 6:56). Notice he didn't say, *if you invite me into your heart I will abide in you and you in me*. In Chapter 11, we will deal with this subject in greater detail.

6:C:2:b:(ii) — Actual Grace:

While the early Church councils clearly distinguished between the two kinds of sanctifying benefits to the soul, the use of the identifying term "actual" seems to have been used for the first time by the Dominican theologian John Capreolus (1380-1446).[186] From a theological standpoint, it became necessary to draw a sharper distinction between the two *gratia gratum faciens* graces (i.e. Sanctifying and Actual). According to Fr. John Hardon, "Terminology is fluid and a variety of synonyms is used for both concepts."[187]

As a sub-classification of the *gratia gratum faciens* category, Actual grace encompasses all grace received that is not a part of the other sub-classification, i.e. Sanctifying grace. An extensive listing of all the various kinds and classifications of actual grace would be impossible to compose; they are too numerous and complex to comprehensively do so.[188] According to Hardon, Actual grace is a "temporary supernatural intervention by God to enlighten the mind or strengthen the will to perform supernatural actions that lead to heaven."[189] Remember, Jesus revealed to St. Faustina that the graces he gives to one soul would overflow and radiate out to another soul. I believe we could characterize Jesus' words thusly: a soul that approaches Jesus with trust will receive so many Sanctifying and Gratuitous graces, that the Gratuitous graces overflow to another soul, who receives them as *external* Actual graces.

While Actual grace is distinct from Sanctifying grace (as discussed above), it is important to note that Actual grace is also sanctifying (small 's'). To clarify the distinction between the two, recall that Sanctifying grace is a direct communication between God and the soul through which that soul is deified. On the other hand, small 's' sanctifying grace is God's communication to the soul through many other means, e.g. preacher, art, music, geographical landscape, etc. Thus we can appreciate a saying used by many of the saints when they exclaimed, "Blessed be the God of all things for sanctifying His elect through one another."[190] There are numerous modes through which this sanctification can occur. The most noticeable modes of sanctification are the following: 1) purification of the heart and body; 2) illumination of the intellect; and, 3) union with God.[191] Let us now turn to the two main sub-types of Actual grace: *internal* and *external*.

6:C:2:b:(ii):I — Internal Actual Grace

The Council of Orange in 529 declared that man is helpless to perform any spiritually worthy act without the illumination and inspiration of the Holy Spirit.[192] Internal Actual grace is defined by Catholic theology as the internal and immediate illumination of the intellect and movement of the will (intellect and will are two faculties of the soul) in response to the Holy Spirit.[193] Important note: the word *immediate* (used above) oes not mean "He dispenses with such external media as preaching, spiritual reading, exhortation or good example. On the contrary, He normally uses such means as the occasion for conferring internal light or strength."[194] What are these internal Actual graces? Some examples of the Holy Spirit's inspirations are as follows: 1) infused ideas and judgments; 2) movements of faith, hope, and charity, and; 3) movements toward other virtues, such as fear of the Lord.[195] This brings us to the subject of *external* Actual grace.

6:C:2:b:(ii):II — External Actual Grace

It is called external (or exterior) grace because it is presented to a person from outside the intellect and will. External graces alone are not capable of sanctifying, but God often uses them as an occasion for giving internal Actual graces, which can be sanctifying.[196] An external Actual grace can be a person, place, or thing. There may exist some confusion as to the distinction between "external Actual" grace and "Gratuitous" grace. A person who receives and acts upon a Gratuitous grace becomes an instrument through which a different person receives an Actual external grace. As the name implies, external grace occurs when the Holy Spirit works from the outside in, so to speak. Using external instruments experienced through our "bodily organs", God causes an influx of Divine causation to inspire movement of the will or mind. Examples of these external instruments include the following: words somebody speaks, miracles, beautiful scenery, beautiful music, ideas communicated and heard, and events.[197]

If I have done my job well, we have gained a better understanding of grace. This should enable us to gain a deeper appreciation of the biblical meaning of the word "mouth". When it comes to understanding man's creation in the image and likeness of God, grace and the "mouth" go indispensably hand-in-hand.

CHAPTER 7 — THE MEANING OF "MOUTH" IN SCRIPTURE

We'll begin by talking about the meaning of being <u>sent</u> using the analogy of a master boat designer. In our analogy, a certain designer possesses the knowledge to design and build the absolutely best boat in the world. His knowledge consists of thoughts. Everything is in his head, so to speak. Unless and until those thoughts are "sent" out by means of some form of expression/gifting, they remain just that — inner thoughts. The designer expresses (sends out) his thoughts fruitfully when, for example, he: 1) goes out and builds the boat; 2) verbally tells someone how to build this boat; 3) draws diagrams of how to build the boat; and/or 4) writes a "How-To" book. Expressions are not limited to verbal words. Any expression that sends out a thought is a *word*, verbal or otherwise. With that in mind, let us proceed with our discussion of the mouth.

7:A — The Mouth of God

Obviously, God does not have a physical mouth. So when we read in Scripture of the "mouth" of God (cf. 1 Kgs 8:15), are we to interpret it as a metaphor that helps us to understand that He is communicating? Let's apply our understanding of being "sent" to the Trinity. In Scripture, it is only the Word of God (Jn. 3:17; 5:23) and the Holy Spirit (Jn. 14:26) who are described as being sent.[198] The Father is <u>never</u> described as such. The Father is always the one who sends. The Father is not expressed; the Father is the one who expresses. In Scripture, it is the *mouth* that sends the Word. In the Word is also sent the Breath, i.e. the Holy Spirit (cf. Jn. 20:21-23; Is. 55:10-11). When a human wishes to say something, the words will not be sent out without the accompanying breath. Scripture tells us that "man does not live by bread alone, but that man lives by everything that proceeds out of the mouth of the LORD" (Deut. 8:3).

7:B — The Breath From the Mouth Dwells in the Heart

The heart of God on fire, i.e. the Holy Spirit, dwells in our hearts. Some theologians do not describe God as having a heart. However, Durrwell writes, "It is there, in our hearts, in the intimate depths of the believer, that the Spirit chooses his dwelling. In God himself the Holy Spirit of God reaches the 'depths' (cf. 1 Cor. 2:10). He is, as it were, the heart of God."[199,200,201] St. Robert Bellarmine, theologian and Doctor of the Church, is known as the father of apologists. In his three-volume work titled, *Disputationes de Controversiis Christianae Fidei adversus hujus temporis Haereticos,* St. Bellarmine tells us that the Holy Spirit <u>IS</u> the heart of God — <u>IS</u> the Spirit of God.[202] St. Hildegard tells us, "<u>In the heart of the radiant</u>

Father ... burns the Holy Spirit [SML]."²⁰³ Furthermore, Jesus tells us that, "out of the abundance of the heart the mouth speaks" (Mt. 12:34). "Mouth" in Scripture refers to that which fruitfully expresses (sends out) the overflow of the heart. Remember, the mouth not only sends out, but it also takes in (in the form of Actual grace) whatever is to reach the heart. If anyone believes that Mt. 15:17-19 contradicts the previous sentence, then I would reply by saying that Matthew's Gospel does not contradict me when I say: in the matter of Actual grace, that which comes into the heart of man comes through the mouth (body) of man. It should be noted, however, in the case of habitual Sanctifying grace, God's power affects the soul directly. In verse 15:2 the Pharisees are accusing the disciples of defiling themselves because they have not performed the prescribed ritual washing of their hands before eating. The Pharisees are clearly talking about organic food, defiled because it was touched by unclean hands, subsequently going through the literalistic biological mouth. So this is the context in which Jesus responds, i.e. whether or not organic food entering the biological mouth and eventually coming out the other end of the body defiles us. This is evident by the wording he uses. In v. 17 he says, "Do you not see that whatever goes into the mouth enters the stomach, and goes out into the sewer. In v. 19-20, Jesus tells the Apostles that adultery, fornication, theft, etc. coming out of the mouth are what defiles us. In a later discussion concerning the "mouth," we will discuss the scriptural basis for believing that the mouth/body play a role in both taking in, and sending out that which truly defiles.

Every thought that is sent, is sent somewhere. Every expression has a destination to which it is sent. Beside the fact of a Triune God that exists in relationship, what was the Father's intended destination for His expression of the Word through His Breath? The answer is — creation. St. Thomas Aquinas writes, "Now the craftsman [*the Father*] works through the word conceived in his mind, and through the love of his will regarding some object. Hence also God the Father made the creature through His Word, which is His Son; and through His Love [*which is associated with the heart*], which is the Holy [Spirit]."[204] As we said previously, all expressions in Love are fruitful. The Father fruitfully expressed the Word through the power of His Breath, and that expression produced the fruit of creation. Hence we read in Scripture, "So shall my word be that goes forth from my mouth [*God the Father*]; it shall not return to me empty, but it shall accomplish that which I purpose, and prosper [*be fruitful*] in the thing for which I sent it" (Is. 55:11). We can conclude that the fruit, which is produced by the expression of the Word by the force of the Father's Breath, will return to that same mouth of God (the Father) who expressed it, where it will be breathed in and become one with God — thus entering into the Trinitarian dialogue (cf. 2 Pt. 1:4).[205] The concept of breathing the Breath through the mouth can also be understood in the light of the Eucharistic discourse (Jn. 6:48-70). Jesus tells the crowd that his flesh is real food and his blood is real drink. He breathes the Breath through his mouth (his body and blood in the Eucharist) and we inhale the Breath when we receive Him in the Eucharist through our mouth/body.

7:C — The Meaning of "Sense-Able" and "Meta-Sense-Able"

Before we proceed further, we need to introduce and define two terms that have been coined by me for use in STOSS. They are *sense-able* and *meta-sense-able*. On February 20, 1980, in his Wednesday audience, JP II said something that I believe is one of his most profound statements regarding the body. He said, "The body, in fact, and it alone is capable of making visible what is invisible: the spiritual and divine. It was created to transfer into the visible reality of the world, the mystery hidden since time immemorial in God."[206] As profound as this statement is, I would nevertheless like to modify it slightly. In order to incorporate STOSS into its understanding, it would read: *The body, and it alone is capable of transferring the spiritual and divine into physical creation, and doing so through the <u>sense-able</u> and <u>meta-sense-able</u> language of the body.*

One of the components of any expression sent via the body is that it is sense-able, i.e. when sent in the presence of a witness, the expression will be perceived by one or more of the witness' five unaided senses. There is also a component of the expression that cannot be heard, tasted, touched, seen, and/or smelled by the naked (unaided) senses. However, it can be sensed, either directly or indirectly, through the aid of instrumentation or sensor. While the word meta-sense-able describes something invisible to the naked eye, it is not to be confused with the "spiritual and divine" to which JP II refers. Something that is meta-sense-able belongs to the classification of physical matter/creation. There are many who fail to make this distinction and it leads them into *serious* error. New-agers and Rosicrucians are only a couple of many other possible examples of those who confuse uncreated and immeasurable Supernatural Life/Light with meta-sense-able light/energy/vibration that is a part of the physical universe created by God. There is nothing in this book which can be classified as New Age! In fact, there is a litmus test that can be applied to determine whether or not something is New Age. You can read about it in Chapter 13 (located in Volume Two of STOSS).

Let me provide some examples of created physical phenomenon that fall into the meta-sense-able category. Gravity can't be sensed by any of the five senses, but the effects of gravity (the apple falling from the tree) are sense-able. However, through the use of a gravimeter, we can measure the strength of a gravitational field. The electromagnetic energy of, say a microwave oven, cannot be sensed (we can hear the unit that produces it, but not EMR itself), but instrumentation exists that will allow us to see and hear electromagnetic waves. We cannot see bacteria, but microscopes provide us with the ability to see them. We cannot sense when a gene from the salt of our DNA is expressing a protein, but with instrumentation, we can see it indirectly. We cannot sense an atom, but through high-powered electron microscopes, we are able to sense individual atoms. Angels/spirits, even though they are created, would *not* fall under the meta-sense-able classification because instrumentation to detect them does not yet exist, to my knowledge.

7:D — The Mouth Cannot Inaccurately Express the Spiritual Heart

It is a commonly held belief in Catholic philosophy that the soul, possessing memory, will (heart), and intellect (part of understanding),[207] are the substantial form of the body.[208] According to Aquinas:

> Now it is clear that the first thing by which the body lives is the soul. And as life appears through various operations in different degrees of living things, that whereby we primarily perform each of all these vital actions is the soul. For the soul is the primary principle of our nourishment, sensation, and local movement; and likewise of our understanding. Therefore this principle by which we primarily understand, whether it be called the intellect or the intellectual soul, is the form of the body.[209]

It's only logical then, to conclude that as the substantial form changes, vis-à-vis a heart that becomes more or less pure, so will the form equally change. God provided St. Catherine with an example of that very thing. She wrote: Because every good or evil consensual thought of the heart is put into action by the body, the resurrected and glorified body will be adorned/imprinted (like cloth adorned with a beautiful painting) with the fruits of the sufferings it underwent (in unison with the soul) during its mortal life. Furthermore, she tells us it is not the body itself that will accomplish this ornamentation. Instead, it is through the fullness of the perfected soul (the substantial form of the body) that this will be accomplished.[210]

The body (mouth) will always accurately express the overflow of the heart. However, because of the sensual component of human expression, an observer of someone else's expression can misinterpret the heart, from which the overflow originated. If one has a lying heart, the sense-able part of the "word" expressed will be an accurate expression of the heart's desire to deceive. Let's look at an example. Jesus said, "Woe to you, scribes and Pharisees, hypocrites! for you are like whitewashed tombs, which outwardly appear beautiful, but within they are full of dead men's bones and all uncleanness. So you also outwardly appear righteous to men, but within you are full of hypocrisy and iniquity" (Mt. 23:27-28). The Pharisees' hearts were prideful and lusted for exaltation. Their sense-able expression was an accurate expression of their heart's lust to be exalted by men. A witness' interpretation of the sense-able expression by a Pharisees was not accurate, but only because they lacked the ability to judge accurately the heart from which the expressions overflowed. This is one reason why Jesus forbids us to judge others (Mt. 7:1-2).

The meta-sense-able expression, however, is quite different. The meta-sense-able part of an expression could never be misinterpreted by anyone who is capable of "perceiving" it. For example, angels, good or bad, could never be fooled by our expressions because they can perceive both the sense-able and meta-sense-able parts of the "word" that comes out of our mouth/body. Satan is incapable of reading our inner hearts and our thoughts,[211] but he can accurately know them by reading the meta-sense-able component (including that which is produced by the biological heart) of a person's expression or by simply reading the condition of our salt and light (Volume Two: Part IV of STOSS will explain this in more detail).[212] Armed with that knowledge, demons seek to tempt us with that which feeds the disordered appetites and attractions of our prideful inner hearts.[213]

St. Catherine of Siena touches on this concept when she informs us there are no real dividing lines between us and our neighbors. She writes, "Keep in mind that each of you has your own vineyard. But every one [sic] is joined to your neighbor's vineyards without any dividing lines. They are so joined together, in fact, that you cannot do good or evil for yourself without doing the same for your neighbors."[214] Most of us have this tendency to think of our body as a fence — a dividing line as St. Catherine calls it. We foolishly believe what happens in the heart stays within the body unless we choose to make a sense-able expression. Through a deeper understanding of STOSS, we can discover the body is not even close to being a fence. In fact, so permeating are the sense-able and meta-sense-able 'words' pronounced by our mouth/body, we would be correct in believing the body is the reason that there is no fence. Through STOSS, we come to understand the body as a veritable transmission tower for the heart. It broadcasts sense-ably (we can, for example, hear the music on our radio), but it also broadcasts the same message meta-sense-ably, i.e. beyond the reach of our sensible faculties. We can't see the radio waves emanating from the very powerful transmission tower.

7:E — The Mouth of Man

In my view, the use of "mouth" in the lexicon of Scripture does not *only* apply to God the Father, but also to man — including the incarnate part of the Second Person of the Trinity, the Word of God. In Scripture, I believe the "mouth" is used to denote that by which is sent out the overflow of the heart (light or darkness) and also takes in that which either enlightens (through the grace of the Holy Spirit) or darkens (feeds the pride and lust of the heart). For man, the mouth is the *entire body*. Depending upon the individual circumstances, various parts of the body may play a more or less prominent role in a particular expression. For example, while the biological mouth may be the most prominent sense-able part of expressing praise for God, the entire body is involved. As JP II wrote, "The body speaks not merely with the whole external expression of masculinity and femininity, but also with the internal structures of the organism, of the somatic [*the entire body and its aggregate parts*] and psychosomatic [*relating to the mind/mental*] reaction."[215] When God speaks or sends forth His Word, He does it with His mouth (Is. 55:11). When man speaks a sense-able and meta-sense-able word (both components are always contributing to the expression), it is his entire mouth/body, through which the word is sent out.

Let's look at a passage that will show us that God is frequently not referring to the literal biological mouth when using the word in Scripture. While the entire scriptural mouth (the body) of a person contributes to any expression, verbal expression through the literal biological mouth may or may not occur. Addressing Himself to his Chosen People about the commandments and the decrees of the Law, God said, "For this commandment which I command you this day is not too hard for you, neither is it far off ... the word is very near you; it is in your mouth [*your body*] and in your heart [*your spirit*] so that you can do it" (Deut. 30:11,14). We "do" with our entire body, not just the biological mouth. JP II writes, "In the text of the prophets the body speaks a 'language'."[216] Where does speech exit the body? Answer: the mouth. According to St. Hildegard, virtues work through the body and soul together;[217] "a virtue is a divine quality that ... fully *incarnates itself* [*SML*]."[218] What does this mean? It means: as the heart is purified, so also is the body. Why is this necessary? So that, in its role as the mouth of the heart, the body can *accurately* express (both sense-ably and meta-sense-ably) virtuous acts and bear good fruit. West writes that the body simply gives expression to the experiences of the heart;[219] the spirit "expresses" itself through a language of the body.[220]

7:F — The Heart and the Mouth of Man, Scripturally Speaking

Jesus told us that the heart speaks through the mouth (Mt. 12:34). Let's take a look at a few examples in Scripture of the inextricable link between the heart and the mouth/body of man:

1) "You brood of vipers! how can you speak good, when you are evil? For out of the abundance of the heart the mouth speaks. The good man out of his good treasure brings forth good, and the evil man out of his evil treasure brings forth evil" (Mt. 12:34-35). Are literal words from the literal mouth the only means by which "good" or "evil" is brought forth? What about burglary? Usually, there are no words exchanged between the thief and the victim, and yet, it is still an expression from the overflow of the thief's heart. What about rape or murder. What is really doing the "speaking" in the commission of these horrendous acts of evil — the literal mouth or the entire body;

2) "Thou wilt find no wickedness in me; my mouth does not transgress. With regard to the works of men, by the word of thy lips I have avoided the ways of the violent" (Ps. 17:3-4). The linkage made between "mouth," "works of men," and "ways of the violent" indicate the expression from the mouth goes far beyond mere verbal speech;

3) "For there is no truth in their mouth; their heart is destruction, their throat is an open sepulcher [*grave*], they flatter with their tongue" (Psalm 5:9);

4) "Then Jacob went on his journey ... he saw a well in the field ... The stone on the well's mouth was large, and when all the flocks were gathered there, the shepherds would roll the stone from the mouth of the well, and water the sheep" (Gen. 29:1-3). Jacob together with the stone well, from which water flows out of its mouth, foreshadows Jesus'

body (NOT his literal biological mouth) from which will flow Living Water. John writes, "So Jesus said to them, 'Truly, truly, I say to you, unless you eat the flesh of the Son of man and drink his blood, you have no life in you'" (Jn. 6:53). "Life" is uncreated Divine Charity, the Holy Spirit;

5) "The mouth of the righteous is a fountain of life, but the mouth of the wicked conceals violence" (Prov. 10:11). Again, see also John 6:51-53;

6) In Ezekiel it is written, "He said to me, 'Son of man, eat this scroll I give you and fill your stomach with it.' Then I ate it, and it was in my mouth as sweet as honey. And he said to me: 'Son of man, go, get you to the house of Israel, and speak with my words to them'" (Ez. 3:3-4). In this passage, the knowledge needed to prophesy (all prophecy comes from the Holy Spirit) is taken in by Ezekiel through his mouth — through his senses, as evidenced by the sweet as honey taste in his mouth. That God's words were written on a scroll and taken into the stomach through the mouth indicates that they had to be "digested" into the physical and spiritual mind so that the spiritual heart could penetrate them[221] and prompt expression through the same mouth by which they were taken in. Commenting on Aquinas' view of this topic, Dr. Magee writes:

> For Aquinas, it is a principle of his epistemology that "nothing is in the intellect which was not first in the senses." Therefore, in order for us to know anything, we must think of it in a sensory sort of way, making use of images (phantasms in Aquinas' terminology) (Summa Theologiae Ia, q. 84, a. 6; 85, 1). Even the most abstract sorts of thoughts involve the use of some sort of phantasm. This applies also to what is the absolute farthest from sense experience, God. Unaided human reason is able to rise to the knowledge of God only by

arguing from sensible effects (and rational principles derived therefrom) to God who is the cause of those effects (ST Ia, q. 2, a. 2). We are not able to know God, or any immaterial thing, perfectly in this way, (ST Ia, q. 88, a. 2) however, since everything we know about God by natural reason is a conclusion from what we know about sensible things because sensible things are what are the first and natural objects of our intellect.[222] And,

7) "The mouth of a loose woman is a deep pit; he with whom the LORD is angry will fall into it" (Prov. 22:14), and "This is the way of an adulteress: she eats, and wipes her mouth, and says, 'I have done no wrong'" (Prov. 30:20). In this passage, the adulteress consumes the man into the "deep pit" described in Prov. 22:14. Then she wipes her mouth (cleans up her body, dresses it in fine clothes, applies makeup and justifies what her mouth/body has done through her own lustful heart by saying I have done no wrong.

Let's look at some Scripture examples of the mouth "breathing in" to the heart.

1) "... the mouth of the wicked devours iniquity" (Prov. 19:28);

2) "Though wickedness is sweet in his mouth, though he hides it under his tongue, though he is loath to let it go, and holds it in his mouth, yet his food is turned in his stomach; it is the gall of asps within him. He swallows down riches and vomits them up again; God casts them out of his belly" (Job 20:12-15). When we compare this passage with Jesus' words about food which is taken into mouth does not defile (Mt. 15:17-19), it becomes clear that Job is not referring to literal food; and,

3) "All the toil of man is for his mouth, yet his appetite is not satisfied" (Eccl. 6:7). This passage also does not refer to the literal mouth or to the appetite for food. If it did, then the hunger hormone, ghrelin, would, in fact, be satisfied.

Adding a non-scriptural component to the discussion, one of St. Hildegard's visions from God can help. In it, she sees, "angels and demons struggle for possession of the soul as it passes from the dying person's mouth."[223] Does anyone think it was necessary for the soul to depart from the dying person's literal anatomical mouth? This is symbolic of the fact that during life the soul expressed itself into the world through the entire body.

7:G — The Language of the Body

STOSS seeks to deepen our understanding of the body's role in man's journey to perfection. How the graces that God gives to us are efficacious for the body as well as the soul. In fact, you cannot perfect one nature without also perfecting the other – in this life anyway. According to the *Catechism of the Catholic Church*, "The unity of soul and body is so profound that one has to consider the soul to be the 'form' of the body: i.e., it is because of its spiritual soul that the body made of matter becomes a living, human body; spirit and matter, in man, are not two natures united, but rather **their union forms a single nature [SML].**"[224] To help us understand, let's imagine that I want to have a custom sheet made as a gift for my wife. I choose to weave yellow and purple colored threads together (I know … I must be color blind). Let's also imagine the weave is very dense (let's say 1,000 thread-count, if that's even possible). So tight is the weave, when looking at the sheet you can't distinguish between the individual colored threads. It is one philosophically substantial sheet, but two thread components. Is it possible to damage, burn or stain a piece of that cloth without equally affecting both colors of thread? Is it possible to clean or soil only the yellow threads … only the purple threads?

So it is with the two components of our single nature. Every sacrament we receive, every exercise of virtue we undertake, every sin we commit, and every choice we make will equally move our body and our soul an equal "distance" toward greater perfection or imperfection. On this journey, there is never a time when the soul has to turn to the body and say — hurry up, you're lagging behind. Each and every step forward or backward that the soul takes, the body takes an equal step in the same direction, and vice versa. We are judged by the fruits we bear, and I'm quite certain that there will never be a situation where the soul is judged by God to merit a higher place in Heaven than the body, or the body has a lower place in hell than the soul, or any combination thereof. God is an infinitely just Judge. Therefore, at our death, in the Light of God's justice, our body and soul will be destined to have the same eternal resting place. Since we are a single nature with two component parts, any grace that God gives us will affect both the soul and the body equally, but with different types of impact on each aspect of our nature. Thus we can see that the body, as the mouth of man, will accurately express the heart.

As was shown previously, the body speaks. The body and it <u>alone</u> is capable of expressing the overflow of the heart — of expressing, in love.[225] According to the tenets of TOB, JP II tells us "the most profound words [*language*] of the spirit ... demand an adequate language of the body."[226] This language of the spirit consists of words of love, giving, and fidelity[227] expressed through the mouth of man — his body.

7:H — The Significance and Gravity of Fruitful Expression

This section will build upon what we have already learned about the 'mouth' in Scripture. We have shown that God is both eternally expressing and, as a result, eternally fruitful. St. Hildegard tells us that the Son of God is the "plenitude of fruition."[228] The Son also expresses fruitfully, for we know that through Him all things were made, especially man who himself is created in the image and likeness of God. The fruitfulness of his Word was desired by the Father, as can be seen in Scripture when He says, "so shall my word be that goes forth from my mouth; it shall not return to me empty, but it shall accomplish that which I purpose, and prosper in the thing for which I sent it" (Is. 55:11). The Son was sent to be fruitful.

We have to ask ourselves, does the fact that we are created in the image and likeness of God — a God whose very nature is to radiate His Light fruitfully — place upon us an inextricable mandate to express fruitfully. Let's answer that question by examining the consequences for not doing so. For modern man, there is probably no subject that is more underappreciated, misunderstood, or out-and-out unknown. God tells St. Hildegard,

> Each person has in himself two callings, the desire of
> fruit and the lust for vice. How? By the desire of fruit he
> is called toward life, and by the lust for vice he is called
> toward death. In the desire of fruit a person wishes to
> do good, and says to himself, "Do good works!' ... But in
> the lust for vice, a person wants to do evil, and says to
> himself, 'Do the work of your own pleasure!"[229]

Scripture contains many passages about the direst of consequences for those who fail to express fruitfully — for those who are lukewarm or tepid. Let's examine some, but not all, of those now.

7:H:1 — Faith Without Works is Dead

In James chapter 2 we read, "What does it profit, my brethren, if a man says he has faith but has not works? Can his faith save him" (v. 14)? "So faith by itself, if it has no works, is dead" (v. 17). On several occasions in this book, we have talked about the Holy Spirit being the life of God, the force by which God breathes in and breathes out the Breath. If one is not exhaling and inhaling, then that person is not in the image and likeness of God, and there is no life within them. Pope Benedict, citing Peter, tells us, "'[God] made no distinction between us and [the Gentiles], but cleansed their hearts by faith' ([Acts] 15:5-11). Faith cleanses the heart ... Faith comes about because men are touched deep within by God's Spirit, who opens and purifies their hearts."230 However, if He is in our heart and we do not breathe out the Breath, then we and our faith are dead. As James also tells us, "For as the body apart from the spirit is dead, so faith apart from works is dead" (v. 26) and, "You believe that God is one; you do well. *Even the demons believe [SML]* — and shudder" (v. 19). These are serious passages, full of meaning. In our discussion on the Trinity we talked about how, if any one Person of the Trinity was missing, God would not be God ... God would not be Love. Being in the image and likeness of God, to deny the promptings of the Holy Spirit, who is divine Charity personified, then we are not in His image and likeness. St. Catherine of Siena likens the soul to a tree which must receive water and nutrients to live, i.e. Divine Love (uncreated Charity ... the Holy Spirit), to live and bear fruit. Without this love, the tree will not only be fruitless, it will also be spiritually dead.231

Luther had it wrong when he said the Catholic Church believes that "works" justify us. That is not what the Church teaches. Works, acts, actions, or any other word that denotes "doing", are all forms of expression. When done in Love, they are fruitful. If we are not doing works in Love, we are not in the image and likeness of God. Furthermore, if we are not fruitful — in the likeness of God — the consequences are dire. Works do not justify us — works are the consequence of being justified through Baptism, and union with the Mystical Body of Christ ... his Church. If, as we learned in our exegesis of James 2:14-17, faith without works is dead, it is because there are no works. No works, no fruit. A thought, an impulse of the Holy Spirit, unexpressed accomplishes <u>nothing</u> for God.

7:H:2 — I Will Spew You Out Of My Mouth

In the first few chapters in Revelations, John is instructed by Jesus to write what he sees regarding the seven churches in Asia. Before being instructed what to write for each church, John hears something along the line of, "He who has an ear, let him hear what the Spirit says to the churches," or, "I know your works," or both. This is significant because it is by the force of the Holy Spirit that all expressions in Love are made; through whom all expressions/works are made fruitful.[232]

John is instructed to write to the church in La-odicea, "I know your works: you are neither cold nor hot. Would that you were cold or hot! So, because you are lukewarm, and neither cold nor hot, I will spew you out of my mouth. For you say, I am rich, I have prospered, and I need nothing; not knowing that you are wretched, pitiable, poor, blind, and naked'" (Rev. 3:15-17). God informed St. Hildegard concerning the meaning of this passage. The "cold" are those who are not entirely given over to the works of evil, while the "hot" are those who are on fire in the Spirit to do good works. She writes that the lukewarm "are one who begins, but not one who finishes; you touch the beginning of good, but you never feed on its perfection, like the wind that blows around a person's mouth and not the food that reaches his stomach."[233] Incidentally, according to St. Catherine, the stomach is a metaphor for something being digested into the heart.[234]

After our long discussion on the scriptural meaning of 'mouth', you probably already have a pretty good idea what is the meaning of the phrase "spew you out of my mouth" (Rev. 3:16). As was said earlier, when the Word of God took on a human body, he took on a human mouth by which he could become one body, one flesh, with man and express the life of God dwelling in his heart, i.e. the Holy Spirit. Remember to whom John was directed to write this message. It was to the church in La-odicea. And what is the Church? It is the Mystical Body of Christ. And who is the Church? We are the Church through the nuptial mystery. So when Jesus tells us that he will spew the lukewarm out of his mouth, he is reiterating what was said in the Gospel of John: "I am the true vine, and my Father is the vinedresser. Every branch of mine that bears no fruit, he takes away, and every branch that does bear fruit he prunes, that it may bear more fruit ... I am the vine, you are the branches. He who abides in me, and I in him [*it is through the Eucharist that we obtain this mutual abiding. See Jn. 6:56*], he it is that bears much fruit, for apart from me you can do nothing. If a man does not abide in me, he is cast forth as a branch and withers; and the branches are gathered, thrown into the fire and burned" (Jn. 15:1-2;5-6). Hmmm, "... thrown into fire and burned." Those are some pretty severe consequences for not using the mouth to express fruitfully.

7:H:3 — Other Passages Regarding the Consequences of Unfruitfulness

I have not attempted to search out every single Scripture passage that deals with the dire consequences for not expressing fruitfully; there are certainly enough here, however, to make the point adequately. Let's proceed:

- "Cursed is he who does the work of the LORD with slackness; and cursed is he who keeps back his sword from bloodshed" (Jer. 48:10).

- "From the fruit of his mouth a man is satisfied; he is satisfied by the yield of his lips. Death and life are in the power of the tongue, and those who love it will eat its fruits" (Prov. 18:20-21).

- **The parable of the sums of money** (last part only) — "Then another came, saying, 'LORD, here is your pound, which I kept laid away in a napkin; for I was afraid of you, because you are a severe man; you take up what you did not lay down, and reap what you did not sow.' He said to him, 'I will condemn you out of your own mouth, you wicked servant! You knew that I was a severe man, taking up what I did not lay down and reaping what I did not sow? Why then did you not put my money into the bank, and at my coming I should have collected it with interest'" (Lk. 19:20-23)?

- **The parable of the fig tree** — "A man had a fig tree planted in his vineyard; and he came seeking fruit on it and found none. And he said to the vinedresser, 'Lo, these three years I have come seeking fruit on this fig tree, and I find none. Cut it down; why should it use up the ground?' And he answered him, 'Let it alone, sir, this year also, till I dig about it and put on manure. And if it bears fruit next year, well and good; but if not, you can cut it down'" (Lk. 13:6-9).

- **The parable of the tenants** — "'He will put those wretches to a miserable death, and let out the vineyard to other tenants who will give him the fruits in their seasons.' ... Therefore I tell you, the kingdom of God will be taken away from you and given to a nation producing the fruits of it'" (Mt. 21:41,43).

• "Even now the axe is laid to the root of the trees; every tree therefore that does not bear good fruit is cut down and thrown into the fire" (Mt. 3:10).

• "Every tree that does not bear good fruit is cut down and thrown into the fire" (Mt. 7:19).

• "But while [the LORD] does not wish the death of a sinner, but only that he should be converted and live, He hates the lukewarm and they quickly cause him loathing."235

As I have already written, if someone is not expressing (sending out) the overflow of a heart wherein dwells the Holy Spirit, that person is still in the image of God, but not in the likeness. If one is not expressing their heart fruitfully, the consequences *are eternal*.

7:H:4 — For Each Tree is Known by its Own Fruit (Luke 6:44)

What is the significance of a tree being known by the fruit that is borne of it? To my mind, it's virtually axiomatic that the significance of fruit in the Bible is with the understanding that the quality of the fruit should be seen as an accurate reflection of the quality of the tree that produced it. Furthermore, we could also surmise that the seed, which is carried within the fruit, is an accurate reflection of the quality of the fruit that bears it, which is an accurate reflection of the tree that bore it.

This would be a good time to pause for a second to talk about the whole concept of fruit. St. Paul tells us, "Now the works of the flesh are plain: immorality, impurity, licentiousness, idolatry, sorcery, enmity, strife, jealousy, anger, selfishness, dissension, party spirit, envy, drunkenness, carousing, and the like ... But the fruit of the Spirit is love, joy, peace, patience, kindness, goodness, faithfulness, gentleness, self-control" (Gal. 5:19-23) and also, "For once you were darkness, but now you are light in the LORD; walk as children of light (for the fruit of light is found in all that is good and right and true), and try to learn what is pleasing to the Lord. Take no part in the unfruitful works of darkness, but instead expose them" (Eph. 5:8-11). It is clear that St. Paul makes a distinction between <u>empty works</u> (works expressed from the overflow of a heart not inhabited by the Holy Spirit) and fruitful works resulting from expressions in love, prompted by the enflaming of the heart by the Holy Spirit. St. Paul uses two distinctly different terms in Ephesians. The word "works" applies to works of the flesh which lead to darkness, while fruits describe the results from the indwelling Holy Spirit in the heart. We will discuss this topic a little further in the next two sub-sections. As we said, Scripture clearly informs us that fruit is an accurate reflection of that which produced it. Otherwise, it would be impossible to tell the tree by the fruit that bore it (cf. Mt. 7:16-20; 12:33; Lk. 6:43-44).

7:H:5 — Multiplication: the "Modus Operandi" of the Holy Spirit

The Holy Spirit always multiplies; He never increases by addition. Fruitfulness that occurs as a result of the inspiration of the Holy Spirit is always multiplicative — always creative (cf. Jdt. 16:14; Ps. 51:10; Is. 65:17; Eph. 2:14-18). God creates through expression; the Father expresses creation through the eternal Word and in the Holy Spirit. In Psalms, we read, "By the word of the LORD the heavens were made, and all their host by the breath of his mouth" (Ps. 33:6). Furthermore, to the degree that each person responds to, and cooperates with, the promptings of the Breath of God, they become co-creators with God.

I don't believe that most people appreciate the distinction between "multiplication" and "addition." The simplest way I can think of to distinguish between the two is this; multiplication results in an increase in the quantity of something without a corresponding decrease in quantity from someplace else. For example, if we have a single tennis ball in a bucket and want to increase the number, we can _add_ more balls by going to the tennis court and gathering up loose balls and dumping them in the bucket. The net result in the total number of tennis balls in existence is zero. We increased the number of balls in the bucket by taking them away from someplace else. Furthermore, the single ball we had in the bucket played no part in the increase in the number of balls in the bucket. Multiplication, on the other hand, is very different. Let's say technology has advanced to the point that we could make exact duplicates of inanimate objects by taking samples of their molecules and making them "grow" at a rapid pace until — voila! we have a duplicate object. So we take the single tennis ball that is in the bucket and we put it in the duplicator and produce five more balls from the single ball that we scanned. We could say that the single ball was multiplied. Why? First of all, the net number of balls in existence increased because we didn't take any of the five newly created balls from someplace else. Secondly, the original tennis ball was fruitful because _IT_ was what was multiplied.

Let's look at some scriptural passages that serve as examples of the Holy Spirit's involvement in fruitfulness accomplished through multiplication, i.e. the multi-regeneration of that which was already in existence.

1) "For thus says the LORD the God of Israel, 'The jar of meal shall not be spent, and the cruse of oil shall not fail, until the day that the LORD sends rain upon the earth.'" And she went and did as Eli'jah said; and she, and he, and her

household ate for many days" (1 Kgs 17:14-15). In this passage, Elijah possessed the power [*Actual grace--SML*] of the Holy Spirit, as symbolized by his possession of the mantle of sheepskin (cf. 1 Kgs 19:13, 19; 2 Kgs 2:8, 13-14).[236] We should also note that God revealed to St. Hildegard that the flesh of fallen man was referred to as sheepskin. She writes, "In place of his luminous garment, Adam was given a sheepskin, and God substituted for Paradise a place of exile."[237] Similar to the previous passage, see also 2 Kgs. 4:2-6.

2) After feeding five thousand using only that which was produced from five barley loaves and two fish, Jesus "told his disciples, 'Gather up the fragments left over, that nothing may be lost.' So they gathered them up and filled twelve baskets with fragments from the five barley loaves" (Jn. 6:12-13).

3) "Then he brought me back to the door of the temple; and behold, water was issuing from below the threshold of the temple ... Going on eastward with a line in his hand, the man measured a thousand cubits, and then led me through the water; and it was ankle-deep. Again he measured a thousand, and led me through the water; and it was knee-deep. Again he measured a thousand, and led me through the water; and it was up to the loins. Again he measured a thousand, and it was a river that I could not pass through" (Ezek. 47:1, 3-5). This occurs in a dream that Ezekiel received concerning the coming re-built and eternal Temple. The new Temple that Ezekiel dreamed about was actually the risen and glorified body of Jesus Christ, which was to be the Temple wherein dwelt the fullness of the Triune God in the New Covenant. The water that flowed from the opening (<u>mouth</u>) of the Temple signifies the Living Water that Jesus promised to give to us. In the dream, this water did not have any other contributory. The

water coming from the mouth of the Temple was not being "added" to by any other water source. The Living Water was being multiplied, becoming deeper and deeper as it flowed further and further out from its source, i.e. the threshold of the Temple. This multiplication of grace (Living Water) of the Holy Spirit can be seen more clearly and more profoundly by reading what John had to say on the subject. He writes, "'If any one thirst, let him come to me and drink. He who believes in me, as the scripture has said, 'Out of his heart shall flow rivers of living water.' Now this he said about the Spirit, which those who believed in him were to receive; for as yet the Spirit had not been given, because Jesus was not yet glorified" (Jn. 7:37-39). We become one Mystical Body with Jesus in Baptism; we become one flesh, one body with Jesus in the Eucharist. When this occurs, we become a new creation and a new channel of grace to others around us. Thus, the water coming from the Temple gets deeper and deeper.

Our mouth will fruitfully express our heart and the resulting fruit and the seeds it contains will accurately reflect that which produced it — good or bad. In Part IV (in Volume Two of this book) we will discuss in much greater detail how the salt and light (cf. Mt. 5:13-14) of our "mouth" changes in order to accurately express the overflow of our heart. As a prelude to that, Part III will be devoted to exploring the contributions that salt, stone, and water make toward gaining an even deeper understanding of the NC Temple and its relationship to the salt of man.

CHAPTER 8 — THE HOLY SPIRIT: POST-FALL TO REDEMPTION

Before proceeding to Part III, I want to first talk about the activities of the Holy Spirit prior to His being "given" as described above in John 7:37-39. Drawing from John, it would seem the Holy Spirit said adios to physical creation after the fall of Adam and Eve. All of creation, from the fall of man onwards, was subject to the bondage of decay (Rom. 8:21). As was amply discussed, the Spirit has no part of decay; the Holy Spirit is life. The presence and activity of the Holy Spirit in material creation did NOT cease after the fall. Let's explore this further.

8:A — Action of the Holy Spirit in Material Creation

Pope Leo XIII tells us that the Holy Spirit, who is Divine Goodness, is the <u>ultimate cause</u> of all things, including the completion of man's salvation.[238] God created all things in the eternal 'now', but it unfolds progressively and gradually until the fullness of time (Eph. 1:10) has arrived; when all creation will have been sanctified (which is the "job" of the Holy Spirit). We can see this work already occurring in the earliest passages of the creation narrative in Genesis. We read, "The earth was without form and void, and darkness was upon the face of the deep; and the Spirit of God was moving over the face of the waters" (Gen. 1:2). Notice that it wasn't the Father or the Son who was moving over the waters; it was the Spirit, the Personification of action. Durrwell writes,

> The Spirit is God in his characteristic attribute, God himself in his infinite action. For Christian faith the Spirit is a person; it can, therefore, be said that he is the personification of action, that he is the 'working'

member or person in the Trinity [St. Cyril of Alexandria says, "The Spirit is the power and natural action of the divine substance. He performs all the works of God." *Thesaurus*, assert. 34 (PG 75, 580; cf. 72, 608)]. Whenever, then, God is active, when he creates, intervenes in history, enters through the incarnation into creation, raises Christ from the dead, establishes a covenant between himself and a people ... it is in the Spirit that all this is brought about, for the Spirit is the power and action of God.[239]

And also,

The Spirit, who is infinite reality, forms the link between God and finite beings. Through him, holiness penetrates right into our world and even becomes incarnate there (cf. Lk 1:35); through him, God lives in man as in a temple (cf. 1 Cor. 3:16; 6:19). The heavenly Spirit is the intimacy of God with the earth, the hand of God touching this world: If it is through the finger of God ...'(Jesus says, according to Lk 11:20), 'if it is through the Spirit of God' (Jesus says, according to Mt 12:28) that I cast out devils ...'[240]

Before the fall of man, the Holy Spirit dwelt in the hearts of our first parents, moving their souls in holiness; sanctifying them from the inside out, so to speak. After the fall, however, this was no longer possible; the Spirit had to work from the outside in; working in the material of physical creation, with the effects radiating inward to the immaterial heart (the soul). Scripture tells us this is so. According to Durrwell, "The strength of the Spirit is the strength of God; it comes down on man from above, seizes hold of him (cf. 1 Sam 16:13) and *clothes him [SML]* with itself (cf. Jg 6:34): 'The Spirit of God will seize on [*but not dwell in*] you (Saul) ... and you will be changed into another man' (1 Sam 10:6). The Spirit of 'counsel and power' will rest on the new

David (Is 11:2), who thenceforward will have as his name 'Wonder-Counsellor, Mighty-God' (Is 9:5)."[241] Remember our earlier discussion on the deeper meaning of circumcision. It was a sign on the flesh of a covenant written in the flesh and the heart of the Chosen people.

8:B — Power of the Holy Spirit on Fallen Man

We mentioned above that the Holy Spirit is the personification of God's action. He is also the personification of God's power. Durrwell provides us with a brief list of only some of the Scripture passages that inform us of this. He writes:

> Throughout the story of the Church the union of the two notions of Spirit and power is invariably maintained. The Gospel is spread 'as power and as the Holy Spirit' (1 Th 1:5); preaching is a 'demonstration of the power of the Spirit' (1 Cor 2:4): people submit to the 'obedience of faith' by the power of 'signs and wonders', by the power of the Holy Spirit (cf. Rom 15:19; 2 Cor 12:12; Gal 3:2-5). The apostles 'boldly' bear witness to Jesus, filled with the power of the Spirit (cf. Acts 4:31 and passim). Among them, Stephen is 'filled with grace and power ... filled with the Holy Spirit' (cf. Acts 6:8; 7:55). The faithful are 'powerfully strengthened by the Spirit' (cf. Eph 3:16) who gives them 'power' to confess the Lord Jesus (cf. 1 Cor 12:3) and to observe God's law (cf. Rom 8:2f.). 'The power of the Holy Spirit will remove from them all bounds to hope' (Rom 15:13), a hope which will be fulfilled when they rise in power ... in a spiritual body (cf. I Cor 15:43f.) through the Spirit living in them (cf. Rom 8: 11). This is a lengthy list of testimony to the power of the Spirit, but it is not exhaustive. We can draw from it a firm, fundamental conclusion: the Spirit is the omnipotence of God.[242]

How does the power of God manifest itself in the time of fallen man? In this first and most important way, God maintains our existence. Patrick Toner writes, "God the Creator of the world — the producer of its whole being or substance — and in the next place, supposing its production, that its continuance in being at every moment is due to His sustaining power. Creation means *the total production of a being out of nothing,* i.e. the bringing of a being into existence to replace absolute nonexistence."[243] In the sense-able realm, he also shows us his power through Gratuitous graces. Aquinas writes:

> The Holy [Spirit] provides sufficiently for the Church in matters profitable unto salvation, to which purpose the gratuitous graces are directed. Now just as the knowledge which a man receives from God needs to be brought to the knowledge of others through the gift of tongues and the grace of the word, so too the word uttered needs to be confirmed in order that it be rendered credible. This is done by the working of miracles, according to Mark 16:20, "And confirming the word with signs that followed": and reasonably so. For it is natural to man to arrive at the intelligible truth through its sensible effects. Wherefore just as man led by his natural reason is able to arrive at some knowledge of God through His natural effects, so is he brought to a certain degree of supernatural knowledge of the objects of faith by certain supernatural effects which are called miracles. Therefore the working of miracles belongs to a gratuitous grace.[244]

Aquinas tells us the power of God, manifested through fallen man, is not dependent on the person's holiness. In fact, "even the wicked can work miracles"[245] through the power of the Holy Spirit, despite the absence of an indwelling. I submit that the salt of DNA was designed by God to be an effective instrument/conduit for the manifestation of the power of God in both the Old and New Covenants. Let's examine some examples in Scripture.

8:B:1 — Scriptural Evidence that the Power of God Works Through the Salt of DNA

There are many instances throughout Scripture where the power and grace of the Holy Spirit are made manifest. Interestingly, the salt of DNA is often associated with the mediation or translation of that power into the physical world. JP II's words bear repeating: "The body, in fact, and it alone is capable of making visible what is invisible: the spiritual and divine. It was created to transfer into the visible reality of the world, the mystery hidden since time immemorial in God."[246] It doesn't even have to be human DNA for this phenomenon to occur. It seems DNA, together with bio-living water (in man), was specifically created by God to serve this very purpose; to function as the mouth which accurately expresses the overflow of the heart wherein the Holy Spirit dwells (2 Cor. 1:21-23). Scripture tells us of how the Lord took some of Moses' spirit (possessive case) and gave it to the seventy elders after which they prophesied (Num. 11:16-17, 24-25) — remember that all true prophecy comes from the power of the Holy Spirit (cf. 2 Pt. 1:16-21) and is part of the classification of Gratuitous grace. We also read that Moses gave Joshua his spirit by laying hands upon him (Deut. 34:8-9).[247]

Let's look at some specific examples. Jesus and his Apostles can attribute their healings (Acts 10:38; Mt. 10:1; Lk. 5:17), exorcisms (Lk. 4:36, 9:1), and other miracles (Rom. 1:4) to the power of the Holy Spirit. In the case of healings, Jesus also attributes them to the faith (which is openness to the gifts and power of the Holy Spirit) of the sick person. So let's examine the contribution of the salt of DNA in manifesting the power of God. Two very powerful examples of such passages deal with Elijah and Elisha resurrecting the dead in a seemingly peculiar way.

8:B:1:a — Elisha's Bones

In Scripture, one of the best examples of my hypothesis is in 2 Kings. It reads, "So Eli'sha died, and they buried him. Now bands of Moabites used to invade the land in the spring of the year. And as a man was being buried, lo, a marauding band was seen and the man was cast into the grave of Eli'sha; and as soon as the man touched the bones of Eli'sha, he revived, and stood on his feet" (2 Kgs. 13:20-21). Remember, Elisha was dead. His soul had long ago left his body. Since it was only Elisha's <u>bones</u> that were present in the grave, we can conclude his death occurred a long time prior to the present events described in this Scripture passage. Remember, only Elisha's salt of DNA was in the grave. The dead man that was dumped there came back to life <u>only</u> after touching Elisha's bones. The soul of the dead man dumped into the grave was not present. Consequently, the question of faith and free will played no part in this miracle. I believe it is clear that the power of the Holy Spirit used Elisha's salt of DNA as an instrument of His power. The Holy Spirit didn't have to use the salt of DNA that formed Elisha's bones, but he chose to. Let's look at another example.

8:B:1:b — The Hemorrhagic Woman

Mark tells us about the woman who had a flow of blood for twelve years. He writes, "She said, 'If I touch even his garments, I shall be made well.' And immediately the hemorrhage ceased; and she felt in her body that she was healed of her disease. And Jesus, perceiving in himself that power had gone forth from him, immediately turned about in the crowd, and said, 'Who touched my garments?'" (Mk. 5:28-30). Based on Jesus' words we know that she hadn't touched Jesus' flesh. She only touched the garments he wore. Keep in mind there were no synthetic garments in those days. Consequently, all clothes worn by people at that time were made of animal or plant DNA. So in this case, the power of Jesus' Spirit was mediated by the salt of Jesus' DNA and through the DNA of the garments in very close proximity to his DNA. The power of the Holy Spirit left him and was received by the salt of DNA of the woman, resulting in the healing of the dysfunction of her DNA. It would almost seem as though this whole event caught Jesus by surprise — which would be impossible. I think that Jesus asked the question, "who touched my garments," as a way of emphasizing the role of her faith (her openness to the power of the Spirit) together with the instrumentality of the salt of DNA in manifesting the power of the Holy Spirit.

8:B:1:c — The Burning Bush

In the 3rd chapter of Exodus, We read how Moses climbed Horeb, the mountain of God, and came upon the glory of God radiating through a burning bush which was not consumed. It is my belief the bush was nothing more than a multitude of cells containing the salt of DNA and structured bio-living water. The bush was mediating the glory of God through its salt of DNA and cellular water. The bush was not the _source_ of that glory; it was only manifesting it. Moses was not yet engaged in a face-to-face encounter with God.

It was not a direct encounter with God' glory; rather, it was mediated through a biological life. One of the signs of the difference between types of encounter is described in Exodus. After Israel's exodus from Egypt, they traveled to Sinai and camped in the surrounding wilderness. In the 33rd chapter Moses pleads with God not to abandon the people because of their great sin. After doing so, he asks God to show him His glory. God decides to grant his request and explains to him how he will accomplish it (v. 18-23). The entire 34th chapter details the following day and, among other things, the encounter Moses had with God's glory (Durrwell tells us that the Holy Spirit is the glory of God[248]) — not mediated through the bush, but directly when the Lord descended in a cloud (v. 5). When Moses' came down from the mountain his face shone with the light of the glory that he had encountered, which was a great shock to the people who saw it. After Moses had spoken, he put a veil over his face to hide this phenomenon because it caused the people to fear (v. 29-35). You may be asking; since the veil would have also contained DNA, why didn't it also show the effects of the glory of God? The reason is because Moses was not the source of the glory, i.e. the radiating light of the Spirit; his salt of DNA only mediated it. You will understand this phenomenon better after reading Part IV (contained in Volume Two of STOSS).

8:B:1:d — The Transfiguration

Scripture tells us, "And after six days Jesus took with him Peter and James and John his brother, and led them up a high mountain apart. And he was transfigured before them, and his face shone like the sun, and his garments became white as light" (Mt. 17:1-2). This is another example of the power and glory of the Holy Spirit being mediated through a mortal human body (one not yet glorified), the body of Jesus. Not only was his body transfigured, but also the salt of DNA of his garments, which were either touching or in close proximity to his body. There is no mention in the passages describing anything else in close proximity to Jesus (e.g. anything inorganic, dirt or rocks) undergoing a similar transformation.

Hmm, are we beginning to see a common theme emerging from these passages? Is there more to this whole 'we are salt and light thing' (Mt. 5:13-16) than meets the eye? Isn't it interesting that the transfiguration of Jesus and the miracle at Cana are both included in JP II's Mysteries of Light, and both accounts are strongly associated with the salt of DNA and water? The transfiguration may not, on the surface, have anything to do with water, but later we will show that it does —

and dramatically so.

8:B:1:e — Moses' Rod/Staff

The book of Exodus is a veritable cornucopia of types and foreshadowings indicating what will come to be in the New and everlasting Covenant of Salt. As it is with many topics in this book, time and space limitations prevent me from writing as extensively as I believe is warranted. Consequently, we will focus only on Moses' rod, or staff, of God. The rod was cut from an almond tree[249] and consisted, therefore, entirely of cells containing the salt of DNA. When God commissioned Moses to lead His people out of bondage, he told Moses it would be through the rod/staff that he would perform the signs of what we now describe as Gratuitous grace, i.e. all of the miracles (Ex. 4:17). It was through the salt of DNA of the rod that the Holy Spirit would show the power of God. Of all the miracles that were performed, the first one Pharaoh's magicians were <u>not</u> able to mimic occurred when the Lord told Moses to instruct Aaron to stretch out the rod and strike the dust, turning plain ordinary dust into living gnats. Only God, <u>through the power of the Holy Spirit</u>, can cause organic life (containing the salt of DNA) to come from inorganic matter. This miracle is reminiscent of man's creation. We were, after all, created from the inorganic dust of the earth (Gen. 2:7). More precisely, Adam was likely made from the inorganic dust of the earth, while the rest of us received our organic dust from Adam and Eve. Upon witnessing the miracle of dust being transformed into gnats, "the magicians said to Pharaoh, 'This is the finger of God'" (Ex. 8:19). Now in Luke, we read the words of Jesus. Talking to the Pharisees he says, "... by the finger of God that I cast out demons" (Lk. 11:20). In Matthew's version of the exchange it was written, "But if it is by the Spirit of God that I cast out demons ..." (Mt. 12:28). Clearly, the term "finger of God" is in reference to the Holy Spirit, and this interpretation is shared by

Augustine.[250] It seems obvious to me that the power of Moses' (or Aaron's) Holy Spirit was mediated through the salt of DNA of his staff.

Throughout Scripture, there has been much written linking the actions of the Holy Spirit with water. I would add: between the Holy Spirit, water, and the salt of DNA. We will cover this three-part relationship more extensively in Chapter 16:C (located in Volume Two of STOSS). I have come to believe, with some uncertainty, that within creation the relationship of water to the Holy Spirit is akin to the relationship the salt of DNA has to the Son of God. It seems as though it is through the instrumentality of water and salt that God acts within material creation; using physical water the Holy Spirit acts within — produces effects on — material creation in conjunction with the firstborn of all creation, i.e. Jesus Christ (cf. Heb. 1:6, Col. 1:15, Ps. 89:27). I believe the parting of waters (Gen. 1:6-7; Ex. 14:15-22; Josh. 3:5-17 through 4:1-18; 2 Kgs. 2:5-9, 12-15) intimates the necessity for a deeper penetration of Jesus' salt and light discourse (Mt. 5:13-14). Emphatically, I am not saying the salt of DNA, and/or the relationship of water with light, can or should be construed in any way as being Supernatural in essence. However, the linkage leads us to a discussion of some very intriguing miracles with water accomplished by the power of the Holy Spirit, and in conjunction with the salt of DNA of both the staff/rod of God and Elijah's sheepskin mantle. I am referring to the miracles relating to the parting of waters.

In the book of Joshua, we read how the Ark of the Covenant proceeded before the people of the nation of Israel in crossing over the Jordan River into the land to which God had led them. When the feet of the priests that bore the Ark rested in the waters of the Jordan, the river ceased to flow and *the waters divided [SML]* so that all of the people crossed over to the other side on dry land (Josh. 3:12-17). Interestingly, inside the Ark was: 1) Moses' staff which was budding (a miracle attributable to the life-giving power of the Holy Spirit giving new life to the salt of DNA in the previously lifeless rod). Perhaps this was a 'type' of the resurrected body of Jesus, who is often represented by wood. Flavius Josephus (37-100 AD) who was a historian and eyewitness to much of the earliest events in Church history, described Moses/Aaron's rod as growing new branches upon which were also growing almonds, which is the type of tree from which the rod had been cut.251); 2) the two stone tablets which were written by the finger of God, i.e. the Holy Spirit; and 3) a gold urn containing some of the manna from heaven (Heb. 9:4). In my opinion, the two stone tablets represent the salt of DNA (the dust of the earth) of our flesh upon which the Law is written (and also in the heart). They also represent the unchangeable Truth and Justice of Jesus, the incarnate Son of God252 (who took upon himself the *heaviness* of a mortal body). The manna represents the salt of DNA of Jesus in the Eucharist through whom we receive an increase of the purifying gifts of the Holy Spirit. In other words, all three items represent the coming of the newly rebuilt Temple (from Ezekiel's dream), which is the final and everlasting Covenant of salt. So what happens when the feet of the priests carrying the Ark enter the waters of the Jordan: the waters divide! This is a deep mystery upon which I hope to shed some light during the remainder of this book.

8:B:1:f — Elijah and Elisha's Mantle

We have already discussed in some detail Elijah and Elisha in Part 'I' of this book. I now want to discuss the mantle and how it relates to our discussion of the Spirit's power being mediated through the salt of DNA. The story of Moses' encounters with God and Elijah's are quite similar. Both went through a forty day and forty night fast on a journey that led them to Mt. Horeb (the mountain of God) and an intimate encounter with God: for Moses, the burning bush; for Elijah, the still small voice when the Lord passed by. During the encounter with God, both men had in their possession an object composed of the salt of DNA; for Moses, it was the wooden staff/rod; for Elijah, it was his sheepskin mantle. After their encounters with God, both of the objects (staff and mantle) were used by the Spirit to mediate the power of God. We have already discussed Moses' rod/staff. Now let's look at Elijah's mantle. This mantle is what Elijah used to cover his face when he encountered the Spirit and Word of God on Horeb, the mountain of God (1 Kgs. 19:8, 11-13). St. Seraphim tells us, "The grace of the Holy Spirit acting externally [Gratuitous grace] was also reflected in all the Old Testament prophets and saints of Israel."[253]

After this encounter, the Lord commanded Elijah to go and *anoint* Elisha to be his successor. After finding Elisha, Elijah threw his mantle over him. Immediately Elisha left what he was doing and ran after Elijah with the desire to follow him (1 Kgs. 19:19-20). This desire, this immediacy of response, is indicative of the presence of the Holy Spirit. It represents the "call", the "attraction" we discussed in Chapter 6:C:ii. In Scripture, to anoint is to convey upon them the Spirit of God (cf. Acts 10:38; Lk 4:14-21; Jn 9:11). Obviously, Elisha's "call" is directly attributable to his anointing through Elijah's mantle. From the Council of Trent, we see that Jesus was anointed and given the gifts of the Holy Spirit necessary to fulfill his function of Prophet, Priest, and King.[254] In Isaiah we read, "The Spirit of the LORD GOD is upon me, because the Lord has anointed me to bring good tidings to the afflicted" (Is. 61:1).

How was Elisha anointed with the Spirit? It was through Elijah's mantle being thrown on him. Let me emphasize, I am talking about the power of God (Gratuitous grace), but not Sanctifying grace. The next example of Elijah and Elisha's Spirit being mediated from them and through the salt of DNA of the mantle are detailed in 2nd Kings. In (2:8) we read how Elijah rolled up his mantle and struck the waters of the Jordan. Upon doing so, the waters divided and the two prophets crossed it on dry land. Just as the power of the Holy Spirit was mediated through Moses' staff when he parted the Red Sea, and the Jordan parted when the feet of the priests bearing the Ark came to the edge of the water, so also the same Jordon was parted through the power of the Holy Spirit mediated through Elijah's mantle.

As Elijah was being taken up in the chariot of fire, his mantle fell from him to Elisha. This signified Elisha's receiving of a double portion of Elijah's Spirit, for which he had asked Elijah. What does Elisha immediately do? He rents his old garments (remember the deeper meaning of garments in Scripture) in two and takes up the mantle, goes to the Jordan and strikes the water with it, and the waters part (2 Kgs. 2:9, 11-15). As was mentioned before, Elijah's mantle, which became Elisha's 'new garment' and through which the power of the Holy Spirit was dramatically manifested, was made of *sheepskin*.[255] The mantle was made of the salt of DNA from a sheep. The inside (or the meat) of a sheep is generally referred to as lamb (we never eat sheep, we only eat lamb).

There is additional significance to the symbolism of the sheepskin. It is not just a garment; it is also the symbol of the body of fallen man. St. Hildegard writes, "In place of his luminous garment, Adam was given a sheepskin."[256] Remember, 'garment' is used in Scripture and other writings as another word for flesh/body. Interpreting Hildegard: in place of a body that was in perfect harmony with a pure and holy spirit, God gave us a sheepskin as a sign of a "garment" that was no longer luminous. It now becomes even clearer that the power of the Holy Spirit can and does work through the garment of our fallen body, symbolized by the sheepskin mantle used by both Elijah and Elisha.

Are there any theological light bulbs coming on for you? The symbolism of the mantle is thus pointing to a meta-sense-able reality. Jesus is never referred to as a sheep; he is referred to as a lamb; more specifically, he is referred to as The Passover Lamb — the Paschal Mystery. Only his followers are referred to as sheep. He is the Passover lamb that, according to Mosaic Law, <u>must</u> be consumed (Ex. 12:8, 34:25). Remember, Jesus told Peter to feed his sheep (Jn. 21:17). Our food is the "lamb" that is meant to be consumed. When we consume the food of the Paschal Lamb death passes us by; we receive the Holy Spirit. The Holy Spirit sanctifies our inner heart which causes our mouth/body/outer garment (foreshadowed by Elijah and Elisha's mantle) to radiate grace and the power of the Spirit.

I don't know about you, but I find the interconnectedness of Moses, Elijah, John the Baptist, the waters of the Jordan River, the baptism of the incarnate Son of God, and the rebuilt NC Temple, to be fascinating and more than coincidental. The Transfiguration of Jesus seems to be the biblical event around which these interconnections coalesce; more to come, later.

Tertullian, a second-century ecclesiastical writer, reinforces the value of our dust. He writes,

> Now, if all things are subject to the soul through the flesh, their subjection is equally due to the flesh ... there is not a soul that can at all procure salvation, except it believe [and acts upon the promptings of the Holy Spirit] while it is in the flesh, so true is it that the flesh is the very condition on which salvation hinges [SML] ... it is the flesh which actually renders it capable of such service. The flesh, indeed, is washed, in order that the soul may be cleansed; the flesh is anointed, that the soul may be consecrated; the flesh is signed (with the cross), that the soul too may be fortified; the flesh is shadowed with the imposition of hands, that the soul also may be illuminated by the Spirit [SML]; the flesh feeds on the body and blood of Christ, that the soul likewise may fatten on its God. They cannot then be separated in their recompense, when they are united in their service.[257]

Tertullian believes that our bodies ... our dust of DNA are the mouth through which the human soul inhales and exhales the spiritual and the divine. He simply uses different wording than I do.

PART III — SALT IN THE NEW TESTAMENT (NT)

After reading Part III, it will be easier to understand and agree with St. Hildegard, who tells us we are made with "great glory" from the _dust_ (salt) of the earth.[258] Expanding further: from dust God made our salt of DNA with great glory and in an awe-inspiring way! In light of Hildegard's words, and in consideration of our discussion of the body's role in being created in His image and likeness, it can be seen that the flesh is, by God's design, a valuable part of man's being.

The New Covenant _is_ a covenant of salt. More precisely, Jesus is the new and everlasting covenant of salt, through which our salt of DNA can be redeemed, purified, and perfected — provided it is our desire and we act upon that desire. Remember, the New Covenant is hidden and foreshadowed in the Old Covenant. In the OC, all offerings had to be salted (Lev. 2:13).[259] We overlook the fact that the offering itself, owing to its organic nature, was also salt. So we can accurately say, the offering of salt had to be salted with salt. The unblemished first fruit offering (salt #1) was an OT 'type' of the perfect offering of Jesus Christ in the Garden of Gethsemane and also on the cross. The salt (salt #2) which salted the salt (#1) was a 'type' of redeemed man who, by uniting his salt of DNA (salt #2) with the Savior's salt of DNA (salt #1) in Baptism and in the Eucharist, would become one NC Temple. By becoming one with the new Temple of Salt (Jesus' resurrected body), the heart is purified to the degree we earnestly seek union with Jesus. Additionally, our flesh (salt) will proportionally cease to be the soul's tempter, becoming instead, the "mouth" which accurately expresses the overflow of the increasingly purified heart (cf. Mt. 23:26).

In the OT salt was external. It was used in the context of both good and bad circumstances and consequences. In the NT it begins to take on a more personal and internal meaning. For example: "You are the salt of the earth" (Mt. 5:13); "Salt is good; but if the salt has lost its saltness, how will you season it? Have salt in yourselves" (Mk 9:50) and, "Let your speech always be gracious, seasoned with salt, so that you may know how you ought to answer every one" (Col. 4:6). When reading these verses, we may also start to realize that there's more to salt in Scripture than its use as a simple metaphor for the salt of DNA. The components of flavor (saltiness and seasoning), wisdom (know how you ought to answer), and expression (speech seasoned with salt) have been added to the mix.

Exploring the interior aspect of salt brings us to our next topic: since all covenants are covenants of salt, what exactly does the New Covenant look like? What was it that Jesus set out to accomplish? Obviously, he set out to redeem us, but he also tell us, "Lo, I am with you always, to the close of the age" (Mt. 28:20). Ok then, how is he with us? Let's examine that further. As it turns out, Jesus, through the prompting of his mother, was kind enough to show us, in advance, what was to be accomplished at the end of his public mission. He showed us the new and everlasting Covenant of Salt. It was through the changing of water into wine at the wedding feast at Cana that we can see it. In order for us to gain a fuller understanding of this, and other, mysteries in Scripture, we first need to return to a topic we touched on in Part I, i.e. the deeper meaning of stone.

CHAPTER 9 — SYMBOLISM OF STONE/ROCK RELATIVE TO JESUS

In Part I of this book we established that the salt of DNA is actually the dust of the earth — particles of extremely small grains of stone. In this, and subsequent sections, we are going to extrapolate on its significance relative to certain Scripture passages. More specifically, we will be focusing our attention on Jesus, who is: the NC Temple; both salt and light; and, the source of Living Water, which leads to bio-living water, which is nothing less than an instrument of grace. Through a closer examination of stone in both the OT and NT, a general trend can be detected regarding how stone is used in reference to Jesus versus how it is used to denote a man.

9:A — Stone: the Symbol of the Son of God Incarnate

The scriptural use of the word "stone" is often a reference to the Word of God incarnate. In Scripture, a natural rock formation is generally referred to as a rock and any piece of that natural rock formation that becomes separated is generally, but not always, referred to as a stone.[260] I believe this is why, in Exodus, Christ is symbolized by a 'rock' (cf. Ex 17:6; 1 Cor. 10:4) instead of a 'stone.' He had not yet become incarnate and, thus, not yet been sent into material creation as a mortal man. As a Person of the Trinity, the Son of God can never be separated from God. However, by taking on a mortal body, the 'man' Jesus could not ascend back to the Father until his redemptive mission had been accomplished (cf. Jn. 12:24). This return to the Father was essential for our salvation. As we read in John, Jesus had to "go to the Father" so that His _body_ could enter into the Trinitarian dialogue, the result of which is the giving of the gift, i.e. the Holy Spirit (Jn. 16:5-10), to his bride, the Church.

This is why, prior to Jesus' ascension, his body (dust of the earth) could accurately be represented by a stone instead of a rock. After the bodily ascension of Jesus, it would be more appropriate to refer to the incarnate Jesus as a rock again; Hildegard tells us the Church sits on the strongest of rocks, i.e. the risen Christ.[261]

Different places in Scripture refer to a foundation stone, a cornerstone (cf. Is. 28:16; Zech. 10:4; and Ps. 118:22, for example). This cornerstone is actually the body of Jesus — the NC Temple. This is confirmed by St. Paul when he writes, "Christ Jesus himself being the cornerstone, in whom the whole structure is joined together and grows into a holy temple in the Lord; in whom you *also are built into it* [*SML*] for a dwelling place of God in the Spirit" (Eph. 2:20-22). That which *grew* into a holy Temple was his body — his soul didn't grow and his divinity didn't grow either. The reason Paul says "grew" is this: through matrimony with his bride (the Church), *we are living stones built into that Temple* (1 Pt. 2:5), thus making it *grow*.

Scripture makes a direct link between the Temple, the cornerstone, and Jesus' body (Jn. 2:21). This same direct linkage can be made with the story of Jacob (Gen. 28:11-19). Taking the stone upon which he had slept the night of his dream (he dreamt of angels ascending and descending a ladder), Jacob erected it as a pillar. According to God's inspiration, Hildegard wrote that: 1) a stone is the very symbol of the Temple; 2) Jacob's erection of the stone was a foreshadowing of the Son of God becoming *incarnate,* and; 3) the stone is the symbol of Truth incarnate.[262] St. Cyprian of Carthage also makes a *direct link between Jesus and stone* by citing the following Scripture passages: 1) Is. 28:16 (the foundation stone from Zion); 2) Dt. 10:1-3 (the two stones tablets hewed after the first two were broken — the two that ended up in the Ark); 3) Jos. 24:25-27 (the witness stone); 4) Acts 4:10-11 (the rejected cornerstone); 5) Gen. 28:11 (Jacob's stone 'pillow' and pillar); 6) Ex. 17:12 (the stone seat Moses sat on during the battle with Amalek); 7) 1

Sam. 17:49 (the stone to the forehead of Goliath); and 8) 1 Sam. 7:12 (the stone that helpeth — called Ebenezer — set up by Samuel after conquering the Philistines).[263]

St. Peter tells us, "Come to him, to that living stone, rejected by men but in God's sight chosen and precious; and like living stones be yourselves built into a spiritual house, to be a holy priesthood, to offer spiritual sacrifices acceptable to God through Jesus Christ" (1 Pt. 2:4-5). In other words, the members of the body of Christ, i.e. the Church, are also living stones and the spiritual house is the Temple.[264] How do we know the spiritual house referred to in this passage is the Temple and not some synagogue-type meeting place? As was said before, only the Temple was the location in which perfect and unblemished offerings were made to God (perfect salt, salted with imperfect salt) by priests.

9:B — Stone: the Symbol of Jesus Who is Truth and Justice Incarnate

An appropriate way to interpret and understand Jesus as Truth and Justice incarnate[265] is in the context of the body's function as the mouth which *accurately* expresses the overflow of the heart. It is in the *language of the body,* issuing forth from the mouth, that this divine reality is expressed into the sense-able and meta-sense-able world.

Jesus is referred to as a stone not only because he is the Person of the Trinity who can be seen and touched, but also because he is Truth incarnate ... and Truth is unchangeable.[266] Hence, the appropriateness of "stone" as a symbol for Jesus, who is Truth incarnate. However, in the word's use, relative to the heart of <u>fallen man</u>, it still reflects a state of unchangeableness, but in a negative way. In Scripture, a heart of stone denotes an intractable unwillingness to follow God's commands and/or repent of our sins (cf. Ex. 7:13, Dt. 2:30, Mt. 19:8); a heart of flesh denotes the opposite (Ez. 11:19). This is why Ezekiel writes, "A new heart I will give you, and a new spirit I will put within you; and I will take out of your flesh the heart of stone and give you a heart of flesh" (Ez. 36:26). After receiving a new 'heart' and a new 'spirit', a heart of flesh (as an integral component of the 'mouth') becomes essential to accurately express the new heart and new spirit. We will learn why this is so, starting in Chapter 14 (located in Volume Two of STOSS). It is very important to remember, however, that referring to Jesus as a stone in Scripture is, sense-ably, *symbolic.* After all, the cornerstone, used in Scripture as a symbol, is governed by the physical laws of inorganic chemistry, while the dust/stone within the human body are governed by the laws of organic chemistry. On a meta-sense-able level, however, referring to Jesus as a stone in Scripture is roughly equivalent to referring to man as dust of the earth — which he actually is.

The difference between Jesus and man is this: Jesus' mouth/body never changes in order to accurately express a heart that has *changed* its degree of purity. To begin with, there is never a speck of impurity in His Sacred Heart that would necessitate a change. Consequently, his body, in its function as the mouth of the heart, never needs to change. This is why he is referred to as a stone, while man's flesh is referred to as a garment or robe. Man's garment is constantly becoming dirty and in dire need of washing. In Baptism man receives a clean new garment, but through sin, it is constantly soiled and needs to be rewashed through the Sacrament of Reconciliation. St. Paul writes, "Christ loved the church and gave himself up for her, that he might sanctify her, having cleansed her by the washing of water with the word" (Eph. 5:25-27).

9:C — Symbolism of Stone Relative to Man

As we just said, Jesus' body is sense-ably symbolized by stone (though meta-sense-ably it is much closer to literal), while man's body is symbolized by garments, robes, sheepskin, and the like. With regard to man, there is one *notable* exception to this scriptural trend. When man is being symbolized in the context of a nuptial relationship to the NC Temple — Jesus' resurrected body — via Baptism and the Eucharist, then man is symbolized by stone. Calling once again upon the "patron saint" of STOSS, we learn from Hildegard that Baptism is the Sacrament through which the Church grows "by the building up of the living stones, who are washed white in the pure font."[267] Not only is man often symbolized by stone in Scripture passages, but he is symbolized by _precious_ stone, e.g. diamond, onyx, and sapphire.[268] Let's look at a few examples.

1) "To him who conquers I will give some of the hidden manna, and I will give him a white stone, with a new name written on the stone which no one knows except him who receives it" (Rev. 2:17). I believe the white stone symbolizes our resurrected bodies in Heaven.

2) "'You were in Eden, the garden of God; every precious stone was your covering, carnelian, topaz, and jasper, chrysolite, beryl, and onyx, sapphire, carbuncle, and emerald; and wrought in gold were your settings and your engravings. On the day that you were created they were prepared.'" (Ez. 28:13).

3) "Take twelve stones from here out of the midst of the Jordan, from the very place where the priests' feet stood, and carry them over with you, and lay them down in the place where you lodge tonight" (Josh. 4:3) and "when your children ask in time to come, 'What do those stones mean to you?' Then you shall tell them that the waters of the Jordan were cut off before the ark of the covenant of the

LORD; when it passed over the Jordan, the waters of the Jordan were cut off. So these stones shall be to the people of Israel a memorial for ever" (Josh. 4:6-7). These twelve stones were a symbol of the twelve tribes of Israel and a type of the twelve Apostles of Jesus.

4) I am going to delay until later quoting Rev. 21:15-21. It is a description of the Heavenly Jerusalem. The imagery of precious stones is used throughout. The significance of these precious stones, gold, and gold's "transparency" will be explained later, at which time I will quote some of its passages. There is a scientific component that leads to a more complete understanding of the passages in question.

We will now begin our examination of the justification for believing that: 1) Jesus' resurrected body is the fulfillment of the covenant of salt that God made with Abraham; 2) salvation comes only through a literal union of the whole man — soul and salt of DNA — with that Temple; and 3) redemption of the body (Rom. 8:23) cannot be achieved without a one-flesh union with the NC Temple. We'll start our discussion with the first miracle that Christ performed in his public ministry, Cana.

CHAPTER 10 — THE WEDDING FEAST AT CANA

A Note Concerning the Real Presence and Transubstantiation

In our discussion of the Wedding Feast at Cana, we will begin to touch on the topic of the Real Presence of Christ in the Eucharist. This discussion will continue in increasingly greater depth throughout the rest of this book. It is a dogma of the Catholic Church that the whole and entire Jesus, in his humanity and Divinity, are truly, really, and substantially present in the Eucharist. This dogma is usually referred to as the "Real Presence". STOSS rises or falls on whether or not the understanding of this dogma would include a justifiable reliance on the belief that the words "truly, really, and substantially present," correctly signifies that his living physical body (though <u>not</u> mortal) — containing his functioning cells, biological water, functioning DNA, proteins, etc. — is present after the consecration of the Communion Host.

Through the dogma of the Real Presence, we know that Jesus is truly and wholly present in the Eucharist. The dogma of Transubstantiation informs us of the mode of his presence.[269] Basically, the dogma of Transubstantiation states: at the consecration of the species of bread and wine during the Mass, the entire philosophical substance of the bread and wine are changed into the entire substance of Jesus' body, blood, soul, and Divinity. While the accidents of bread and wine are still visible, all that makes the bread be bread, and the wine be wine (i.e., their substances), are totally gone ... replaced by the whole and entire substance of Jesus in both his humanity and Divinity. This is often referred to as the "sacramental" presence of Jesus in the Eucharist.

There are those who believe that the body and blood of Jesus are not *physically* present in the consecrated host; that the sacramental presence is not also a physical presence. In an effort to keep (as much as possible) this book accessible to those who are not theologians, and because the subject matter in question is necessarily both theologically and philosophically complex, I have decided to address the concerns of those who are more theologically inclined, to Appendix 'A' of this book. You should read it if ...: 1) you believe that the sacramental presence of Jesus in the Eucharist is not also a physical presence; 2) you believe that Paschasius Radbertus was a heretic; 3) you believe that a mortal body is the **only** type of physical body; or 4) you've read Ludwig Ott's book, *Fundamentals of Catholic Dogma*, especially the chapter titled "The Fact of the Real Presence of Christ," and the sub-section titled "The Heretical Counter-theses". Otherwise, please feel free to continue reading the current section.

Now that we are done with the provisos, let's begin our discussion of the miracle at Cana by citing John. He writes:

> On the third day there was a marriage at Cana in Galilee, and the mother of Jesus was there; Jesus also was invited to the marriage, with his disciples. When the wine failed, the mother of Jesus said to him, "They have no wine." And Jesus said to her, "O woman, what have you to do with me? My hour has not yet come." His mother said to the servants, "Do whatever he tells you." Now six stone jars were standing there, for the Jewish rites of purification, each holding twenty or thirty gallons. Jesus said to them, "Fill the jars with water." And they filled them up to the brim. He said to them, "Now draw some out, and take it to the steward of the feast." So they took it. When the steward of the feast tasted the water now become wine, and did not know where it came from (though the servants who had drawn the water knew), the steward of the feast called the bridegroom and said to him, "Every man serves the good wine first; and when men have drunk freely, then

the poor wine; but you have kept the good wine until now." This, the first of his signs, Jesus did at Cana in Galilee, and manifested his glory; and his disciples believed in him (Jn. 2:1-11).

The miracle at Cana and the setting in which it was performed pre-figures: 1) the bride of Christ, i.e. his Church of which we are members; 2) the groom, i.e. the NC Temple; 3) the marriage of the two, i.e. through Baptism; and 4) the most intimate of nuptial unions (infinitely more intimate than the conjugal embrace experienced in human marriage) through the sacrament of the Eucharist, from which the Church draws her life, i.e. the Holy Spirit.[270] The miracle at Cana also prefigures the sanctifying and purifying effects this nuptial union will have on our inmost heart and on our salt of DNA, i.e. our mouth. Stated another way, this miracle is revealing to the world the consequences resulting from the accomplishment of his redemptive mission. It would appear that Mary was used as an instrument by the Holy Spirit. Through her intercession, Jesus performed this miracle ... and he knew exactly what it would mean. Let's examine the different components of this miracle and how each contributes to a deeper understanding of its meaning.

10:A — On the Third Day

These are the very first words of the story of the miracle at Cana and they are quite significant. On the first day of John's narrative, Jesus is baptized in the Jordan, foreshadowing the baptism of water and the Spirit, which is the rite of initiation into the nuptial mystery that is the Church that Jesus would build. On the third day of his public ministry, he performs the miracle at Cana. The timing of this event coincides with, and specifically points to, another very significant future event that would occur on the "third day": the Resurrection of Jesus from the dead.[271] It was Easter — the third day after His death on the cross. It was the day that he arose from the dead through the power of the Holy Spirit. It was the day when his body was spiritualized and glorified. It was the day of the arrival of the Kingdom of God/Kingdom of Heaven, which is the outpouring of the Holy Spirit[272,273] in the person of Jesus Christ.[274]

The validity of the direct linkage between the two events that occurred on the "third day" is established by Jesus' response to his mother when asked to perform the miracle. He said, "My hour has not yet come" (Jn. 2:4). What does he mean by his *hour*? It is when Jesus dies and passes over to the Father.[275,276] Nowhere else in Scripture are Jesus' miracles directly linked to his coming *hour*. When Jairus begged Jesus to come heal his daughter (she died before Jesus arrived at Jairus' house), did he respond — *what has this to do with me? Don't you know it is not yet my hour* (Mt. 5:23-24 and 38-41)? No, he didn't. We can summarize the significance of the "third day" thusly: 1) on the third day after the start of Jesus' public ministry, he performed a miracle that foreshadowed and summarized the entire purpose of his mission on earth; 2) his mission was the establishment and creation of His Church whom he would take as his bride, who would be purified in the waters of Baptism, through which she becomes one Mystical Body with the new and everlasting Temple; and 3) this mission would be accomplished through his Passover on the third day after the end of His public ministry.[277]

10:B — Fill the Jars With Water

As Scripture describes it, the water in the jugs was meant for the Jewish rite of purification. This informs us of the significance of this component of the miracle. This miracle is not only about purification, but also about <u>how</u> this purification would be accomplished. The water in the jugs foreshadows Baptism through which we are both washed clean and also "married" to the groom, becoming one Mystical Body with him. Through this nuptial union, the OC rite of initiation, i.e. circumcision (itself a sign of purity in both heart and body — see Chapter 4:B) is fulfilled and replaced by the infinitely more efficacious NC rite of initiation, i.e. Baptism. Through Baptism the *guilt* of our sins is washed away. Baptism doesn't purify our hearts, thus we continue to struggle with our fleshly desires and attractions. In other words, it doesn't take away our concupiscence. This is exactly why it is essential to become one flesh with Jesus in the Eucharist, as is also foreshadowed by the miracle taking place in the context of both the wedding <u>*and*</u> the wedding banquet. This will be explained further in the balance of this Chapter and throughout Parts III and IV (in Volume Two).

10:C — Cana: Foreshadowing the Purification of Man

What is the fountain? According to Ezekiel's prophetic dream (Ez. 47:1-12), it is the resurrected body of Jesus, the NC Temple from which life-giving water flows; waters that are living because they represent Divine Charity, the Holy Spirit himself. One of the major components of this miracle is that Jesus changed the water into wine. In the Church, wine is the symbol of grace, and the "new wine" that is described in this miracle has the ability to purify our hearts.[278] This is of critical importance since, according to JP II, all moral disorder stems from the impurity of a lustful heart.[279] As we have discussed previously, the body (our salt of DNA) will accurately express the overflow of the "heart" of man. Consequently, as the heart of man is purified through grace, the salt of DNA of man must also change so that it accurately expresses the increasing purity of the heart/spirit. I'm not going to jump the gun too much, but keep in mind that wine is composed of, primarily, two things: water and the salt of DNA of the grape. As we process further into this book, and especially in Volume Two: Part IV, we will see more clearly and with greater awe, the profound significance of these two substances and how they work in conjunction with each other to purify the salt of man.

According to Hildegard, just as strong wine strengthens human blood, so too does the blood of the Lamb strengthen man, making it possible for him to escape the bondage of sin imposed upon it by the flesh.[280] This reinforces the understanding that Jesus' Salt of DNA — His body and blood — will physically purify us. The genetically oriented *strengthening of human blood* corresponds to and is synonymous with the spiritually oriented *life-giving freedom*.

10:D — Significance of Six Stone Jars

There are multiple layers of significance to the six <u>stone</u> jars which help us to grasp the reason for their inclusion in this miracle. The miracle at Cana is a foreshadowing of what Jesus would accomplish at the end of his mission on earth — at the completion of his "hour". The six stone jars filled with the water (meant for the rite of purification) foreshadows the *rebuilt* NC Temple. When the centurion pierced the lifeless body of Jesus, penetrating all the way into his heart, his blood and water flowed out from the wound (Jn. 19:33-34). The six <u>stone</u> jars represent the "living stone" (dust/stone of DNA) which is the resurrected body of Jesus (1 Pt. 2:4); out of the <u>mouth</u> of these jars (again representing Jesus' body) comes Living Water that purifies.

I want to briefly talk about Jacob. I will reserve greater detail concerning him for Chapter 11. There are three foreshadowing events in the Genesis account of Jacob that relate to stone; they each contribute to a greater appreciation of the significance of the material from which the six jars at Cana were hewn, i.e. stone. They are: 1) The stone pillar that Jacob (a type of Christ[281]) erected, at the place he called Bethel (Gen. 28:18-19), which symbolizes the Word of God incarnate; [282] 2) The heavy stone that covered the well from which his future bride, Rachel (a type of the Church[283]), watered her father's sheep (Gen. 29:9-10), represents the heaviness of Jesus' *mortal* body; and, 3) When this heavy stone is rolled away (hmm, didn't a heavy stone have to be rolled away from Jesus' tomb?) via Jesus' death and resurrection, the 'mouth' of the stone well (representing the resurrected body of Jesus) became the means through which Living Water was able to be drawn for Rachel's sheep. The symbolism of these three events provides us with a deeper understanding of the meaning of the six stone jars at Cana, from which new wine flows.

10:E — The Number 'Six'

The fact that there were <u>six</u> jars (not five, or three, or whatever other number) is also significant (there are no coincidences in God's plans). St. Augustine tells us, "We must not despise the science of numbers, which, in many passages of holy Scripture, is found to be of eminent service to the careful interpreter. Neither has it been without reason numbered among God's praises, 'Thou hast ordered all things in number, and measure, and weight'[Wis. 11:20]."[284] Relative to the number six, Augustine writes, "And this number [six] is on that account called perfect, because it is completed in its own parts ... And Holy Scripture commends to us the perfection of this number, especially in this, that God finished His works in six days, and on the sixth day man was made in the image of God."[285] St. Methodius of Olympus writes that six, "... is a symbol of Christ, because the number six proceeding from unity is composed of its proper parts, so that nothing in it is wanting or redundant, and is complete when resolved into its parts."[286] In six days God made creation perfectly (cf. Gen. 1:31) and the culmination of that perfect creation was man. The meaning of six goes beyond that, however.

As the first creation took place in six "days," the six stone jars at the wedding feast of Cana symbolize the <u>*new creation*</u> that will become reality with the culmination of Jesus' mission — when all things are made new. St. Paul writes, "For neither circumcision counts for anything, nor uncircumcision, but a new creation" (Gal. 6:15). St. Leo the Great writes, "Let God's people then recognize that they are a new creation in Christ."[287] According to Pope Leo, not only people but also "things" have been newly created. In other words, <u>all</u> creation has been made new by Jesus.[288] We will explore a deeper understanding of "new creation" later.

Especially germane to our discussion on the miracle at Cana and the six stone jars, St. Augustine makes a direct link between the number six, the body of Jesus, and the NC Temple (Jesus' body). He writes,

> And not without reason is the number six understood to be put for a year in the building up of the body of the Lord [*within the womb*], as a figure of which He said that He would raise up in three days the temple destroyed by the Jews. For they said, "Forty and six years was this temple in building [Jn. 2:19-21]." And six times forty-six makes two hundred and seventy-six. And this number of days completes nine months and six days ... in that number of sixes the body of the Lord was perfected; which being destroyed by the suffering of death, He raised again on the third day. For "He spake this of the temple of His body," as is declared by the most clear and solid testimony of the Gospel; where He said, so shall the Son of man be three days and three nights in the heart of the earth.[289]

10:F — Tasted the Water Now Become Wine

It is my belief, as it is also Pope Emeritus Benedict XVI's,[290] that the new wine in this miracle foreshadows the Eucharist, in which the bread and wine are transformed into the body, blood, soul, and divinity of Jesus. In this book, I will not be presenting a comprehensive defense for the Catholic teaching concerning the Real Presence of Jesus and Transubstantiation. There are many others who have already done so, quite capably I might add. However, I will refer you to several sources that will provide compelling reasons why the teaching is justified. They are:

- Apologist Tim Staples (a former Protestant) recorded a 4-CD (also available as a download) set titled, *Living Bread — A Defense of Christ's Real Presence in the Eucharist.* He answers virtually every objection with which a non-believer (in Catholic teaching) would confront a Catholic. The set is available on www.catholic.com. I highly recommend it;

- Also on the same site are a couple of tracts about this topic. The link to one of the tracts is: http://www.catholic.com/tracts/the-real-presence. More can be found from there;

- Baptist convert, Steve Ray, has a downloadable MP3 at: http://www.steveraysstore.com/mp3-downloads/. I would also recommend his CDs. And;

- A good website that is free to read is located at: http://matt1618.freeyellow.com/eucharist.html. Clicking on the links within the articles will lead to other good articles.

Let's return to our topic. An interesting aspect of changing water into wine as part of this wedding event is this: it is the only miracle in Scripture (that I have found) performed by Jesus (Jesus did not perform the miracle of changing water into blood in the book of Exodus) in which something inorganic (the water), i.e. having no life, no DNA, was changed into something organic (the wine), i.e. having the blueprint for life, having the salt of DNA. The recognition of the role of DNA in this mystery is critical for understanding the deeper meaning of the miracle at Cana. The wine that Jesus produced in this miracle wasn't just good wine, it was the best wine. In fact, it would be logical to assume the wine's DNA was perfect, without defect, just as Jesus' body and blood are perfect. How could it even be possible that a perfect God could make anything, let alone wine, imperfectly? As we showed in Chapter 6, ALL of creation, all that has being, is an expression of God. God could not be God if He were able to express himself imperfectly. At Cana, changing water into wine (containing DNA) foreshadowed changing bread and wine into the body (salt of DNA) and blood (salt of DNA and water) of Jesus, through which we receive his Holy Spirit to dwell in our bodies', thus becoming living stones built into the NC Temple (cf. 1 Pt. 2:5) through matrimony. It is through this one-flesh relationship with Jesus in the Eucharist and the resulting in-dwelling of the Holy Spirit that we are truly purified. Both participate in this sanctification (cf. 1 Cor. 6:11). Jesus' salt of DNA and bio-living water _heals_ our "sick" body[291] through Gratuitous grace, and his Holy Spirit _purifies_ our "sick" heart through Sanctifying grace.[292]

The original water in the jars was intended for use in an *external* rite of purification. However, after the water was changed into wine, it became part of the wedding banquet. Instead of an external washing of feet, it became that which was meant to be consumed by the guests at the wedding. In the OT, the Passover lamb (prefiguring Jesus in the Eucharist) had to be consumed at the Passover meal. At Cana, the salt of DNA of the wine coupled with water (representing Living Water and the body and blood of the Passover lamb) are consumed and thus dwell within the salt of DNA of our bodies. The nuptial union of the Bridegroom and Bride via Baptism (resulting in our becoming one with the Mystical Body of Christ) together with our partaking in the marriage feast of the Lamb (i.e. the feast at Cana), the Eucharist[293] point to <u>the</u> means of purification, which is more efficacious and more intimate than we could ever imagine.

10:G — Significance of Mary at Cana

I would be remiss if I did not briefly address the significance of Mary's role in this miracle. Much can and should be written on this subject. However, at this time I will only offer up a few sentences in support of the significance of Mary's role at Cana, and it's meaning relative to the Church and the Eucharist. I can think of no better person to help with this endeavor than JP II, who gave us the meditations on the Mysteries of Light, of which the miracle at the wedding feast of Cana is one. In his 2003 encyclical letter, *Ecclesia de Eucharistia*, he specifically details the intimate relationship of Mary to Cana, the Church, and the Eucharist. He writes: 1) "In repeating what Christ did at the Last Supper in obedience to his command: 'Do this in memory of me!' we also accept Mary's invitation to obey him without hesitation: 'Do whatever he tells you'"(*Jn.* 2:5);[294] 2) "*If the Church and the Eucharist are inseparably united, the same ought to be said of Mary and the Eucharist* [SML];"[295] and, 3) "Among the mysteries of light I included *the institution of the Eucharist* (cf. No. 21: AAS 95, 2003, 20). Mary can guide us towards this most holy sacrament, because she herself has a profound relationship with it."[296]

The implications of STOSS for our understanding of Mary's role in creation, and also the economy of salvation, are profound!!!!! In Scripture, we are told Jesus was fully human in ALL things except sin (cf. Heb. 2:17, 4:15).[297] The fact that the *entire* incarnate part of Jesus' human nature came from Mary's salt of DNA — and from hers alone — leads us to some unfathomably deep implications. Knowing what I now know about human nature in light of Scripture, TOB, and science, I find myself asking some intriguing questions. For example, if Mary were not the Mediatrix of all graces (as the secondary efficient cause — Jesus being the primary efficient cause), could it still be accurately stated that Jesus was fully human in all aspects? And if he were not fully human, could he still have redeemed man without dramatically altering the very nature of all mankind? Other facts, which will be revealed later, will open up our minds to further ponderings.

CHAPTER 11: — NOW IS THE NEW AND EVERLASTING COVENANT OF SALT

In the Old Covenant of salt, Jewish life was centered on the Temple and the synagogue. In the NC of salt, Christian life is centered on the Temple and the Church; the relationship between the two is markedly different than it was between the Temple and the synagogue. A short description of each would be helpful.

11:A — The Synagogue

The synagogue is sort of a Jewish community center. Primarily, it provided a place for people to gather for the reading and systematic interpretation of Scripture. It also served as a place for various functions, such as funerals, business gatherings, ceremonies, educational activities, and other types of meetings.[298] The synagogue is kind of like a modern-day parish hall or worship center, perhaps containing a pulpit. It was also a place where Bible studies and meetings could be held. However, there were no altars of holocaust and no offerings made to God in the synagogue. The Ark of the Covenant was not present in the synagogue, i.e. it was never considered to be the dwelling place of God on earth. In the synagogue, there is no "godes" (the Holy) or "debir" (the Holy of Holies).[299] In ancient Judaism, there were multiple synagogues existing at one time, but always and only one Temple. There is no place in the Bible where the synagogue is described as eternal; even as a dwelling place of God! Jesus never said: *Destroy this synagogue and in three days I will rebuild it.* John never clarifies, telling us that the synagogue Jesus was referring to was his body.

11:B — The Old Covenant Temple

In the Bible, the word "Temple" signifies a sanctuary, a place sacred to the Divinity, a house (dwelling place) of God.[300] In all of historical Scripture, there has always been only one place at any given time where God dwelt within creation in a special way. Arguably, the first place was the "tree of life" in the Garden of Eden. The second place would be Mt. Horeb (the mountain of God) (Ex. 3:1). The third place was the Ark of the Covenant (Ex. 25:10). The fourth place was the stone Temple (built to house the Ark). The 'stone' Temple of Jesus' glorified body would be the fifth and final one, destined to exist for all eternity.

To the Israelites, the Temple in Jerusalem was called Bet Yehovah (house of Jehovah).[301] While the building of the first Temple was in the heart of King David, who had already begun accumulating all of the materials and furnishings necessary to accomplish his heart's desire, its accomplishment was reserved by God for David's son, Solomon (1 Chron. 28:1-6). The chronology of the Temple is this: "The temple which Solomon erected to the Lord about 966 B.C. was destroyed by Nabuchodonozor in 586 B.C. After the return from captivity, Zorobabel raised it again from its ruins (537 B.C.), but in such modest conditions that the ancients who had seen the former Temple wept. In the eighteenth year of his reign, which corresponds to 19 B.C., King Herod destroyed the Temple of Zorobabel to replace it by another which would equal, if not surpass in splendour, that of Solomon."[302] Just as there were never two places where God simultaneously dwelled, there also were never two Temples existing at one time. The location of the Temple and each rebuilt Temple was located around the exact same location, i.e. the *sacred rock*, which was the foundation for the altar of holocausts in the Temple of Jerusalem.[303] The location of the sacred rock is significant because it is at the location where David, who had become prideful, saw an angel sent by God make ready to strike the people of the city. The angel was stayed when David humbled himself before God. In gratitude, David built an altar upon this rock. It is the same location where ancient tradition holds that Abraham made ready to sacrifice his son, Isaac. The fact that the sacred rock was not only spared in each rebuilding of the Temple, it was the very center of each design.[304] Perhaps, and this is only conjectured on my part, the sacred rock provides us with a deeper understanding of Jesus' words to Peter when he said, "And I tell you, you are Peter, and on this rock I will build my church, and the powers of death shall not prevail against it" (Mt. 16:18).

The important point is this: it was ordained by God that there be one — and _only_ one — _special_ dwelling place for God, continuously existing from the time of David onward. Starting with Solomon's time and continuing until the resurrection of Jesus, that dwelling place of God was within the literal stone walls[305] of the Temple. It was always located in the same place and according to the same structural layout.[306] The Temple was the center of the Jewish world, as can be seen by the three great national festivals in Judaism (the Passover, Pentecost, and the Feast of the Tabernacles) which were all celebrated at the Temple in Jerusalem. So important were these festivals, all males were expected to travel there for their celebration.[307] According to Ezekiel's prophetic dream, this solitary Temple (dwelling place for God) was meant to exist for *all eternity* (Ez. 43:7). In Haggai, we read, "I will fill this house with splendor, says the LORD of hosts. The silver is mine, and the gold is mine, says the LORD of hosts. The latter splendor of this house shall be greater than the former, says the LORD of hosts; and in this place I will give prosperity, says the LORD of hosts" (Haggai 2:7-9). In other words, the glory of the NC Temple will far exceed that of the OC Temple and this glory will exist forever.

11:C — What is a Covenant of Salt?

We have already given a very brief and general definition of the biblical understanding of a 'covenant' between God and man (Chapter 4:B). Scripture also refers to salt covenants or covenants of salt. What, if any, is the difference between a covenant, and a covenant of salt?

In the Biblical sense, a covenant is <u>much</u> more than is a civil covenant. It is a solemn oath and a gift of persons — a gift that is also a unity.[308] Dr. Scott Hahn tells us the Trinity is a covenant relationship of three Persons in one God.[309] A covenant forms a sacred kinship with God.[310] Nowhere in Scripture can a passage be found in which God is cited as establishing a covenant with man that is specifically referred to as a salt covenant. Yet, we know that salt covenants exist. There are three passages that refer to them (2 Chron. 13:4-5, Lev. 2:12-14, Num. 18:18-20). Why is that? There is also no specific text in Scripture defining a covenant of salt.

Due to their eternal nature (among other reasons, as well), all covenants are also salt covenants.[311] In Genesis we read, "You shall be circumcised in the flesh of your foreskins, and it shall be a sign of the covenant between me and you" (Gen. 17:11); and, "So shall my covenant be in your flesh [*salt of DNA*] an everlasting covenant" (Gen 17:13). In other words, circumcision was only a <u>sign</u> of the covenant that God made with Abraham and his people, but it was not, itself, the covenant. The covenant was 'in the flesh,' i.e. a covenant of salt. In the OC, purification of the heart was affected from the outside of the person, penetrating inward to the heart[312] (cf. Rom. 7:23-24). This was because of man's fall from grace. The Holy Spirit could never dwell in an impure and disordered heart. In the NC, purification/sanctification occurs from the inside of the person (the inner heart ... the spirit),[313] simultaneously affecting the outside (the flesh). In the NC, this inner sanctification is accomplished solely through the union of our salt together with the salt of our Redeemer, Jesus Christ.

Scripture tells us salt covenants are multigenerational (e.g. 2 Chron. 13:4-5). Any time succeeding generations are included in a covenant, it follows that man's seed is involved; it cannot be otherwise. Anytime man's seed is involved, man's salt/dust of DNA is inevitably involved. Elaborating on 2 Cor. 6:16-18, Dr. Scott Hahn teaches that a covenant with God creates kinship[314] and forges a family bond[315] deeper than we can imagine. What do families have in common? The answer is a closely shared salt of DNA. The very use of the word "covenant" reinforces the interpretation of the scriptural word "salt" as meaning the salt of DNA ... the salt we all (including Jesus) share with our first parents. We are all fruits from the same tree of Adam.

In all of God's promises to man, the fulfillment of the promise is conditioned on man fulfilling his end of the bargain, so to speak. This is what constitutes the 'salt' component of a covenant with God. In OC days, in addition to keeping God's Laws and Commandments, all Israelites were expected to make themselves an offering to God.[316] What are we? We are salt and light (Mt. 5:13-16). We are also told that all of Israel's offerings had to be salted.[317] It is written in Leviticus 2:13, "you shall not let the salt of the covenant with your God be lacking." God's part of any covenant could **never** be lacking. Within Scripture, especially the OT in which Leviticus is contained, God is never symbolized by (or linked to) salt in any way (the human part of Jesus would be an exception, but not in the context any Trinitarian "lacking"). Consequently, Leviticus 2:13 *cannot* be interpreted in such a way as to imply that God has a linkage to salt, and that it could be lacking. In Leviticus, it was man's salt that could be lacking. Only man is salt. Only man's part of the 'deal' can be lacking. It is only man's salt that could be lacking from what would otherwise be an acceptable and pleasing sacrificial offering to God.

How does man express the overflow of his inner heart? It is

through the mouth, i.e. his body. What is his body? Salt. Any offering to God would, by necessity, be accomplished through man's scriptural "mouth". We know all prescribed offerings to God by the Israelites were organic in nature. Therefore, we can accurately say this: all offerings of salt to God had to be salted. That which was being offered (e.g. meat, cereal, non-water drink) was a 'type' of the suffering incarnate Jesus who made himself an offering to our Father. We know this because all offerings had to be both unblemished and also first fruits. Only the incarnate Son of God could ever be identified as being without blemish. Therefore, the salt that had to be <u>added</u> to the salt of the offering is our salt (of DNA). Our sufferings/offerings are 'acceptable and pleasing' (cf. Malach. 1:10-11, Is. 64:6, 1 Pt. 2:4-5) to the Father *only* when we unite them with the Son's infinitely and eternally perfect offering. After an oblation was offered to God on the altar, it then <u>*had*</u> to be eaten (the offering was not valid otherwise). It was believed that by eating the offering, the offeror would become one with that offering and thus participate in the benefits of the altar sacrifice.[318] Perhaps we can understand a little better why Jesus tells us, "Truly, truly, I say to you, unless you eat the flesh of the Son of man and drink his blood, you have no life in you; he who eats my flesh and drinks my blood has eternal life, and I will raise him up at the last day. For my flesh is food indeed, and my blood is drink indeed. He who eats my flesh and drinks my blood abides in me, and I in him (Jn. 6:53-56). Pope emeritus Benedict XVI writes,

> In the Old Testament the shared enjoyment of bread and salt, or of salt alone, served to establish lasting covenants (cf. Num 18:19; 2 Chron 13:5; cf. Hauck, TDNT I, p. 228). Salt is regarded as a guarantee of durability. It is a remedy against putrefaction, against the corruption that pertains to the nature of death. To eat is always to hold death at bay — it is a way of

preserving life. The "eating of salt" by Jesus after the Resurrection, which we therefore encounter as a sign of new and everlasting life, points to the risen Lord's new banquet with his followers. It is a covenant-event, and in this sense it has an inner association with the Last Supper, when the Lord established the New Covenant. So the mysterious cipher of eating salt expresses an inner bond between the meal on the eve of Jesus' Passion and the risen Lord's new table fellowship: he gives himself to his followers as food and thus makes them sharers in his life, in life itself.[319]

According to Fr. Martin von Cochem,

And [the Eucharist] is indeed that clean oblation which cannot be defiled by any unworthiness or malice of those that offer it, which the Lord foretold by Malachias was to be offered in every place clean to His name (Session xxii, Ch. 1). The offering of this clean oblation was predicted by the prophet Malachias in the following words: "I have no pleasure in you, saith the Lord of hosts; and I will not receive a gift of your hand. For from the rising of the sun even to the going down My name is great among the Gentiles, and in every place there is sacrifice, and there is offered to My name a clean oblation." (Malach. 1:10-11). All the Fathers of the Church consider this passage to refer to the Sacrifice of the Mass [*in which the accidents of bread and wine are changed into the physical body and blood of Jesus, together with his soul and his divinity*]. For this prophecy does not find its fulfillment in the Old Testament, but in the New, wherein also are fulfilled the words which were spoken by God the Father to His Son: "Thou art My Son, this day have I begotten Thee. Ask of Me, and I will give Thee the Gentiles for Thy inheritance." (Ps. 2:7-8) ... The sacrifice here predicted by Malachias cannot be that which was offered by Christ on the Cross, as non-Catholics assert; for that was made in one place only, on Calvary, not in every place, as the prophet declares. Nor can the supposition be entertained that the prophecy refers to a sacrifice of praise or of good works, for these are no oblation in the proper sense of the word, nor are they always a "clean oblation;" [the] prophet says: "All our justices are before Thee as a filthy rag." (Is. 64:6).[320]

According to Von Cochem, "oblation" is defined as, "The act of making an offering, especially the act by which the victim of a sacrifice is offered to God or a false deity. Any offering for religious or charitable uses." Jesus, in the eternal "now" is definitely a victim of a sacrifice to God.

The NC is in fact, a covenant of salt. With the birth of Jesus, the task that was assigned to the Jews was completed. At the conclusion of the OT, the salt of DNA that would "build" Jesus' body had been preserved from irreparable corruption and decay through obedience to the Law and reception of Actual and Gratuitous grace. The promises God made to the chosen people with the covenant of salt were fulfilled. Because of our one-body, one-flesh union with Jesus, the family of Adam also became the family of our Messiah. With His birth, Jesus *became* the everlasting covenant of salt. No longer in need of a chosen people within a chosen lineage to preserve Abraham's seed, redemption in the NC became available to all men — Jews (who would still remain the firstborn of the covenant, the first fruits if you will) and gentiles alike. It is through Jesus and His Church that man's body and soul will be purified and perfected. While Jesus is the fulfillment of the covenant of salt, it will be fully accomplished on the last day when perfected souls will reunite with the perfected body and then be glorified through Jesus who is the resurrection and the life.

11:D — The New Covenant Temple

As we have already stated, the NC is hidden in the OT, and OT is fully revealed in the NT. When Jesus tells his listeners to destroy this Temple and in three days he will rebuild it, he is telling them that the era of the "literal" geological stone Temple is ending,[321] and the new and everlasting covenant of salt — the Temple which is his mystical and literal body — is about to begin. Since the geological constructed Jewish Temple was destroyed circa 70 AD[322] and was never re-built, the only way that Ezekiel's dream of the rebuilt Temple (Chapters 40-47 in Ezekiel, esp. 47) could not be judged as wrong is if his words are right _and_ the words of both Jesus (Jn. 2:19) and John (Jn. 2:21) are true. Jesus did not refer to his body as the synagogue. He did say it about the _one and only_ Temple.

Let's incorporate our deeper understanding of stone in Scripture together with events described in Genesis chapters 17 through 29. In (17:1-14) God makes a covenant with Abraham — a covenant of salt (of DNA), as signified by circumcision. In (19:26) God also shows us the consequence for breaking the covenant by allowing Lot's wife to become a pillar of salt (of DNA) deprived of bio-living water. In chapters 28 and 29 we learn about Jacob, who was the son of Isaac, who was the son of Abraham, which makes him the third generation living under the covenant of salt between God and man. I find it more than mere coincidence that during the third generation, God chose to give us a sign of the fulfillment of that covenant of salt. The resurrection of Jesus occurred on the third day after his death. The Temple was rebuilt when the body of Jesus was resurrected in glory. The Scripture account of Jacob confirms that the NC Temple will be built of a new kind of stone — a living stone. Let's elaborate.

11:D:1 — The Story of Jacob and the Stone Pillar

After receiving the blessing of his father, Jacob is sent to find a bride. When he came to a "certain place" he took a stone and laid his head upon it and went to sleep. As he slept, he dreamed of a ladder upon which angels ascended and descended. Then the Lord spoke to Jacob saying, "... your descendants shall be like the dust of the earth" (Gen. 28:14). We know what dust of the earth means. When he awoke, he set up the stone upon which he slept as a pillar and anointed it with oil, and called the place Bethel (Gen. 28:28-29). Bethel is the Hebrew word for "house of God,"[323] which the Temple is. The stone pillar Jacob calls the house of God foreshadows the incarnate Jesus,[324] the Anointed One [*recall that Jacob poured oil on the stone pillar*], whose resurrected <u>body</u> will be the eternal Temple that will replace the old Temple.[325] This rebuilt Temple will become the dwelling place of God on earth (cf. Col. 1:18-20).

When Jacob awoke from his dream he said, "How awesome is this place! This is none other than the house of God, and this is the gate of heaven" (Gen. 28:17). What is meant by the phrase "gate of heaven?" According to Hildegard, it is the heavenly Jerusalem — the NC Temple of the Living God.[326] The stone pillar is an appropriate symbol of the meta-sense-able reality of the "certain place" because Jesus is Truth. Catherine of Siena specifically links the 'gate of truth' with Truth incarnate (the embodied Son of God) and tells us the Father is one with this gate.[327] When we go through this gate, we find ourselves in the Father.

The stone pillar represents the Temple, but the gate is that which we pass through to enter into the Temple — but the two are one in the same. The gate represents the salt of DNA of his body present in the Eucharist through which we receive Living Water.[328] Jacob's stone pillar, <u>the gate</u>, foreshadows the meta-sense-ably literal cornerstone of the rebuilt Temple of eternal life and is the scriptural counterpoint to the meta-sense-ably

175

literal salt pillar of death, which is what Lot's wife became. The location where Lot's wife became a pillar of salt is of no small significance. Lot's escape route was from Sodom (Gen. 19:1) to Zoar (Gen. 19:22-23). The entire trip kept them relatively close to the eastern and southern shores of the Dead Sea (see endnote).[329] You may recall from Ezekiel's dream (Chapters 40-47 in Ezekiel, esp. 47), the Dead Sea was used to signify lifelessness and unfruitfulness — a complete deprivation of Living Water.

Jesus often compares himself (and man) to things composed of wood (examples below). He does this to emphasize that we must become one *living* body with him — one literal family — one salt (cf. Mk. 9:49-50) united together receiving his Living (and bio-living) Water. At the time of Jacob, a gate could not have been made of stone. Most likely, it would have been made of wood. So let's look at some Scripture references to a one-salt of DNA unity with Jesus as represented by wood:

1) "I am the vine, you are the branches. He who abides in me, and I in him, he it is that bears much fruit, for apart from me you can do nothing" (Jn. 15:5);

2) In the parable of the ten virgins we read, "And while they went to buy [*oil for their lamps*], the bridegroom came, and those who were ready went in with him to the marriage feast; and the door was shut. Afterward the other maidens came also, saying, 'Lord, lord, open to us.' But he replied, 'Truly, I say to you, I do not know you'" (Mt. 25:10-12). St. Seraphim equates the *door* being shut with *bodily* death.[330]

3) "So Jesus again said to them, 'Truly, truly, I say to you, I am the door of the sheep. All who came before me are thieves and robbers; but the sheep did not heed them. I am the door; if any one enters by me, he will be saved'" (Jn. 10:7-9); and,

4) "If the root is holy, so are the branches. But if some of the branches were broken off, and you, a wild olive shoot, were grafted in their place to share the richness of the olive tree ... They were broken off because of their unbelief, but you stand fast only through faith. So do not become proud, but stand in awe. For if God did not spare the natural branches, neither will he spare you ... For if you have been cut from what is by nature a wild olive tree, and grafted, contrary to nature, into a cultivated olive tree, how much more will these natural branches be grafted back into their own olive tree" (Rom. 11:16-17, 20-21, 24).

We will resume our treatment of the significance of wood in Chapter 11;D;xii. In it, we will explore why Jesus chose to die on a cross, the material of said cross being the salt of DNA of wood. We will also examine the cross' symbolism in light of the Scripture accounts of Elijah, Elisha, the Passover feast, and the Epistles of St. Paul.

Let's continue our discussion of Jacob. The next day (after his dream), Jacob came upon a stone well. A heavy stone covered the mouth of the well. When Jacob saw the approaching Rachel (his future wife), he was struck by her beauty. He then rolled away the heavy stone from atop the mouth of the well and watered her sheep. The heavy stone covering the mouth of the water well represents: 1) the heaviness of Jesus' mortal body, a body meta-sense-ably bound by kinship to fallen man's sinful salt of DNA — even though he himself was without sin; 2) the heavy stone that had to be rolled away from the mouth of Jesus' burial tomb (a symbol of his dust/stone) after his death and resurrection. Rolling the heavy stone from the mouth of Jacob's well was a must in order to access the life-sustaining water (cf. Jn. 7:38-39; 14:16-17, 26; 15:26; 16:7) within the well. Giving this symbolic Living Water to Rachel's sheep through the mouth of the stone well foreshadows the accomplishment of Jesus' mission. St.

Cyprian, one of the early Church fathers, tells us that Rachel was a "type" of the NC Church[331] and that Jacob is a "type" of Christ[332] who is, in turn, the corner*stone* of the rebuilt NC Temple.

11:D:2 — Church + Temple = the Mystical Body of Christ

In OT Scripture, the future cornerstone of the NC Temple (cf. Is. 28:16, Zach. 10:4, Psalm 118:22) is referenced. We now know that Jesus is that cornerstone (Mt. 21:42). We also know the NC Temple will exist forever (e.g. Ez. 37:26-28, 1 Sam. 2:35, 1 Kgs 9:3-5, Tobit 1:4). Further still, we know that Jesus established his Church and upon the "rock" of Peter it would be built (Mt. 16:18). So how do we reconcile Church and Temple? What is the relationship between the two? Paul helps to provide us with the answers in Ephesians 5:22-33. We'll only cite three passages. He writes, "For no man ever hates his own flesh, but nourishes and cherishes it, as Christ does the church, because we are members of his body. 'For this reason a man shall leave his father and mother and be joined to his wife, and the two shall become one flesh.'" This is a great mystery, and I mean in reference to Christ and the church;" (Eph. 5:29-32). The Mystical Body of Christ (MBC) is the result of the marriage of the Bridegroom (Jesus, the rebuilt NC Temple) with the Bride (the Church). Jesus only describes the Church as being built up (Mt. 16:18). Jesus describes the rebuilding of the Temple as being completely accomplished in three days (Jn. 2:19-21). Yet Paul describes the temple as growing. He writes, "Christ Jesus himself being the cornerstone, in whom the whole structure is joined together and grows into a holy temple in the Lord; in whom *you also are built into it* [*SML*] for a dwelling place of God in the Spirit" (Eph. 2:20-22). This seeming inconsistency can be rectified by recalling our treatment of the miracle at the wedding feast of Cana (Chapter 10). Because of this one

Mystical Body union, when the Church grows, the "holy temple" also grows. Peter tells us, "Come to him, to that living stone, rejected by men but in God's sight chosen and precious; and like living stones be yourselves built into a spiritual house, to be a holy priesthood, to offer spiritual sacrifices acceptable to God through Jesus Christ" (1 Pt. 2:4-5).

In an encyclical on the MBC, Pope Pius XII equates the building of a new church in Rome with a temple. He writes, "It tells of those living stones which rest upon the living cornerstone, which is Christ, and are built together into a holy temple, far surpassing any temple built by hands, into a habitation of God in the Spirit."[333] He makes the same comparison when he writes, "For the Divine Redeemer began the building of the mystical temple of the Church when by His preaching He made known His Precepts; He completed it when he hung glorified on the Cross; and He manifested and proclaimed it when He sent the Holy [Spirit] as Paraclete in visible form on His disciples."[334]

Before we talk about the proper understanding of the MBC, let's list what is *not* a correct understanding. The MBC is not purely social (e.g. Knights of Columbus) or juridical (e.g. a group responsible for administering justice) in nature.[335] Nor is it purely spiritual, invisible, or intangible.[336] The MBC is not simply a moral body, a union of people pursuing a common end.[337] Pope Pius writes, "as Christ, Head and Exemplar of the Church 'is not complete, if only His visible human nature is considered, ... or if only His divine, invisible nature ..., but He is one through the union of both and one in both ... so is it with His Mystical Body [cf. *Ibidem*, p. 710].'"[338] He adds:

> We wish to speak in a very special way of our union with
> Christ in the Body of the Church ... this union is very
> close. In the Sacred Scriptures it is compared to the
> chaste union of man and wife, to the vital union of
> branch and vine, and to the cohesion found in our

body.[cf. *Eph.*, V, 22-23; *John*, XV, 1-5; *Eph.*, IV, 16.] Even more, it is represented as being so close that the Apostle says: "He (Christ) is the Head of the Body of the Church,"[Col., I, 18] and the unbroken tradition of the Fathers from the earliest times teaches that the Divine Redeemer and the Society which is His Body form but one mystical person, that is to say to quote Augustine, the whole Christ.[Cf. *Enar. in Ps.*, XVII, 51 and XC, II, 1: Migne, P.L., XXXVI, 154, and XXXVII, 1159] Our Savior Himself in His sacerdotal prayer did not hesitate to liken this union to that wonderful unity by which the Son is in the Father, and the Father in the Son.[*John*, XVII, 21-23].339

The MBC is a living, organic, and perfectly ordered body.340 How is this so? It is because Christ is its Head of the Body and the Holy Spirit is its soul.341 In philosophy, we know the soul is the form of the body. We also know the Holy Spirit is the unity of God. I could go on, but I think what has been said so far, gives us a 'working' understanding of the MBC.

What does this understanding of the Mystical Body tell us about the link between the Church and the rebuilt Temple? It tells us that the two are one Mystical Body through marriage. The temple has not disappeared in the NC. That which was meant to be in the temple still must be done by his Bride, the Church, which is built into the temple. Offerings to God still must be made; priests must still be present to offer them on the altar to the Father, and; the fullness of God still dwells in this temple. The MBC is compared to the one-flesh relationship that exists in a marriage between a man and a woman. According to Scripture, when a man and woman marry they become one flesh (cf. Gen. 2:24) through the power of the Holy Spirit. They remain distinct persons. The distinctiveness of the two does not undo the one-flesh relationship. Sense-ably, it seems to be a symbolic union (we don't see their two bodies meld together).

Meta-sense-ably, this one-flesh union is as real as created structured light (e.g. laser) and/or energy of all types. In Part IV (in Volume Two), we will begin to see how that is a true statement.

11:D:3 — Billions and Billions of Temples??

In Chapter 6 of the first letter of Paul to the Corinthians, we read, "Do you not know that your bodies are members of Christ (v. 15) ... But he who is united to the Lord becomes one spirit with him (v. 17) ... Do you not know that your body is a temple of the Holy Spirit within you, which you have from God? You are not your own; you were bought with a price. So glorify God in your body" (v.19-20). If each of us is a temple of the Holy Spirit, does that mean there are billions and billions of Temples in the world right now? The answer is, absolutely not. That would be contrary to what Scripture tells us concerning a single dwelling place for God — one Temple. We are *not* separate Temples; we are temples because we are <u>built into</u> the <u>one and only</u> Temple, which is Jesus' body, wherein the Holy Spirit dwells. This is why Paul tells us we are not our own. This is also why the Temple *grows* (Eph. 2:20-22). To help us understand the concept of a growing Temple, let's use the analogy of a human baby named Jane. At birth, Jane is a complete human person. As she gets older, more and more cell division occurs, leading to a great increase in the number of cells in her body. In other words, she grows. It's still the same complete human person named Jane ... but bigger. Let's say that she added a trillion new cells to her body over a span of 18 years. Each cell contains a complete set of genes (i.e. instructions) for building Jane from scratch all over again. Does that mean there are now a trillion new Jane's on the planet? The obvious answer is: no! What we have is a single body containing, let's say, ten trillion cells. Each cell has a more or less different function than any other cell. Each cell comes from the same source (sperm and egg). Every cell communicates with, and effects the cells around it — at lightning speed. Nevertheless, it is still one human person named Jane.

The Church is the body of Christ through marriage. We are meant to be literally, albeit meta-sense-ably, united to His resurrected body through Baptism and the Eucharist. Jesus is not the Temple that becomes the Church, or vice versa. On the contrary, we are the Church (the Bride) that is built into the Temple in a nuptial mystery. The Temple grows because the Church, which is built into the Temple, grows (Eph. 2:20-22). God tells Hildegard He perfects the Church "... for love of the Church *in* [*SML*] His Son."342 Jesus tells Peter, "And I tell you, you are Peter, and on this rock I will build my church" (Mt. 16:18). Why didn't Jesus say; upon this rock I will build my Temple? The answer is — it would be inaccurate to do so. First of all, he can't say I *will* build my Temple, using the future tense, because his resurrected body IS the completely rebuilt Temple. He didn't promise to "start" rebuilding the Temple in three days ... he said it will be rebuilt in three days (Mt. 26:61), implying completeness, which is how the Jews of his time interpreted it. If they had not interpreted his statement thus, there would have been no reason for them to react with incredulity, as they did.

We know the Temple is the dwelling place of God on earth, but what is the Church that he is building? The Catechism tells us that the word "Church" (*ecclesia* in Latin and *ek-ka-lein* in Greek) translates as a convocation or assembly.343 The Church is not a dwelling place; it is an assembly (that dwells someplace or abides in something). This is the overriding difference between the Temple and the Church. In the OC Temple, God dwelled in the Holy of Holies, but the Chosen People (the ekklesia, the OC "church" so to speak) worshiped and sacrificed from outside of the Holy of Holies. In fact, to even enter into the presence of the unveiled Ark of the Covenant, or to look inside of it, or to touch it would result in death (cf. Lev. 16:2; 1

Sam. 5:9-11, 6:19). To my knowledge, there is no unitive language contained in OT Scripture that intimates a one-body or one-flesh relationship with the OT Temple, wherein God, vis-à-vis the Ark, dwelt. Such a relationship is, however, a dominant theme in the NC Scriptures. The last book in the Bible tells us where Jesus was taking us. St. John wrote, "'the marriage of the Lamb has come, and his Bride has made herself ready' ... 'Blessed are those who are invited to the marriage supper of the Lamb'" (Rev. 19:7, 9).

11:D:4 — The NC Temple Offering

As we stated in Chapter 11:C, Scripture clearly indicates that a clean oblation will be offered to God for all eternity. We also know that all sacrifices to God were made on the altar of the Temple. Finally, we know that Jesus' resurrected body is the NC Temple. Scripture reads, "I have no pleasure in you, says the LORD of hosts; and I will not accept an offering from your hand. For from the rising of the sun to its setting my name is great among the nations, and in every place incense is offered to my name, and a pure offering; for my name is great among the nations." (Mal. 1: 10-11), and "We have all become like one who is unclean, and all our righteous deeds are like a polluted garment. We all fade like a leaf, and our iniquities, like the wind, take us away." (Is. 64: 6). Thus, the salt that was added to these unblemished offerings represents the salt of DNA of _our_ bodies joined in a mystical one-flesh relationship to the _man Jesus_ crucified on the cross as both a pleasing (cf. Lev. 1:9, 13, 17; 2:2; Ex. 29:41 and many others) and eternal offering (Lk. 22:19; Jer. 33:17-18; *Didache* 14:1–3[344]) to God.

Nothing happens by chance with God. I do not believe the Son of God was crucified on the salt of DNA of wood by happenstance. It was not a coincidence he was _stretched out fully_ on the cross and then _nailed to it,_ symbolizing the necessity of man to be crucified with Christ so that, by dying with him, we can rise with him (Rom. 6:2-8; Jn. 3:13-15, 12:32).

Through STOSS we gain a deeper understanding of Paul when he writes:

1) "I have been crucified with Christ; it is no longer I who live, but Christ who lives in me" (Gal. 2:20);

2) "Those who belong to Christ Jesus have crucified the flesh with its passions and desires" (Gal. 5:24);

3) "Henceforth let no man trouble me; for I bear on my body the marks of Jesus" (Gal. 6:17); and,

4) "We know that our old self was crucified with him so that the sinful body might be destroyed, and we might no longer be enslaved to sin ... But if we have died with Christ, we believe that we shall also live with him" (Rom. 6:6, 8).

It is by joining our sufferings with Jesus on the wood of the cross that we are crucified with Christ in a mystical one-flesh union with him on the cross. Every mention in Scripture of taking up one's cross is followed by the words: and <u>follow</u> me (Mt. 10:38, 16:25; Mk. 8:34; LK. 9:23). It's not enough for us to simply pick up our cross. We must go where Jesus goes. Where is Jesus going? To Calvary. This is what Paul refers to when he tells us, "Now I rejoice in my sufferings for your sake, and in my flesh I complete what is lacking in Christ's afflictions for the sake of his body, that is, the church" (Col. 1:24). Our offerings can never be acceptable and pleasing to God (cf. Jer. 6:20; Is. 1:11; Mk. 12:33) unless they are joined together with those of Jesus. This is why we salt the salt of the offering with our salt of DNA, as foreshadowed in the OT.

In Exodus we read, "And the LORD said to Moses, "Take sweet spices, stacte, and onycha, and galbanum, sweet spices with pure frankincense (of each shall there be an equal part), and make an incense blended as by the perfumer, seasoned with salt, pure and holy" (Ex. 30:34-35). This sweet incense is made only for God. In fact, he tells Moses that anyone using it for their personal use will be cut off from God's people. The sweet spices are, so to speak, an adjective describing how pleasing to God is the odor of that which is being offered. What is being offered? It is "salt, pure and holy." All of the ingredients listed above as part of the incense are organic and, therefore, comprised of salt of DNA. This foreshadows Jesus' bodily (salt of DNA) death nailed to the wood of the cross. His sacrifice *alone and only* is pleasing and acceptable to God. It is by becoming one-flesh with him (as represented by the salt of DNA of the wood) that our offerings to God become acceptable.

How do we become one body with Jesus on the cross? Remember, the OT/OC foreshadows and enlightens us of the deeper meaning of the NT/NC. To appreciate more fully the meaning of Jesus' Passover (from the meal to the crucifixion ... both were an essential part of the Jewish Passover sacrificial celebration[345]) we must also consider the culture and beliefs surrounding those Feasts at the time. According to the theologian, Gary Burge, Judaism at the time of Christ believed that a meal was a form of fellowship. So when a sacrificial meal was being offered to God, a portion of it was burned up, creating a pleasant odor which symbolically rose up to God. This brought about both fellowship and reconciliation with God.[346] The burnt offering was then consumed because it was believed by eating the offering they would become one with that offering. Thus, they would participate in the benefits of the altar sacrifice.[347] Who/what was the Paschal Lamb killed that day? It was Jesus' body and blood. What was the altar? It was the cross of his crucifixion.[348] When we consume the Paschal Lamb in the Eucharist, we become one with Christ crucified, as represented by the salt of DNA of the wood of that very same cross. According to the Council of Trent, "The Sacrifice of the Cross and the Sacrifice of the Mass are one and the same."[349] This is what is meant when Paul writes about his being crucified with Christ (Gal. 2:20). By uniting ourselves to Christ in a mystical one-flesh union on the cross via the Eucharist, our finite and unworthy offerings (cf. Is. 64:6)350 are intimately joined with Christ's eternal and utterly pure oblation (cf. Mal. 1:11). Thus, our offering is eternal, acceptable, and pleasing to our Father.351 When we crucify our flesh of its passions and desires (Gal. 5:24), our offering is made pleasing to God _only_ because we have joined our blemished suffering salt to the unblemished suffering salt of Jesus Christ.

Now is not the time or place for a lengthy treatment of the subject above. Consequently, a quick peremptory note is in order:

1) No, Catholics do _not_ re-crucify Jesus in a bloody manner;

2) In the Mass, we are made present at his once-for-all sacrifice on the cross;

3) The sacrifice of the Mass is _both_ a memorial and a sacrificial offering; and,

4) See the _Catechism of the Catholic Church_, Paragraphs 1322-1405 for a thorough and documented explanation of the Catholic teaching on the Eucharist.

Scripture accounts of the prophets Elijah and Elisha provide us with examples and additional understanding of Paul's teachings on our being crucified with Christ. Both prophets performed one particular act that profoundly illustrates this fact. Both demonstrate that it is Jesus, through the grace and power of the Holy Spirit, that we will experience resurrection after death. In 1 Kgs., we reads this about Elijah: "And [Eli'jah] cried to the LORD, 'O LORD my God, hast thou brought calamity even upon the widow with whom I sojourn, by slaying her son?' Then he stretched himself [*My note: in the same manner as Jesus was stretched out on the cross, Paul was stretched out for flogging (Acts 22:25 NIV), and the heavens stretched out like a tent (Ps. 104:2)*] upon the child three times, and cried to the LORD, 'O LORD my God, let this child's soul come into him again.' And the LORD hearkened to the voice of Eli'jah; and the soul of the child came into him again, and he revived" (1 Kgs. 17:20-22). Then the woman said to Elijah, "Now I know that you are a man of God, and that the word of the LORD in your mouth is truth" [*recall that the mouth/body expresses the heart/Holy Spirit*] (1 Kgs. 17:24). By stretching himself out upon the dead child three times, Elijah shows us three things. They are: 1) The necessity of a one-body relationship (via the Mass and Eucharist) with our Savior on the cross; 2) Jesus' resurrection from the dead on the third day is prerequisite to any other resurrection; and, 3) Through mystical one-flesh relationship with Jesus, via Baptism, we can take comfort in his words to Martha, "I am the resurrection and the life" (Jn. 11:25).

Let's turn to Elisha. He also brought life back to a dead child. Even though the circumstances surrounding Elijah's and Elisha's accounts are extraordinarily similar, the belief that both grace and life (through the *Power* of the Holy Spirit in the form of Gratuitous and Actual graces) are expressed through the salt of DNA can be seen even more forcefully in Elisha's story. Similarities of special interest existed between these two prophets. They are: 1) Elisha was Elijah's successor, and 2) Elijah had a special encounter with the Holy Spirit on the Mountain of God during which Elijah used his sheepskin mantle to cover his face (1 Kgs. 19:8, 11-13); and, 3) Elisha asked for and received, a double portion of Elijah's Holy Spirit (2 Kgs.. 2:9, 11-15) symbolized by taking possession of the same mantle of sheepskin that Elijah had used to shield his face from the presence of God on the aforementioned mountain. We know Jesus was resurrected through the power of the Holy Spirit — as are <u>all</u> resurrections.

Scripture tells us, "When Eli'sha came into the house, he saw the child lying dead on his bed. So he went in and shut the door upon the two of them, and prayed to the LORD. Then he went up and lay upon the child, putting his mouth upon his mouth, his eyes upon his eyes, and his hands upon his hands; and as he stretched himself upon him, the flesh of the child became warm. Then he got up again, and walked once to and fro in the house, and went up, and stretched himself upon him; the child sneezed seven times, and the child opened his eyes" (2 Kgs 4:32-35). This account is even clearer concerning the necessity of a one-Mystical Body relationship with Jesus, both on the cross and in Baptism. This union is necessary for resurrection from the dead through the power of the Holy Spirit. In His dialogue with St. Catherine, God adds a few details to this Scripture account. God provided St. Catherine with a deeper understanding of 2 Kgs 4:32-35 (see text above). She wrote (Note: like Hildegard, Catherine is simply writing what God is telling to her),

> [The mission of the incarnate Word] was prefigured in the Old Testament when Elisha was asked to raise up the young man who was dead. At first he did not go. Instead he sent Gehazi with his staff, telling him to put it on the boy's back. Gehazi went and did as Elisha had told him but the boy did not rise. When Elisha realized that he had not risen, he went himself and member for member laid himself out on the boy [*symbolizing a meta-sense-able one-flesh union with Jesus. (SML)*]. He breathed sharply seven times [gifts of HS] into the boy's mouth and the boy took seven breaths as a sign that he had come back to life.
>
> Gehazi was prefigured in Moses, whom I sent to lay the staff of the Law on the dead human race. But this law did not give you life. So I sent the Word my only-begotten Son, who was prefigured in Elisha [SML]. He laid himself out on this dead child by joining the divine nature with your human nature. Member for member he joined this divine nature with yours: my power, the

wisdom of my Son, the mercy of the Holy Spirit-all of
me, God, the abyss of the Trinity, laid upon and united
with your human nature. After this union the gentle
loving Word accomplished the other by running like one
in love to the shameful death of the cross, where he laid
himself out *[above, Elisha is said to have "laid himself
out"; in the this sentence, Jesus "laid himself out" on
the <u>cross</u>. (SML)]*. And after this union he gave the
seven gifts of the Holy Spirit to this dead child, blowing
into the soul's mouth of desire and driving out death in
holy baptism. The soul breathes as a sign that she has
life, casting out of herself the seven deadly sins. Thus
has she become a garden adorned with sweet, mild
fruits.352

Notice the extraordinary similarity of Jesus' laying himself
out fully on the salt of DNA of the wood of the cross and the
prophet Elijah's laying himself out fully on the dead children.
Interestingly, this passage is almost identical to the story of
Elijah resurrecting a dead child in 1 Kgs 17:17-24. In that
passage, Elijah stretched himself out on the dead child three
times before the child's spirit returned to his lifeless body.
Hmm! Three days was the number of days in which Jesus
would rebuild the Temple, i.e. be resurrected from the dead
through the Holy Spirit.

11:D:5 — All Grace Flows Through Mystical Body of Christ

We have already discussed how the Mystical Body of Christ
came about as a result of the marriage of the Bride (the Church)
with the Bridegroom (the NC Temple which is Jesus'
resurrected body — see Jn. 2:19-21) in the Holy Spirit. Jesus
Christ, through his Mystical Body, is the primary efficient
source of all created grace of the Holy Spirit that comes to

mankind.[353] When we combine: 1) the passages about our being built into the holy temple (Eph. 2:20-22, 1 Pt. 2:4-5); 2) the passages telling us that rivers of living water will flow from our hearts (Jn. 7:38-39); and, 3) Ezekiel's dream of the rebuilt Temple (Chapters 40-47 in Ezekiel, esp. 47), we can see ample evidence of the above. Let's unpack Chapter 47 of Ezekiel.

11:D:5:a — Ezekiel's Rebuilt Temple

In Chapter 47 there are two points made that I think are very apropos to this topic. The first point concerns the water (representing the Living Water which is the grace of the Holy Spirit) that proceeds out from the threshold of the "resurrected" salt/stone Temple. In his dream, as the water travels further and further away from the Temple threshold, it actually becomes deeper and deeper (v. 3-5). There is no way, factoring into the equation the laws of any branch of the physical sciences, that this could take place without the presence of some other modifying physical factor, such as a dam or an additional water contributory. The laws of gravity and fluid dynamics would not allow it. So there must be a spiritual significance attached to it.

What seems to be occurring is some sort of multiplication (remember that Living Water, i.e. grace, is always fruitful/multiplicative when accepted and acted upon); the kind of multiplication at play in this phenomenon is analogous to a candle and flame. The candlestick is the human being and the flame is the fire of Love, which is the Holy Spirit. The original flame burning on the original candlestick is the Holy Spirit dwelling in the Sacred Heart of the incarnate Word of God. When another candlestick touches the flame of the original candle, it, too, catches fire. It's the same flame, but it now burns on two candles. I believe the increasingly deepening waters detailed in this account are not symbolizing a multiplication of Holy Spirits, but a multiplication of those people in whom the Spirit now dwells, through a one-flesh union with the Bridegroom. This union causes rivers of living water to flow from their hearts (cf. Jn. 7:38-39) and out their mouth. I believe this Living Water is communicated from its source (the Mystical Body of Jesus) to the members of the "swarm" via the Sacraments, Gratuitous, and Actual graces. The basis for this interpretation comes from what Ezekiel writes a few passages later. We read, "And wherever the river goes every living creature which swarms will live" (v. 9). There are several conclusions that can be reached from this one sentence.

I'm not going to go into any great depth in exploring v. 9, but here are a few of the more important points:

- Everything that occurs is directly related to contact with Living Water (grace of Holy Spirit) from the Temple;

- There are two references to life in this passage and each has a distinctly different meaning. The context of the phrase "every living *creature*" seems to indicate every form of biological life; while the last reference in the phrase "every living creature which swarms will *live*" seems to be indicative of the indwelling presence of the Holy Spirit as a consequence of contact with the river of Living Water; and,

- We must answer the question: why is it that only a "creature that swarms" will live? The answer comes by understanding the characteristics of a swarm. A swarm lives and functions coherently through interaction, and only through interaction (i.e. expression in one form or another). For example: a single ant finds a sugar cube and a little while later, a multitude of ants are following the pheromone trail (as also do cockroaches) to that sweet delight;[354] bees inside a hive, watch the "dance" of another bee and acting on the basis of that dance are led to a source of food;[355] the six or seven birds surrounding a lead bird will modify their flight trajectory based on the sudden movements of a startled bird;[356] and, a locust transforms to swarming mode because of increased levels of serotonin brought on by tactile stimulation and other types of contact.[357] One might be tempted to think that the use of swarming in Scripture is simply implying living together through a sort of group coherence. That would be a reasonable interpretation were it not for the context in which it was used, i.e. the *multiplication* of <u>grace</u> among largely non-hierarchical "creatures" and the consequences thereof. While the Temple from which the Living Water proceeds has a hierarchy (a ministerial priesthood), the swarm does not. Grace is the communication of Living Water to man; Calling him to communion with the Father, through the Son, and in the Holy Spirit. When man follows the "call/communication/grace" that triggers the "swarming" instinct, he finds life.

• Through the reception of the Sacraments of the Church, especially Baptism and the Eucharist, we are enabled to communicate the Living Water of the Holy Spirit (in the language of the body) to those around us. The symbolism of "living *creature*" indicates this communication of grace occurs through man's mouth/body when in a nuptial union with the resurrected NC Temple. The Spirit is the force of the unity of God.[358] Consequently, the linkage between creatures that swarm and life through grace are not, I think, coincidental at all.

11:D:5:b — Role of Body/Flesh

We have already shown how Jesus' body, i.e. unchangeable Truth incarnate, is symbolized by stone (i.e. the collective 'dust' of trillions and trillions of copies of DNA in our body). God himself makes this link by referring to the Son of God as a fire-producing flint.[359] Flint is a stone (symbolizing unchangeable Truth incarnate). Furthermore, according to God, this stone — this body — plays a direct role in "producing" fire. What is the fire? It is the Holy Spirit![360]

Remember Tertullian's words, "Flesh [*the salt of DNA*] is the very condition on which salvation hinges ... the flesh feeds on the body and blood of Christ that the soul likewise may fatten on its God. They cannot then be separated in their recompense."[361] Their "recompense", in this case, is grace, the outpouring of the Spirit. Jn. Paul II tells us,

> Through our communion in his body and blood, Christ also grants us his Spirit. Saint Ephrem [the Syrian of the 4th century] writes: "He called the bread his living body and he filled it with himself and his Spirit ... He who eats it [*through the 'mouth'*] with faith, eats Fire and Spirit ... Take and eat this, all of you, and eat with it the Holy Spirit. For it is truly my body and whoever eats it will have eternal life (*Sermo IV in Hebdomadam Sanctam*: CSCO 413/Syr. 182, 55)." The Church implores this divine Gift, the source of every other gift, in the Eucharistic epiclesis.[362]

JP II tells us, "man cannot, in a certain sense, express this singular language of his personal existence and of his vocation without the body ... words of the spirit — words of love, of giving, of fidelity — *demand an adequate language of the body [SML]*. Without that they cannot be fully expressed."[363] West tells us that spiritual love <u>cannot</u> be separated from this language of the body.[364] We will talk a great deal about the language of the body in Part IV, contained in Volume Two of this book.

In his book, *Jesus of Nazareth*, Pope Benedict XVI talks about Jesus' <u>body</u> being the NC Temple from which flow cleansing, purifying Living Water. During the course of this discussion, he quotes from the apocryphal Gospel of Thomas. Normally I would not use an apocryphal Gospel as a source to support this STOSS, but I figure that if it's good enough for the Pope to quote, then it's good enough for me. Quoting the words of Jesus, Thomas writes, "Whoever drinks from my mouth shall become as I am (Barrett, *Gospel*, p.328)."[365] In other words, it is from the NC Temple of salt/stone,[366] i.e. the mouth of the resurrected Jesus, that we receive Living Water — the life of God, the Holy Spirit. Wherever this living stream of water flows, the result is cleansing and fruitfulness.[367] Furthermore, the Pope tells us that when we become one with Christ, we too, become fountains of the fruitful and Living Water — the Holy Spirit [cf. Jn. 7:37-39].[368]

Durrwell writes, "The gift of the Spirit tends to make the believer what Christ is: 'a life-giving spirit'. Grace enables him to be a source of grace; each believer shares in the sanctification of others according to the power of the Spirit who sanctifies him. In Christ he shares in the union of the Trinity."[369] How does the believer share this grace? It is through the mouth/body. JP II tells us that grace (the radiation of God's love) is God's Spirit breathed into our dust and, in turn, radiated (expressed) outwards through our bodies.[370]

CHAPTER 12: — REDEMPTION OF THE BODY VIA MYSTICAL BODY OF CHRIST

According to JP II, the redemption of man, i.e. the body and soul, was the entire mission of Jesus in the created world.[371] So what is the redemption of the body? Let's look at what St. Paul tells us. He writes, "... creation itself will be set free from its bondage to decay ... We know that the whole creation has been groaning in travail together until now; and not only the creation, but we ourselves, who have the first fruits of the Spirit, groan inwardly as we wait for adoption as sons, the redemption of our bodies. For in this hope we were saved. Now hope that is seen is not hope. For who hopes for what he sees? But if we hope for what we do not see, we wait for it with patience" (Rom. 8:21-25).

12:A — Redemption is a Process of Purification, Culminating in Purity of "Heart"

Paul's "redemption of the body" is not just an event accomplished by Jesus some two thousand years ago; it is a process that starts now. It won't be completed, however, until the return of Jesus, the resurrection of our bodies, and the general judgment. Jesus' Passion and death on the cross purified us of the *guilt*[372] associated with our sins, but he did **not** purify the heart of man, as anyone who is not blind can observe by looking at the condition of the world from the time of Jesus' death forward. In both Ephesians 1:7 and Col. 1:4, St. Paul identifies redemption as the forgiveness of sins. And yet our body, which is nothing more than the mouth of our inner heart, is in need of, and is waiting for, redemption (Romans 8:23). Consequently, the redemption *of the body* is simply the process of purification of the body by means of the inner purification of the heart. Both are accomplished through a one Mystical Body (through Baptism) and a one-flesh relationship (the Eucharist) with Jesus.

Jesus informs us there is work left for us to do; that the process of redemption of the body is not finished. He said, "You, therefore, must be perfect, as your heavenly Father is perfect" (Mt. 5: 48). This statement of Jesus occurs as part of a longer sermon commonly referred to as the Sermon on the Mount in which Jesus is perfecting Old Testament Laws; updating them to reflect the arrival of the Kingdom of God. According to Pope Benedict XVI, Jesus in his sermon gave us a new Torah to replace the old.[373] This new Torah was given in order to inform us that we must now be purified from the inside out, i.e. we must purify the heart which will, in turn, heal and purify the body. Nowhere in this sermon does Jesus tell us to wait until later to comply with the new Torah of the heart; it demands immediate discipleship and must be acted upon by following Jesus in his footsteps.[374] JP II sees the Sermon on the Mount in precisely the same way. He directly links purity of the heart with the redemption of the body, because, in his view, love cannot exist without purity of the heart.[375]

Further illustrating the role of the heart in the redemption of the body, Pope Benedict XVI tells us that in order for man to see God, the body and soul must interact harmoniously; we see God through the eyes of the spiritual and physical heart.[376] Archbishop Luis Martinez expresses that sentiment by saying, "nature and souls sing to the same Beloved, saying the same thing, each in its own language. To live spiritually is to sing because living spiritually is loving. For the song to be perfect, all the human faculties must be rectified and harmonized, like the strings of a lyre, and the Holy Spirit must inspire the unique song of a unique love."[377] Scripture tells us, "Who shall ascend the hill of the LORD? And who shall stand in his holy place? He who has clean hands and a pure heart" (Ps. 24:3-4). So the passage could be re-phrased thusly: *he whose heart is pure and whose acts, expressed through the mouth, are an accurate expression of that pure heart, can ascend the hill.* The redemption of the soul is the forgiveness of the guilt of our sins. The redemption of the body is killing the love of sin existing in the human heart.

It is by no means coincidental that, in direct context to this new Torah of the heart, Jesus brings up salt. Jesus tells us during the course of this very same Sermon, "You are the salt of the earth; but if salt has lost its taste, how shall its saltness be restored? It is no longer good for anything except to be thrown out and trodden under foot by men" (Mt. 5:13). In other words, if our salt of DNA (our body/mouth) is no longer doing that for which it was created by God to do, i.e. express fruitfully the overflow of a pure heart (one full of the Spirit), then our salt has lost its taste.

12:B — Means To Attain Redemption of the Human Heart

Because redemption of the body is a process of purification of the spiritual heart and a corresponding purifying/harmonizing of the body/mouth, God designed the body to change (via quantum and molecular changes in the salt of our DNA and the "bio-living" water — more on that later — existing in the human cell) so that the language of the body accurately expresses the language of the spiritual heart; as the heart is purified, so too, is the body correspondingly purified. Furthermore, as the body is purified it is increasingly freed from the bondage (cf. Jn. 8:34) to decay that St. Paul refers to (cf. Rom. 8:1-3). We will be offering more evidence of the validity of this statement when we discuss The Incorruptibles later in Section D of this Chapter.

Some non-Catholics hold views close to that of Catholics. William Porcher Dubose, who is probably the most original and creative thinker the American Episcopal Church has ever produced, believes that through Baptism: we become one with Jesus; one with his redemptive act; one with his death to sin; and one with his life in the Father.[378] Our redemption is not simply due to Jesus' salvific act, it is also due to the fact that he is in us. This oneness places us in a condition of grace that is essential to salvation. However, being in the condition for salvation is not the same as salvation itself. It is only as the actions of Christ become, also, "our act through participation, that we are actually saved."[379]

Pope Benedict XVI tells us that purification of the heart is a consequence of becoming one with Jesus Christ.[380] JP II tells us that the Eucharist is the source and summit of the sacramental life, and is the most efficacious means through which the Holy Spirit is communicated to man.[381] Jesus says, "Salt is good; but if the salt has lost its saltness, how will you season it? Have salt in yourselves, and be at peace with one another" (Mark 9:50). In Chapter 1 of this book, we discussed Pope Benedict's treatment of salt in Acts 1:3-4. Luke very specifically used the word "synalizômenos". The literal translation of the description of the resurrected Jesus' eating with the Apostles is, "... eating *salt* [*SML*] with them." When we eat anything organic we are, literally, eating organic salt, i.e. DNA. Benedict further makes the case that Luke intentionally chose this wording. While all baptized Christians, in general, are part of the Mystical Body of Christ, Luke was telling us that an even more personal one-flesh relationship existed with Jesus in the Sacrament of the Eucharist, which was established at the Last Supper.[382,383]

The peace that Jesus refers to, is the indwelling of the Spirit. By the joining of our salt with Jesus' salt, we are "salted with fire [*remember the fire in Jesus' Sacred Heart?*]" (Mk. 9:49). In other words, we must have Jesus' salt in us so that we can also have the peace of the Holy Spirit in us. In *Ecclesia de Eucharistia*, JP II tells us that the Son of God and the Holy Spirit work inseparably in the Church and in the Eucharist; it is through this joint activity (impossible to separate) that we are sanctified in soul and body.[384]

12:C — Redemption is Freedom From "bondage to decay" (Rom. 8:21)

We should be able to easily understand the "bondage" part of St. Paul's words. We know that sin enslaves us (Jn. 8:34, Rom. 6:12-22); and, from our discussion of STOSS relative to original sin, we know why and how it enslaves us. So what does the "decay" part mean? As was discussed previously, sin is not something — it is nothing; it is the absence of something; it is non-being. More precisely, all creation decays when it has ceased to be "newly" expressed by God (see also Chapter 6). When creation ceased to be "good," it ceased to be part of the Trinitarian dialogue.

The Word of God is expressed/begotten by the Father and through the Son creation is fruitfully expressed and it is called "very good" (Gen. 1:31). _Only_ God is good (Mt. 19:17). From this, we can surmise that only the part of creation that is good will be eternally and unceasingly expressed. Our God is a living God — always breathing in and out without cessation. This eternal and continuous "dialogue" of the Trinity IS the life of God. In Psalms David writes, "You are my son, today I have begotten you" (Ps. 2:7) and, "When thou hidest thy face, they are dismayed; when thou takest away their breath, they die and return to their dust. When thou sendest forth thy Spirit, they are created; and thou renewest the face of the ground" (Ps. 104:29-30). David is telling us: when the Breath (Holy Spirit) is withheld we decay and die; when the Breath is sent out, i.e. expressed together with the Word, we are newly created (begotten, in the case of the Son) and have life. The Son is eternally and unceasingly begotten,[385] and all that is created is created through the Son and in the Holy Spirit[386] (Jn. 1:1-4). Therefore, since all creation is made through the Son in the Holy Spirit, and since the Son is eternally begotten, so MUST it be that all which is "good" in creation is also eternally expressed/created. Furthermore, since the Son CANNOT express anything that is bad (he wouldn't be God if he could), it can be concluded that sin is non-being,[387] nothingness,[388] and death (Gen. 2:17, Rom. 5:12). As we all know, that which is dead (not alive) decays.

In John, the Pharisees were criticizing Jesus for "working" on the Sabbath. He tells them, "My Father is working still, and I am working" (Jn. 5:17). To understand what is meant when Jesus says that the Father is working, we only need to read the creation account in Genesis. "Work", for God, means expressing/creating and it was from this activity that He rested on the seventh day (Gen. 2:1). JP II tells us that, "This cooperation in the creative activity of God is what work is."[389] Citing Scripture (Acts 7:49-50; cf. Is 66:1-2), Pope Benedict makes the link between where God dwells — the Temple of stone in the Old Covenant, and the Temple of Jesus' body in the New Covenant — with where God *rests*.[390]

This is what JP II meant when he wrote, "this is the human dimension of the mystery of the Redemption. In this dimension man finds again the greatness, dignity and value [*i.e. the 'goodness' of God*] that belong to his humanity. In the mystery of the Redemption, man becomes newly 'expressed' and, in a way, is newly created."[391] Through the blood of Jesus, we were "re-created" in grace,[392] i.e. newly expressed by God. As a result of a vision concerning the happiness of God, Faustina tells us that even though this happiness never changes, it is, at the same time, always new.[393] In Scripture, we read, "The steadfast love of the LORD never ceases, his mercies never come to an end; they are new every morning; great is thy faithfulness" (Lam. 3:22-23). To help understand this passage, it helps to remember that fruitful expression is an indispensable "component" of Divine Love/Charity.

12:D — The Incorruptibles

I assert that the redemption of the body is a process that begins in the present. It is inextricably linked to the purification of the heart and, therefore, the body. Why? The body <u>must</u> also be correspondingly healed and redeemed in order to accurately express the overflow of the increasingly purified heart? St. Paul directly links the bondage to decay with the absence of the redemption of the body. Is there any evidence that decay of the body is halted or slowed down as a consequence of the purification of the heart through the indwelling of the Holy Spirit? The answer is a resounding, yes!

The term "Incorruptibles" refers to saints within the Catholic Church who have died and experienced a very significant lack of decay — lasting, in some cases, for centuries. Preserved bodies fall into three classifications: the deliberately preserved, the accidentally preserved, and the Incorruptibles. Examples of the first two classifications have been discovered from before Egyptian times. The incorruptible saints have only existed since early Church times.[394] This makes sense, since the Mystical Body of Jesus, through which we receive an indwelling of the Holy Spirit, did not exist before that. To my knowledge, the phenomenon of the Incorruptibles exists <u>only</u> within the ranks of the saints of the Catholic Church. This, too, makes sense since it is <u>only</u> the Catholic Church, through an unbroken apostolic succession, that obeys Jesus' teachings about literally eating his flesh and drinking his blood in the Eucharist. In Volume Two: Part IV we will discuss the science that I believe is behind the Gratuitous grace the Holy Spirit employs to accomplish the phenomenon of incorruptibility.

It is important to distinguish between the characteristics of the deliberately and the accidentally preserved bodies versus those of the Incorruptibles. The Incorruptibles have been classified as natural mummies, but that is an incorrect classification. Without exception, preserved bodies of the deliberate or accidental classification are rigid, very dry and discolored. Most, but not all, of the Incorruptibles are moist and perfectly flexible despite the passage of centuries (up to 1600 years). This is true despite burial environments that were very hostile to the preservation of a body.[395] For example, deliberate attempts to speed up the decaying process by covering the body with quicklime which, by the way, had no negative impact on their incorruptibility.[396] Corruption of the internal organs was halted, despite the fact that their internal organs contained materials that were highly corrupting.[397] Incredibly, virtually all of the Incorruptibles listed in Joan Carroll Cruz's book, *The Incorruptibles*, underwent no deliberate means to preserve their bodies from decay.[398] Of the slightly over one hundred Incorruptibles that she details in her book, only one percent underwent some sort of deliberate intervention and those cases are well documented and not hidden from the public.[399] Every legitimate case of an incorruptible is examined by physicians and scientists who are independent of the Church. In order for the Church to accept the deceased person as a true incorruptible, the conclusions of the medical and scientific experts must be that the reason for the preserved state is unaccountable, mysterious, and miraculous.[400] Another phenomenon associated with the vast majority of Incorruptibles is the presence of a sweet scent around the body, and the exuding of blood and oils from the body, despite decades or centuries of time since their death.[401]

There are detractors (there always are detractors to any spiritual miracle) who try to debunk the authenticity of the Incorruptibles. They claim that the Incorruptibles have wax masks and gloves to make them look better than they really are. They claim that the Incorruptibles have been preserved through exposure to radiation, and so on. There is a well-worn axiom that goes something like this: for those who have faith, no proof is necessary; for those who lack faith, <u>no proof will</u> <u>suffice</u> ... even if they have to conjure up an argument against whatever proof presented (e.g. remember, the Apostles were widely accused of stealing Jesus' body). To avoid an exercise in futility, I will not waste the reader's time by embarking on a defensive tangent. However, with very little effort and the presence of an objective intellect, any and all such claims of fraud can be quickly dispatched to the trash heap.

St. Cyril of Jerusalem declared that, "Even though the soul is not present, a virtue [*indicating the* unmistakable *presence of the Holy Spirit and, therefore, an absence of decay-SML*] resides in the body of the saints, because of the righteous soul which has for so many years dwelt in it, and used it as its minister."[402] All saints have exhibited heroic virtue, but not all saint's bodies' are found to be incorruptible. I believe saints who have achieved the highest degrees of purity of heart, through their holy desire for union with Christ, are the ones whose bodies' are found to have substantially or partially escaped the "bondage to decay" that St. Paul writes about.

After reading all of Part IV (contained in Volume Two of STOSS) you might like to read *Appendix B-Incorruptibles Revisited*. In 'Appendix B' I delve into some biological processes that may come into play as instruments used by the power of the Holy Spirit in accomplishing incorruptibility. Without first reading Part IV, one might not fully understand the explanation I give. This miracle of incorruptibility would fall under the category of Gratuitous grace.

APPENDIX A — IS JESUS PHYSICALLY PRESENT IN THE EUCHARIST

Introduction to Appendix

It is a dogma of the Catholic Church that the whole and entire Jesus, in his humanity and Divinity, are truly, really, and substantially present in the Eucharist. This dogma is usually referred to as the "Real Presence". The Theology of the Salt rises or falls on whether or not the correct understanding of this dogma would include a justifiable reliance on the belief that the words "truly, really, and substantially present," signifies that his living physical body — containing his functioning cells, biological water, DNA produced proteins, etc. — is present.

Through the dogma of the Real Presence we know that Jesus is truly and wholly present in the Eucharist; the dogma of Transubstantiation, however, informs us of the correct understanding of how — or in what mode — he is really present. Basically, the dogma of Transubstantiation says: at the consecration of the species of bread and wine during the Mass, the entire substance of the bread and wine are changed into the entire substance of Jesus' body, blood, soul, and Divinity. While the accidents of bread and wine are still visible, all that makes the bread be bread, and the wine be wine (i.e., their substances), are completely absent ... replaced by the whole and entire substance of Jesus in both his humanity and Divinity. This is often referred to as the "sacramental" presence of Jesus in the Eucharist. We will talk more about this sacramental presence later.

Without going into great detail, let's very briefly define two philosophical terms that relate to our understanding of Transubstantiation, i.e. substance and accident.

Substance — as defined by De Munnynck "signifies being

as existing in and by itself, and serving as a subject or basis for accidents and accidental changes."[403] An example of a corporeal substance is a rock. It exists in and of itself. A rock is still a rock regardless of its shape, weight, color, density, location, etc. He goes on to write:

> The Scholastics ... also distinguished primary substance
> (substantia prima) from secondary substance
> (substantia secunda): the former is the individual thing
> — substance properly so called; the latter designates the
> universal essence or nature as contained in genus and
> species. And, again, substance is either complete, e. g.
> man [body and soul], or incomplete, e. g. the soul
> [without the body]; which, though possessing existence
> in itself, is united with the body to form the specifically
> complete human being. The principal division; however,
> is that between material substance (all corporeal things)
> and spiritual substance, i.e. the soul and the angelic
> spirits ... An attempt has recently been made by
> representatives of physical science to reconstruct the
> idea of substance by making it equivalent to "energy".
> The attempt so far has led to the conclusion that energy
> is the most universal substance and the most universal
> accident (Ostwald, "*Vorlesungen uber
> Naturphilosophie*", 2nd ed., Leipzig, 1902, p. 146).[404]

Accident — as defined by Dr. Joseph Magee, "are the modifications that substance undergo, but that do not change the kind of thing that each substance is. Accidents only exist when they are the accidents of some substance. Examples are colors, weight, [and] motion."[405] Using the example of man, we can say a substantial man remains a substantial man (body and soul) regardless of whether he is fat or skinny, moving or resting, black or white, tall or short, etc.

To my knowledge, the Church has never formally defined

whether a man is: 1) a being composed of two "incomplete" substances (i.e. corporeal and spiritual) which, together, form a complete man, or 2) a being composed of a single substance of which a body and soul are included.[406] Aquinas made the case that it was the latter[407] and Augustine the former.[408] Regardless of which is correct, we can safely say this: if the resurrected Jesus was a complete man (he is), then his entire substance in the Eucharist would include a corporeal body (though glorified, of course) and a human soul. If any of the two were missing, he would not be a complete man and, therefore, his entire substance would not be present. Likewise, this can be said of his Sacramental presence in the Eucharist and of the presence of his proper species (that species which occupies three-dimensional spaces, i.e. his dimensive quality, which is philosophically categorized as an "accident") in Heaven.

STOSS stands or falls on a correct understanding of both the Real Presence and Transubstantiation; for it is a basic tenet of STOSS that our body and our soul are changed as a direct result of becoming one Mystical Body with Jesus through Baptism, and a one flesh union with him in the Eucharist. In this Appendix, however, we will only be discussing the latter.

We will be attempting to arrive at a correct understanding of Transubstantiation through a discussion of four different subjects. They are:

1) An examination of a Eucharistic controversy that occurred in the 800s between, primarily, Paschasius Radbertus and the Monk Ratramnus of Corbie;

2) An examination of the meaning of "substantial presence" using sense-based arguments;

3) An examination of the doctrine through the writings of others; and,

4) A brief examination of a deeper understanding of "light" as it relates to the "substance" of our human nature.

Early Eucharistic Controversy

The aforementioned controversy I want to discuss in this section also happens to be the first Eucharistic controversy in the history of the Church. It was ignited by Paschasius Radbertus. We will discuss the content of his treatise and the background surrounding it a little later. First, however, I want to tell you the reason it is so important relative to STOSS.

Radbertus' views regarding the presence of Jesus in the Eucharist are highly compatible with the views that I espouse in my exposition of STOSS. Consequently, if his writings are judged to be theologically credible, then the credibility of STOSS will also be bolstered. If his writings are not credible, or worse, judged to be heretical, the acceptability of STOSS will suffer. I personally know of three young priests who believe that Paschasius Radbertus and/or his views are heretical. All three have one thing in common: they cite Ludwig Ott's book, *Fundamentals of Catholic Dogma* as either a direct or indirect source for that belief. Ott's book is popular among many younger people who are trying to gain a deeper understanding of theology. Many seminarians and priests working towards their degrees in Theology also read his book. In general, I believe the book is good, but it has some serious flaws that must be understood before attempting to use it as a basis for judging the writings of others. I believe Ott has, perhaps inadvertently, perpetrated a grave injustice to Radbertus.

Let's discuss the history and teachings of Radbertus. In 831 he composed a treatise titled *De Corpore et Sanguine Domini*[409] (translation: Of The Body and Blood of the Lord). It is important to note that, while Radbertus wrote the original work of this title, there are at least two additional works (both of which are responsive to Radbertus' work) written by different authors that use the exact same title. Consequently, one must be very careful to ascertain which author's work is being referenced. In 844 the treatise was revised and sent to

Emperor Charles the Bald.[410] According to Joseph Pohle, "The emperor commissioned the Benedictine Ratramnus of Corbie to refute certain questionable assertions of Paschasius, and when Rabanus Maurus joined in the discussion (cf. Ep. Iii ad Egilem, P.L., CXIII, 1513) there occurred the first controversy on the Eucharist, which continued up to the tenth century and even later."[411]

What did Radbertus teach? According to Dr. Mark Armitage:

> Taking his lead from St Ambrose of Milan, Radbertus insisted that the true, historical body of Jesus Christ is literally present in [the] Eucharist, in such a way that, in receiving Christ's true body and blood, the communicant is united with Christ <u>physically and directly [SML]</u>. Agreeing with St. Irenaeus of Lyon, Radbertus affirmed that the image of God is located in the whole human person — body and soul (and not just soul) — with the result that salvation is to be seen in terms of union between the whole human person and the whole person of Christ (body, blood, soul and divinity) who makes himself efficaciously, literally and physically present (and communicable) in the Eucharist ... [Radbertus rejected] the dualistic separation of body and soul (which some Latin theologians had imported from Greek theology).[412]

Quick note: in Chapter 6:A, we answered the question of where, in man, the image and likeness of God resides. Radbertus was not suggesting there was some sort of hypostatic union in person or in nature. In my view, he was suggesting something more along the lines of JP II's works on the Nuptial Mystery of man. Some felt Radbertus meant it is Jesus' mortal body that was present[413] and that he must be understood to be sensibly present in the Eucharist.[414] Both of these interpretations of his writings are incorrect.

Were Radbertus' teachings right or wrong? Let's list a few reasons why we can absolutely believe he was <u>not</u> wrong.

1) "[Radbertus] defended himself with some skill against the attacks of his critics, especially in his *"Epistola ad Frudegardum"*. But a more thorough vindication of St. Paschasius was made by Gerbert, afterwards Pope Sylvester II (d. 1003), who, in a work bearing the same title *"De corpore et sanguine Domini"*, contended that the doctrine of <u>St. Paschasius was correct in every particular</u> [SML]."[415]

2) Paschasius was canonized a saint. If he were an unrepentant heretic, he would never have been canonized. I am not aware of any record of him ever having repented of, or recanted his teachings; this because he had nothing in his teachings to recant or repent of. [*Note: St. Paschasius Radbertus (9th century) should not be confused with St. Paschasius (6th century). I have read the work of others that were attributing information that should have been attributed to the former, but were incorrectly attributed to the latter*].

3) Emperor Charles the Bald, who originally had difficulty accepting Radbertus' treatise, eventually came to accept the truthfulness of his writings.[416]

4) Radbertus' adversary (Retramnus of Corbie) "was determined to be heretical and placed on the Index of Prohibited Books in 1559, but was removed in 1900. Both wrote in imprecise wording."[417]

5) According to Elizabeth Francis Rogers, "His book *Of the Body and Blood of the Lord* was the first to elaborate for western Europe the doctrine of the miraculous conversion of the elements in the Eucharist, which in the twelfth century received the name of transubstantiation [See Gore, *Dissertatiōns on Subjects Connected With the Incarnation,*

p. 236. "Paschasius appears beyond all reasonable question to teach a doctrine of transubstantiation"]."[418]

6) Noted theologian, Fr. John Hardon writes, "After eleven centuries, Pius XII has 'canonized' Paschasius' teaching by incorporating it, almost verbatim, in the *Mediator Dei*."[419]

7) In OSV's Encyclopedia of Catholic Doctrine, Jordan Aumann, O.P. writes, "In the ninth century, Paschasius Radbertus stated clearly the Catholic teaching on the Real Presence."[420] Aumann wrote this sentence in a sub-section titled, "Transubstantiation".

Clearly, St. Paschasius and his writings are not heretical; so why the perception, on the part of so many younger theologians, that he is? I place much of the blame squarely on Ott's book. Let's look at his book and examine what he writes.

In a Chapter titled "The Fact of the Real Presence of Christ," and in a sub-section titled "The Heretical Counter-theses," Ott writes,

> *The Book of John Scotus* on the Eucharist, invoked by Berengarius of Tours in support of his [heretical] error, and which was condemned by the Synod of Vercelli (1050) probably was written by the Monk Ratramnus of Corbie († after 868), *De corpore et sanguine Domini*. Ratramnus, it is true, did not deny the Real Presence, but in contrast to Paschasius Radbertus († about 860), who maintained the complete identity of the sacramental body with the historical body of Christ, [Ratramnus] strongly emphasized the different way in which the Body of Christ was manifested in the Eucharist, and applied to the Eucharist the expressions, similitudo, imago, pignus. Others who attacked the exaggerated realism of Paschasius Radbertus were Rabanus Maurus, in a lost letter to the Abbot Eigil of Prüm , and the Monk Gottschalk, in the *Dicta cuiusdam*

sapientis de corpore et sanguine Domini adversus Ratbertum, which is erroneously ascribed to Rabanus Maurus ... Berengarius of Tours († 1088) denied the Transubstantiation of the bread and wine and the Real Presence of Christ. He saw in the Eucharist merely a figure (figura, similitudo) of the body and blood of Christ transfigured in Heaven.[421]

There is absolutely nothing in Ott's text wherein he accuses Radbertus of being heretical. Instead, he is made to appear guilty by ...: 1) association, i.e. when he includes him in a section on heretical counter-thesis without mentioning that he was never declared a heretic; 2) listing two others who were opposed to his views w/o providing those in favor of his views (as we did above); 3) failing to mention that during the canonization process, this saint's writings would likely have been closely scrutinized. He would not have been canonized were his writings found to be problematic; and 4) failing to mention that St. Radbertus was merely reiterating the teachings of other Church Fathers such as St. Ambrose, St. Augustine, and St. Chrysostom.[422] I am not accusing Ott of intentionally misleading his readers, but he does so nonetheless. In my opinion, any schools using Ott's book should take steps to guard against the 'trashing' of St. Paschasius Radbertus' writings.

Sense-based Arguments Favoring Transubstantiation and a Physical Presence of Jesus in the Eucharist

Let's now spend a few minutes talking about whether or not a dogmatically appropriate understanding of Transubstantiation would also allow for the belief that Jesus is physically present in the Eucharist. In the next section, we will look at what other writers and theologians have to say. In this section, however, we'll approach it from a sense-based standpoint.

In the 6th chapter of John's Gospel, Jesus repeatedly tells his followers that they must eat his flesh and drink his blood if they wish to have life within themselves. Any objective and detailed reading of Jesus' bread of life discourse in that Gospel would lead to the understanding that Jesus' listeners were interpreting his words literally, and they were interpreting them carnally. As a result, they were: 1) repulsed by what he was saying (v. 52, 60); 2) murmuring and complaining among themselves about what he was saying (v. 41, 52, 60); and, 3) ceasing to follow him (v. 66). In response, Jesus tells them his words are spirit and life (v. 63). By these words, Jesus was not contradicting what he had so emphatically spoken of in the preceding verses. He wasn't saying that his meaning is not physical — not carnal — he was simply telling them not to focus on that aspect of his teaching; not to let it cause them to lose sight of the bigger salvific meaning of his words. Why? God in his infinite wisdom knows our frailties and would take that into account in dictating the form and matter of the sacrament of the Eucharist.

Aquinas, too, tells us the reason God hides the physical and carnal (but also glorified and transcendent) body and blood of Jesus under the accidents of bread and wine. He writes, "Why see we not the flesh? Because, if the flesh were seen, it would revolt us to such a degree, that we should be unable to partake of it. And therefore in condescension to our infirmity, the mystical food is given to us under an appearance suitable to our Minds."[423] I would add: but it is physical flesh and blood, nonetheless.

Again, but from a more authoritative source, let's read what God revealed to St. Hildegard about this. She wrote, "[The consecrated host] appears in human eyes to be bread and wine, for human frailty is so delicate that people would shudder at receiving bleeding flesh and trickling blood."[424] Hmm! This wording doesn't exactly convey the message that the substance of Jesus hidden in the Eucharist is only an ethereal or spiritual representation of his physical body. The idea that Jesus' corporeal body was somehow transformed into a spiritual body cannot even be entertained.[425] The truth of God's revelation to Hildegard can be seen by the reaction of the disciples listening to Jesus when, as described in John's Gospel, he told them what they must do regarding his body and blood.

So the question is this: Why would there even need to be a veil (a term often used to describe the philosophical accidents of bread and wine) under which the body and blood of Jesus are hidden, unless what is hidden is, in fact, the true physical and corporeal Jesus — blood and all? If that described by God as being hidden, i.e. physical "bleeding flesh and trickling blood," were not there in the first place, then saying they needed to be hidden would be ridiculous, deceptive, and completely unnecessary.

It is important to note here that the resurrected and glorified physical and corporeal Jesus is not a <u>mortal</u> Jesus, but an immortal Jesus. His glorified human nature is now transcendent; he is not bound by space or time; he cannot be physically affected by the cosmos or anything in physical creation. However, consider these facts: 1) weight is a function of mass times the gravity of the planet; 2) Jesus' glorified body can no longer be affected by the gravitational pull of earth; 3) in Eucharistic miracles where the veil of the consecrated host is lifted, the flesh and blood that is present can be weighed and measured. What does this mean? Created gravity is no longer capable of exerting a force on Jesus' physical glorified body, but the accidents that inhere to the substance of his mortal body — including his weight — still concomitantly exist in Jesus' complete substance, which is what the Eucharist is. It is impossible for us to understand the infinite mystery of the Transubstantiation to any measurable depth. If any of us believe we have achieved that depth, then I would say that person's god is too small and too weak. We are not able to see the physical presence of Jesus in the Eucharist because of his glorified and transcendent state, and because God knows it would be an obstacle to our receiving him. Importantly, when God lifts the sacramental veil, when we see his flesh and blood, it is not, as Aquinas tells us, an illusion or a hallucination; God is not deceiving us.

Aquinas tells us that when the appearance of consecrated host is miraculously lifted to reveal the real flesh and/or blood of Jesus,

> The same reverence is shown to it as was shown at first, which would not be done if Christ were not truly there, to Whom we show reverence of latria. Therefore, when such apparition occurs, Christ is under the sacrament ... as was said already, this is not deception, because it is done "to represent the truth," namely, to show by this miraculous apparition that Christ's body and blood are truly in this sacrament. And thus it is clear that as the dimensions remain, which are the foundation of the other accidents, as we shall see later on (Q. 77, A. 2), the body of Christ truly remains in this sacrament.[426]

Keeping in mind that God does not deceive us when we see the physical body and blood of our Lord in the Eucharist, let's look at some examples of God allowing us to see the physical Jesus in the Eucharist:

1) I'll start by simply recalling the four miracles (at Lanciano, Sokolka, Buenos Aires, and Legnica) listed in Chapter 14 (located in Volume Two of STOSS) in which a consecrated host was seen to transform (sacramental veil removed) into actual physical heart tissue. There has been a total of approximately one-hundred-thirty-five such Eucharistic miracles recognized by the Church.[427] In the case of the miracle at Buenos Aires, Columbia University Professor, Frederick Zugibe, perhaps the greatest expert in the field of cardiac pathologies and forensic medicine of the heart, said that, at the time the Eucharistic tissue samples were delivered to him, the cells of the heart muscle tissue were actually beating.[428] This is consistent with what the Catholic Encyclopedia tells us about Jesus' glorified body. Pohle writes, "The glorified Christ, Who 'dieth now no more' (Rom, vi, 9) has an animate Body through whose veins courses His life's Blood [*SML note — I would also add: His blood flows because of the beating of his heart (which produces electromagnetic energy*[429])] under the vivifying influence of soul."[430]

2) In the writings of Cesar of Heisterbach, the story is told of a recluse who had devoted herself to a life of penance and prayer. She had a special devotion to the Holy Mass. The devil had succeeded in planting severe doubts in her mind about the truth of Transubstantiation. God had compassion for this humble servant and allowed a miracle to take place. When the priest was saying Mass, he carelessly overturned the chalice after the Consecration. To the priest's horror, the "accident" of wine had assumed the appearance and color of blood. After Mass, the priest tried every way he could think of to clean the blood-stained corporal. But to no avail. The following week the priest, in tears, held the corporal up for the congregants to see and explained what had happened. He was convinced that God allowed this to happen to firm up the faith of those who entertained doubt

about the truth of the dogma of Transubstantiation: so he made a point to take the corporal around to show to others. Eventually, he went to the dwelling of the recluse. At seeing the blood-stained corporal she fell to her knees and wept bitter tears of regret for her disbelief. Then, with these words she made a public confession of faith: "I steadfastly believe that in the consecrated chalice the true, <u>natural</u> [SML] Blood of Christ is really present, the same that was shed for us upon the Cross." After returning home and again putting the corporal into water, he was amazed to see the stain immediately disappear. It seems obvious that it was for the benefit of the recluse that this miracle had occurred.[431]

3) Fr. Peter Cavagnelas, a monk of the Order of St. Jerome, was having terrible doubts as to whether or not the Blood of Christ was really present in the sacred host. One day he was saying Mass. After saying the words of the Canon in which the angels are asked to carry these gifts to the altar, a cloud descended and completely surrounded both the Host and the chalice, blocking the view of Fr. Cavagnelas. Alarmed, he made a sincere act of contrition and lifted his heart in prayerful petition. When the cloud lifted, the Sacred Host was suspended in midair above the chalice. While he starred at the Host, blood began to drip from the Host into the chalice. This continued until the exact same amount of Blood was in the chalice as there had been wine prior to the Consecration.[432]

4) Blessed John of Alvernio was known to have celebrated Mass very devoutly. At a High Mass on the feast of the Assumption, he was overcome with love for Christ. At the Consecration, Blessed John beheld a smiling infant — the baby Jesus — in his hands. At the sight of this Most Holy Infant, Fr. John's heart was pierced and his bodily strength was sapped; he fell into a state of ecstasy.[433]

I could cite very many other examples of this miraculous revelation in which the "veil" is lifted so that mortal eyes can behold the sacred reality of what was already there ... the true and real presence of the body and blood of the risen and glorified Jesus in the Eucharist, but I think the point has been sufficiently made.

Writings of Others Relating to Transubstantiation and the Physical Presence of Jesus in the Eucharist

<u>**Pope Pius XII**</u> – In his papal encyclical *Mystici Corporis Christi*, Pope Pius XII seeks to explain the meaning of the term "Mystical Body of Christ" in referencing the Church. Further, to distinguish the body of Christ in the Church from the body of Christ in the Eucharist, he writes, "by it we may distinguish the Body of the Church, which is a Society whose Head and Ruler is Christ, from *His physical Body* [*SML*], which, born of the Virgin Mother of God, now sits at the right hand of the Father and is *hidden* [*SML,* i.e. his physical body is there, but hidden] under the Eucharistic veils [by veils is meant the sacred species of bread and wine]."434 That's right: it is Jesus' physical/natural body which is present in the Consecrated Host.435 The point is this: a glorified body is NOT a spiritual body; a glorified body does not cease to be a physical body; it's just NOT a mortal body and it IS a spiritualized physical body. Another point that can be extrapolated by the Pope's words is this: while Jesus' "proper species" are in Heaven and seated at the right hand of the Father, his physical body is still sacramentally present in the Eucharist.

According to prominent saint/theologians, there are two formal operations of quantity. Joseph Pohle writes:

> The simplest treatment of the subject was that offered by the Schoolmen, especially St. Thomas (III:76:4), They reduced the mode of being to the mode of becoming, i.e. they traced back the mode of existence peculiar to the Eucharistic Body to the Transubstantiation; for a thing has to so "be" as it was in "becoming", Since [by the power of words] the immediate result is the presence of the Body of Christ, its quantity, present merely [concomitantly], must

follow the mode of existence peculiar to its substance, and, like the latter, must exist without division and extension, i.e. entirely in the whole Host and entirely in each part thereof. In other words, the Body of Christ is present in the sacrament, not after the manner of "quantity", but of "substance", Later Scholasticism (Bellarmine, Francisco Suárez, Billuart, and others) tried to improve upon this explanation along other lines by distinguishing between internal and external quantity. By internal quantity ... is understood that entity, by virtue of which a corporeal substance merely possesses "aptitudinal extension", i.e. the "capability" of being extended in tri-dimensional space. External quantity, on the other hand ... is the same entity, but in so far as it follows its natural tendency to occupy space and *actually* extends itself in the three dimensions. While aptitudinal extension or internal quantity is so bound up with the essences [aka, substance] of bodies that its separability from them involves a metaphysical contradiction, external quantity is, on the other hand, only a natural consequence and effect, which can be so suspended and withheld by the First Cause, that the corporeal substance, retaining its internal quantity, does not extend itself into space.[436]

St. Hildegard of Bingen – as quoted earlier, tells us, "Out of clay God so shaped humanity that through this tiny spark of the soul we become flesh and blood out of clay ... [we] would have remained only clay unless the soul had transformed it."[437,438] When we talk about man, it is evident from the last sentence that our substance includes our flesh (dust/clay of the earth) and blood (clay contains water). Without the soul, our substance would have consisted only of "clay", but with the breath of the soul, it becomes one substance containing both clay (and the water that is part of clay) and soul. Hence, when we talk about the "substance" of Jesus in the Eucharist, we are talking about his glorified physical body and blood (clay) together with the human soul hypostatically united in Person to his Divinity.

St. Thomas Aquinas – Aquinas tells us, "Those sacramental species [of bread and wine] are indeed accidents, yet they have the act and power of substance [but without the substance – SML]."[439] What Aquinas is referring to is this: consecrated wine can still, for example, get us intoxicated; the consecrated bread can still go stale. It retains this power because God miraculously maintains the <u>act and power of the substance</u> of bread and wine in the accidents of bread and wine. It can be surmised through his words that the power and act of the substance, through its accidents, affects other physical bodies (i.e. those receiving the Eucharist). Are we foolish enough to believe that the act and power of the substance of bread and wine in the Eucharist (while the accidents are miraculously maintained, their substances are no longer present) are more powerful than the act and power of the substance of Jesus, *which is actually present* in the Eucharist? Let me make one point crystal clear: the substance of bread and wine no longer exist in the consecrated host. However, God miraculously maintains the act and power of the substances of bread and wine in these accidents, despite their substantial absence.

It is logical, therefore, to believe that the substance of Jesus' body, blood, and soul united to his Divinity in the Eucharist will affect other bodies, those who receive him in that Sacrament. The fact that various components of the many Eucharistic miracles, i.e. unveiled specimens of Jesus' flesh and/or blood, available for study are able to be quantified by physical means (i.e. obtained from scientific examinations using various testing equipment/apparatus) indicate that the "substance" of Jesus in the Eucharist is both physical (body and blood) and spiritual (soul and Divinity). If the glorified body was not physical, then it would not produce an effect on testing equipment. To help us understand how this occurs, allow me to restate what Pohle wrote. Both the internal and external quantity of the substance of Jesus' body in the consecrated host are present, but the external is usually miraculously suspended by God for reasons we have already discussed. However, when it suits God's purposes, he can very easily 'un-suspend' the external.

Keeping in mind what Aquinas told us about these miracles, i.e. they do not deceiving us because they convey the truth, let us ask the question: is the substance of Jesus hidden under the sacred species different from the substance of Jesus immediately after the miraculous visual revelation? Is the substance of Jesus that is capable of affecting scientific equipment and also equipment for quantifying weight in the physical world different from the substance of Jesus hidden in the Eucharist? The answer is: absolutely not. There are not two Jesus'; not two substances. The glorified substance of Christ is unchangeable and indivisible.

Quoting Pope Alexander, Aquinas writes, "Pope Alexander III, who says (Conc. Later. iii): 'Since Christ is perfect God and perfect man, what foolhardiness have some to dare to affirm that Christ as man [*body, blood, and soul — SML*] is not a substance?'"[440] He also tells us, "since the substance of Christ's body is not really deprived of its dimensive quantity and its other accidents, hence it comes that by reason of real concomitance the whole dimensive quantity of Christ's body and all its other accidents are in this sacrament [SML note: and I would add (as Aquinas said earlier): and also retain the act and power of Jesus' substance]."[441] He also says, "By the power of the sacrament there is contained under it, as to the species of the bread, not only the flesh, but the entire body of Christ, that is, the bones, the nerves, and the like,"[442] in other words, all those things necessary to have a living body that radiates grace to those who become one body, one Spirit with him (1

Corinthians 6:16-18; Ephesians 2:17-19) in the Eucharist.

Based on this, a logical question to ask is whether or not Jesus has physical movement in the Consecrated Host. Aquinas responds by saying, "In Christ, being in Himself and being under the sacrament are not the same thing, because when we say that He is under this sacrament, we express a kind of relationship to this sacrament. According to this being, then, Christ is not moved locally of Himself, but only accidentally, because Christ is not in this sacrament as in a place, as stated above (A. 5)."443 Theologian Fr. John Hardon comments on these words of Aquinas by writing:

> All the standard commentators on the *Summa*
> understand St. Thomas to mean that there is only an
> *extrinsic* difference between the Eucharistic and natural
> Christ when he says that in one case the mode of being
> is natural and in the other sacramental. Thus [St.
> Robert] Bellarmine, in commenting on this part of the
> *Summa* and also explaining the pertinent words of [the
> Council of] Trent, says: "The Body of Christ, because of
> its special mode of existence in the Eucharist, does not
> express any *relation* to surrounding bodies. Therefore,
> we can truly say that <u>the Body of Christ, as it is in the
> Eucharist, is true, real, natural, living, quantified,
> having color, and that His flesh is corporeal, not
> spiritual</u> [<u>SML</u>]. But we do not say that the Body of
> Christ in the Eucharist is sensible, visible, tangible, or
> extended, although it is such in heaven. The reason is
> because these names imply a *relation* to surrounding
> bodies, which the Body of Christ does not have in the
> Eucharist." [Bellarminus, "*De Sacramento
> Eucharistiae*," V, lib. 1, cap. 2 (Naples, 1858), 250].444

Aquinas further states, "The substance of Christ's body is in this sacrament by the power of the sacrament, while dimensive quantity is there by reason of real concomitance, consequently Christ's body is in this sacrament substantively, that is, in the way in which substance is under dimensions, but not after the manner of dimensions."[445] This can, perhaps, be more easily understood by examining one particular aspect of the Eucharistic miracle at Lanciano. In addition to the visual transformation of the consecrated bread into heart muscle tissue, from the consecrated wine there also appeared five globules of blood of varying sizes. Despite the varying sizes (dimensive quantity) of the globules, any combination of globules weighs the exact same as the remaining other globules; one globule weighs as much as the remaining four globules weighed collectively or individually; put another way, a very small globule weighs exactly the same as a larger globule or a multiple of globules.[446]

Fr. John Hardon – Fr. Hardon is a well-known and well-respected Jesuit priest, theologian, and teacher. He was an aggressive defender of Catholic orthodoxy. In fact, during his studies at Pontifical Gregorian University in Rome (circa 1950), it was his duty to collect all the heretical books that had been checked out of the library by graduate students. He became known as an agent of orthodoxy and an enemy of the modernists who were striving to update the Church to their views of the faith.[447] At the request of Pope Paul VI, he wrote the 1975 edition of *The Catholic Catechism*.[448] He also wrote the *Modern Catholic Dictionary* and a detailed catechetical study program for the Holy See when Pope John Paul II requested that Mother Theresa's Missionaries of Charity be trained in catechesis. He served as a consultant for the drafting of the Catechism of the Catholic Church promulgated by Pope John Paul II. He received the Papal Medal in 1951 and the St. Maximilian Kolbe Award in Mariology in 1990.[449] Hardon died in December of 2000. Cardinal Raymond Burke initiated the Cause for Hardon's canonization in 2005 and obtained the imprimatur of the Congregation for the Causes of Saints in Rome; Fr. Robert T. McDermott is the Postulator for the Cause.[450] All of his writings have been given a nihil obstat.[451] Below are quotes from different articles that Hardon has written.

- In his discussion of the Real Presence of Jesus in the Eucharist relative to the Encyclical *Mediator Dei*, Hardon quotes Pope Pius XII who says, "the faithful bear witness to and solemnly avow the faith of the Church that the Word of God is <u>identical</u> [SML] with the Son of the Virgin Mary, who suffered on the Cross, who is present in a hidden manner in the Eucharist, and who reigns upon His heavenly throne [*Acta Apostolicae Sedis* (trans: Acts of the Apostolic See), XXXIX, 570]."[452] Hardon then proceeds to more precisely define what the Pope means by the word: *identical.* He writes, "When Pius XII identifies this body, so minutely described, with the Real Sacramental Presence, he is attributing to the Lord's humanity in the Eucharist all the *intrinsic* properties and perfections, qualitative and quantitative, which are attributable to His historical body, once mortal and passible on earth, and now glorified and immortal in heaven."[453]

- "Shortly after Trent, Pope St. Pius V authorized the publication of the *Roman Catechism* which built on the Council of Trent ... Regarding the Real Presence, the pastors were told to explain that 'in this sacrament is contained not only the true Body of Christ-and that means everything that goes to make up a true body, such as bones, nerves, and so on-but also Christ whole and entire.' Consequently the Eucharist contains Jesus Christ in the fullness of his divinity and the completeness of his humanity ... when we speak of *transubstantiation*, we mean that the whole substance of bread and wine, its 'breadness' and 'wineness,' is replaced by the living and glorified Jesus Christ ... Is there any real difference between Jesus in heaven and Jesus in the Eucharist? No, it is the same Jesus ... The living, breathing Jesus Christ is in the Blessed Sacrament."454

• "[Jesus] is in the Eucharist with His human mind and will united with the Divinity, with His hands and feet, His face and features, with His eyes and lips and ears and nostrils, with His affections and emotions and, with emphasis, with His living, pulsating, physical Sacred Heart [SML]. That is what our Catholic Faith demands of us that we believe. If we believe this, we are Catholic. If we do not, we are not."455

• "When we pray before the Blessed Sacrament, we are adoring Christ in the fullness of His human nature, including His physical properties, which include His heart of flesh, now glorified but living and, we may add, pulsating out of love for us [Remember the Eucharistic miracle in Buenos Aires--SML] [Hardon, John A. *Advanced Catechists Course, Explanations of Questions, Vol II: The Sacraments;* Kensington, MD, Inter Mirifica, 1994. P. 84. #61]."456

Pope Pius XII — In his Encyclical *Mediator Dei*, the Pope writes, "From what We have already explained, Venerable Brethren, it is perfectly clear how much modern writers are wanting in the genuine and true liturgical spirit who, deceived by the illusion of a higher mysticism, dare to assert that attention should be paid not to the historic Christ but to a 'pneumatic' or glorified Christ ... these false statements are completely opposed to the solid doctrine handed down by tradition. 'You believe in Christ born in the flesh,' says St. Augustine, 'and you will come to Christ begotten of God.'[Saint Augustine, *Enarr. in Ps.* 123, n. 2]"457

St. Irenaeus — "In the same manner in which you ascribe to the Eucharist only the value of a symbol, so also the incarnation is reduced (by you) to mere appearance: there is not more flesh in the one than in the other. The incarnation does not differ from the Eucharist [*Adv. Haereses V, 2*]."458

St. Leo the Great — "What was visible in our Savior has entered into the sacraments [*Homily* 74, 12]."459

Spiritual and Material Light and the Substance of Man

Let us now briefly touch on the subject of "light" as it relates to the substance of Jesus' humanity (both before and after his death and resurrection) in the Eucharist. We know that: 1) the substance of man is both spirit (the soul) and corporeal (the body and blood); 2) in the substance of man, there can't be a body without a soul (note: the philosophical/theological subject of the body-soul separation in death and how that fits within a correct understanding of the substance of man is not one we will be dealing with in this book); and 3) spirits are created light, as can be seen in Genesis wherein it is written, "And God said, 'Let there be light'; and there was light" (Gen 1:3).[460] Our souls, too, are light. In a letter from St. Hildegard to Abbot Helmrich she writes, "Don't allow it to happen that you put out the light of your soul which has so much merit in heaven above."[461] This light of the spirit is actual light that can be seen by human eyes when God permits it, such as occurred with Jesus' Transfiguration.

Too often we subconsciously think of light and knowledge of Truth as two different things; they are not. God IS Light. Jesus is Light from Light — Truthfully expressed by the Father. Through Jesus all things were made; made perfectly ordered and in harmony.[462] One of the major themes of STOSS is the role of electromagnetic energy (light) in the formation and functioning of the human body, and also the expression of the soul's light through the "mouth" of our body. So a logical question arises: is the spiritual light which is the spirits (angels and souls) the same as electromagnetic radiation? I believe the answer to that question is: no! To begin with, most, if not all, electromagnetic radiation reaching earth comes from the sun which, as Genesis tells us (1: 14-16), came after the "light" that is descriptive of the angels. Therefore, material light (electromagnetic energy, the light of the sun, etc.) is almost certainly different from spiritual light (the spirits).

This leads to an additional conundrum. It is well accepted in theological circles that the body is the form of the soul. Prof. Eleonore Stump is an expert on Aquinas' philosophical views. On the subject of "configuration", she wrote that Aquinas believed that the body is configured/ordered by the spirit, while the soul/spirit is a "configured configurer."[463] Hildegard tells us that prior to the fall, man's body was a luminous garment.[464]

A good portion of Volume Two: Part IV of this book is devoted to exposing the role that material light, i.e. electromagnetic radiation, plays in the functioning and organization of living organisms — including humans; so I'm not going to duplicate that discussion in this Appendix. It is my belief that the spiritual soul uses material light as an agent in its "work" as the configured configurer, as Aquinas puts it. Hildegard tells us that the sun [more specifically, light] gives power and mass to the human organism[465] and influences the functioning of the body.[466] When we talk about the substance of Jesus in the Eucharist, we must remember (as was shown above) that his body is living and functioning underneath the veil of bread and wine. Consequently, we should not ignore the possibility that material light plays a role in that functioning.

As a very brief example of the potential agency of material light used by the spirit in the functioning of the body, I want to give a very brief description of an experiment performed by one research team headed by Luc Montagnier. He is no scientific hack. He won the Nobel Prize in biology for discovering the HIV/AIDS virus. He also performed experiments that seem to suggest a role of morphogenetic fields of electromagnetic radiation in configuring living organisms. This is how the experiment was performed: 1) test tube "A" of hydrated DNA of bacteria was subjected to a magnetic field resonating at close to the earth's frequency (7.8 Hz); 2) scientists observed an electromagnetic signal coming from the water in test tube "A"; 3) approximately 18-24 hours after placing a second test tube (test tube "B") containing only water next to test tube "A", researchers noticed that the water in test tube "B" began to emit the same electromagnetic signal as the water in test tube "A"; and, 4) the DNA building blocks (absent actual DNA strands) needed to create a new strand of DNA were placed into the water in test tube "B". As a result, the water nanostructures and their electromagnetic resonance caused a new DNA strand to be formed in test tube "B" that was virtually identical to the strand in test tube "A". If a shield that effectively blocks electromagnetic radiation is placed between the two test tubes, the results are not duplicated.[467]

An article detailing this experiment was published in the *Journal of Physics*.[468] Further information can also be found at: <http://www.rexresearch.com/montagnier/montagnier.htm>

It should be noted that, at the time of this writing, the experiment performed by Montagnier had not been peer reviewed or duplicated by other scientists. However, experiments performed by others involving memory of water nanostructures have been shown to be repeatable. In the book *Water and the Cell,* the two opposing camps on this topic are dealt with much more extensively.[469] There is some controversy swirling around Montagnier's results. His results contradict what some scientists say is settled science. In fairness to Montagnier, he has added other variables to the experimental model that could produce the results he has achieved.

An important question needs to be answered: if material light is integral to the order and function of the human body, does a glorified body still need the sun. The short answer is no. Hildegard writes that "[Jesus] came as one sent by God to bear witness to the One who is the true Light that gives light to all lights."[470] I don't know the particular way in which it is accomplished, but suffice it to say that God, who gives light to all, will have no problems in keeping the glorified body ordered and "living".

EPILOGUE

We now come to the close of Volume One (V.1) of The Science and Theology of Salt in Scripture. STOSS was written in four parts. The first three parts are contained in V.1. In V.2, introducing and unpacking Part Four, which is titled, The Science of the Salt and the Light (Mt. 5:13-14), will be the primary focus. As a short recap, in V.1 we discussed the following main points:

- Salt refers to the salt of our DNA;

- Salt and dust are one in the same in the Bible, though the word 'salt' seems to be used more often in the context of its impact on the 'language of the body';

- Using our newly gained understanding of salt and dust, we were able to reveal twelve, out of the thirty-four, mysteries of advanced science that relate to man;

- As a result of the above, we should have gained a better understanding of why the body (salt and dust) is an integral part of how we are created in the image and likeness of God;

- Building upon this, we acquired a better understanding of why God was so harsh on the OT peoples. It was a necessary step in order to preserve the seed of Abraham up until the time of Jesus; no righteous DNA from Mary, no human Jesus from the line of David, no Jesus being a member of the family of man;

- We learned that the body is the biblical mouth through which the heart expresses its overflow into the visible world;

- We showed that a deeper knowledge of salt, dust, and stone in the Bible leads us to understand, more fully, Jesus' mission on earth; and lastly,

- Through STOSS it was revealed, to a greater degree, what were some of the effects brought about as a consequence of the completion of His mission, upon the world — past, present, and future.

Clearly, V.1 was primarily concerned with the theological and biblical aspects of salt in the Bible, though some science was discussed. This is why only twelve of the available thirty-four mysteries were revealed. In V.2, the focus will be switched. Science will dominate the discussion, but theology will also be incorporated as well. In V.2 we will go into much greater detail as to how and why God created man to be the mouth through which the spiritual heart speaks — doing so accurately via the language of the body, despite hearts that are constantly changing that which it treasures and desires. In V.2, we will come to understand, with great amazement, why St. Hildegard tells us that of all of creation, God considers man as His most glorious. There may be times when you, too, shed tears in awe of our infinitely good and Omnipotent God. We will learn why God is not against scientific exploration and discovery. In fact, quite the opposite is true. God is the quintessential scientist.

Here are some of the questions that will be discussed and answered in V.2:

- What are the other twenty-two scientific mysteries hidden in plain sight in the pages of the Bible;

- Why is both the spiritual and biological heart so important to God;

- Why did 'both' Adam and Eve have to eat the apple before their eyes were opened;

- Why did Jesus choose the wedding feast at Cana to perform his very first public miracle — A miracle which signaled the beginning of his public ministry;

- Why does there seem to be an inextricable link between the Holy Spirit and water;

- Why does Jesus tell us we have no life in us if we don't eat his flesh and drink his blood;

- Similarly, why does Jesus tell us his flesh is real food and his blood is real drink;

- Why and how do so many of our deceased saints have incorruptible bodies, even after the passage of centuries;

- Why and how did Jesus leave his image on his burial cloth, i.e. The Shroud of Turin?

- Was Eve's creation exactly the way it was described in Genesis, and;

- How does the manner of Eve's creation affect every single woman ever born — making them very different from men (I'm not speaking only biologically)?

These questions, and many more, will be explored in V.2. It should be available sometime around October of 2017 (just in time for Christmas; wink, wink).

ENDNOTES

1. St. Hildegard of Bingen, *Scivias* (Mahwah, NJ: Paulist Press, 1990), 499 (© Paulist Press; all rights reserved; all quotations from Hildegard's book, *Scivias*, are used with permission of Paulist Press)

2. Ibid., 61

3. Ibid., 60

4. Ibid., 17

5. Copyright 1965-6, Division of Christian Education of the National Council of the Churches of Christ in the United States of America. Accessed on www.biblegateway.com. Used with permission.

6. Albert Einstein. BrainyQuote.com, Xplore Inc, 2017. https://www.brainyquote.com/quotes/quotes/a/alberteins161289. html, accessed May 20, 2017

7. J. D. Watson, Crick, F. H. C., with commentary by Tom Zinnen, "A Structure for Deoxyribose Nucleic Acid," *Nature* (Access Excellence @ the National Health Museum) 171,737 1953 (April 1953)

8. Ibid.

9. cf. James D. Watson, *The Double Helix: A Personal Account of the Discovery of the Structure of DNA* (New York, NY: Touchstone, 2001), 80, 88, 160, 204

10. S. M. Perepelytsya and S. N. Volkov, "Counterion vibrations in the DNA low-frequency spectra," *The European Physical Journal*

E-Soft Matter (Spinger Berlin / Heidelberg) 24, 3 (November, 2007)

11. Maxim D. Frank-Kamenetskii, *Unraveling DNA: The Most Important Molecule of Life* trans. Lev Liapin, Revised ed., (Reading, MA: Perseus Publishing, 1997), 60, http://www.questia.com/PM.qst?a=o&d=85769698

12. Florida State University, "How life may have first emerged on Earth: Foldable proteins in a high-salt environment," *Science Daily*, http://www.sciencedaily.com/releases/2013/04/130405064027.ht m: Science Daily LLC, April 4, 2013 (accessed 04/07/2013); — **Journal Source**: M. Longo, J. Lee, M. Blaber. "Simplified protein design biased for prebiotic amino acids yields a foldable, halophilic protein."*Proceedings of the National Academy of Sciences*, 2013; 110 (6): 2135 DOI:10.1073/pnas.1219530110

13. Weir, Kirsten. "20 Things You Didn't Know About ... DNA." *Discover*. June 13, 2011. Accessed April 8, 2017. http://discovermagazine.com/2011/apr/20-things-you-didnt-know-about-dna.

14. Christine L. Haskin, Gary D. Fullerton, and Ivan L. Cameron, "Molecular Basis of Articular Disk Biomechanics: Fluid Flow and Water Content in the Temporamandibular Disk as Related to Distribution of Sulfur," in *Water and the Cell*, Pollack, Gerald H., Cameron, Ivan L., Wheatly, Denys N (The Netherlands: Springer, 2006), 64.

15. Hildegard, 98

16. Christopher West, *Theology of the Body Explained* (Boston, MA: Pauline Books and Media, 2003), 350

17. West, *Theology of the Body Explained,* 85, 99

18. St. Seraphim of Sarov. (2010-06-25). *On Acquisition of the Holy Spirit* (Kindle Locations 175-179). Kindle Edition

19. St. Thomas Aquinas. *Summa Theologiae* (Third Millennium Media L.L.C., The Faith Database L.L.C., 2008). I, q. 75, a. 4

20. Pope Benedict XVI, (2011-03-10). *Jesus of Nazareth Part Two, Holy Week: From the Entrance Into Jerusalem To The Resurrection* (Kindle Locations 3436-3437). Ignatius Press. Kindle Edition

21. cf. Aquinas, *Summa Theologiae,* I, q. 99

22. Hildegard, *Scivias,* 163

23. Dr. Michael Pidwirny. "Composition of Rocks". *Fundamentals of Physical Geography*, 2nd Edition (2006), http://www.physicalgeography.net/fundamentals/10d.html, 05/07/2009 (accessed 10/10/2011)

24. Ibid.

25. Yinon Bentor, "Periodic Table: Sodium", in *Chemical Element.com,* http://www.chemicalelements.com/elements/na.html (accessed 10/11/2011)

26. Ibid.

27. Watson, *The Double Helix: A Personal Account of the Discovery of the Structure of DNA,* 165-166; 183; 193; and 113-114

28. Ibid., 68-69, 167-168

29. University of Georgia, "Light Shed on Ancient Origin of Life," *Science Daily,* http://www.sciencedaily.com/releases/2013/03/130307110644.ht

m: Science Daily LLC, March 6, 2013 (accessed 03/08/2013); —
Journal Source: F. Sarmiento, J. Mrazek, W. B. Whitman.
"Genome-scale analysis of gene function in the hydrogenotrophic
methanogenic archaeon Methanococcus maripaludis." *Proceedings
of the National Academy of Sciences*, 2013; DOI:
10.1073/pnas.1220225110

30. David Lyle Jeffrey, Klyne Snodgrass, "Stone," *A Dictionary of
Biblical Tradition in English Literature* (Grand Rapids, MI.: Wm.
B. Eerdmans Publishing Co., 1992), 736

31. MineralTown, "Soil, Sand and Dirt,"
http://www.mineraltown.com/infocoleccionar/How_rocks_minera
ls_are_formed.htm#Crystals, (accessed 10/11/2011)

32. Hildegard of Bingen. *Hildegard of Bingen's Book of Divine
Works: With Letters and Songs*. Translated by Robert
Cunningham, Jerry Dybdal, and Ron Miller. Edited by Matthew
Fox. (Santa Fe, NM: Inner Traditions International/Bear &
Company, ©1987) All rights reserved.
<http://www.Innertraditions.com> Reprinted with permission of
publisher. Kindle Locations 2430-2431

33."Clay," *Wikipedia, The Free Encyclopedia* (Wikimedia
Foundation, Inc.), http://en.wikipedia.org/wiki/Clay, (accessed
10/17/2012)

34. Ron Milo, Rob Phillips, "How Big Is A Human Cell," *Cell
Biology By The Numbers*, http://book.bionumbers.org/how-big-is-
a-human-cell/, (accessed 08/23/2016)

35. Stacy A. Trasancos, *Particles of Faith: A Catholic Guide to
Navigating Science* (Kindle Locations 588-589). Ave Maria Press.
Kindle Edition.

36. Ken Ham, "Millions of Years and the 'Doctrine of Balaam,'" *Answers in Genesis*, https://answersingenesis.org/the-word-of-god/millions-of-years-and-the-doctrine-of-balaam/: June 1, 1997 (accessed 05/07/2017)

37. cf. Peter Abelard (circa 1100 AD), "The Story of My Misfortunes," (Third Millennium Media L.L.C., *The Faith Database* L.L.C., 2008).

38. *Dogmatic Constitution on Divine Revelation,* http://www.vatican.va/archive/hist_councils/ii_vatican_council/documents/vat-ii_const_19651118_dei-verbum_en.html, Chapter IV, n. 16

39. St. Augustine, *Christian Doctrine*, (Third Millennium Media L.L.C., The Faith Database L.L.C., 2008), Book IV, Chapter 21, Section 45

40. John Hardon,"Types (Scriptural)," *Modern Catholic Dictionary*, http://www.catholicculture.org/culture/library/dictionary/index.cfm?id=36970, (accessed 02/25/2012)

41. John Hardon,"Antitype," *Modern Catholic Dictionary*, http://www.catholicculture.org/culture/library/dictionary/index.cfm?id=31869, (accessed 02/25/2012)

42. Augustine, *Christian Doctrine*, Book IV, Chapter 21, Section 45

43. Aquinas, *Summa Theologiae,* I, q. 99

44. Ibid.

45. St. Catherine of Siena, *The Dialogue*, trans. Suzanne Noffke, O.P (Mahwah, NJ: Paulist Press, 1980), 86

46. Aquinas, *Summa Theologiae,* I, q. 76

47. Dr. Norman Doidge, *The Brain That Changes Itself*, (New York, NY, Penguin Books, 2007), 107

48. Hildegard, *Scivias*, 113

49. Ibid., 417

50. Ibid., 257-258

51.Christopher West, *Theology of the Body Explained*, 43

52.Aquinas, *Summa Theologiae,* I, q. 95, a. 1.

53. Hildegard, *Scivias*, 113

54.Tristan Lavender, "No more shame?," *Universiteit Leiden*, http://www.leidenuniv.nl/en/researcharchive/index.php3-m=&c=319.htm: Universiteit Leiden, May 8, 2007 (accessed 10/21/2008)

55. Wendy Zukerman, "Stress Gives Reef Fish Wonky Ears," http://www.abc.net.au/science/articles/2009/04/27/2553465.htm: *ABC Science*, April 27, 2009 (accessed 04/27/2009)

56. Doidge, *The Brain That Changes Itself*, 114

57. Hormone Health Network, "Hormones and Health," *Endocrine Society*, http://www.hormone.org/hormones-and-health/what-do-hormones-do, January 1, 2008 (accessed May 29, 2008)

58.Doidge, *The Brain That Changes Itself*, 119

59. Ibid.

60. Aquinas, *Summa Theologiae*, III, Q. 1, Art. 4

61. Ibid.

62. Francois Jamart, *Complete Spiritual Doctrine of St. Therese of Lisieux* (New York, NY: Alba House, 1996), 109

63. University of California – Berkeley, "Social Scientists Say Compassion Is Humans' Strongest Trait", *News-Medical*, http://www.news-medical.net/news/20091210/Social-scientists-say-compassion-is-humans-strongest-trait.aspx, December 10, 2009 (accessed 04/30/2012)

64. Leen, Rev. Edward. *The Holy Spirit*. (New York, NY: Sheed & Ward, 1939; Sceptor Publishers, 1998, 2008), 15-16, 18

65. Trinity Communications, "Christian obedience, like family unity, is based on love, Pope says," *CatholicCulture.org*, http://www.catholicculture.org/news/headlines/index.cfm?storyid=2697: Trinity Communications, April 23, 2009 (accessed 04/27/2009)

66. Scott Hahn. (2011-07-18). *A Father Who Keeps His Promises: God's Covenant Love in Scripture* (p. 24). St. Anthony Messenger Press, Servant Books. Kindle Edition

67. Ibid., 29

68. Ibid., 27

69. Hildegard, *Scivias*, 332

70. J. Tierney, "Circumcision," *The Catholic Encyclopedia* (Third Millennium Media L.L.C., The Faith Database L.L.C., 2008)

71. Aquinas, *Summa Theologiae,* III, q. 66, a. 1.

72. Dr. Brian J. Morris, "Circumcision: An Evidence-Based Appraisal," *Circinfo.net*, http://www.circinfo.net/why_the_foreskin_increases_infection_risk.html:2008 (accessed 10/23/2008)

73. Ibid.

74. cf. Hildegard, *Scivias*, 79

75. Catherine of Siena, *The Dialogue*, 130

76. Aquinas, *Summa Theologiae* II-I, q. 98, a. 1.

77. The Holy See, e-text version on USCCB website, *Catechism of the Catholic Church*, http://www.usccb.org/beliefs-and-teachings/what-we-believe/catechism/catechism-of-the-catholic-church/epub/index.cfm: ©Libreria Editrice Vaticana, 1994, n. 2515

78. Kennedy, D. (1912). "Sacraments," In *The Catholic Encyclopedia*. New York: Robert Appleton Company. Retrieved October 20, 2008 from New Advent: http://www.newadvent.org/cathen/13295a.htm

79 . Rabbi Moshe Yoseph Koniuchowsky, written in an email to 'heb_roots_chr@hebroots.org, "Children of Salt," Covenant of Salt, http://www.hebroots.org/hebrootsarchive/0209/0209b.html: (accessed 4/08/2008)

80. Rabbi Moshe Shamah, Rabbi Ronald Barry, "Parashat Nisabim Part I," http://www.judaic.org/bible/nisabim1.pdf: Sephardic Institute, 2008 (accessed 04/29/2009)

81. Hillary Mayell, "Three High-Altitude Peoples, Three Adaptations to Thin Air," *National Geographic News*, http://news.nationalgeographic.com/news/2004/02/0224_04022 5_evolution.html: National Geographic Society, February 25, 2004

82. University of California - Santa Cruz, "How epigenetic memory is passed through generations: Sperm and eggs transmit memory of gene repression to embryos," *Science Daily*, www.sciencedaily.com/releases/2014/09/140918141448.htm: ScienceDaily, September 18, 2014 (accessed 09/20/2014); **Journal**

Source: L. J. Gaydos, W. Wang, S. Strome."H3K27me and PRC2 transmit a memory of repression across generations and during development." *Science*, 2014; 345 (6203): 1515 DOI:10.1126/science.1255023

83. Hildegard, *Scivias,* 269

84. The Wake Forest University Baptist Medical Center, "Molecular Fingerprint Of Cocaine Addiction Revealed," ScienceDaily, http://www.sciencedaily.com/releases/2008/05/080527113200.ht m: ScienceDaily L.L.C., May 29, 2008 (accessed 05/29/2008)

85. Doidge, *The Brain That Changes Itself,* 107

86. Max-Planck-Gesellschaft, "Childhood Trauma Leaves Mark On DNA Of Some Victims: Gene-Environment Interaction Causes Lifelong Dysregulation Of Stress Hormones," *Science Daily*, http://www.sciencedaily.com/releases/2012/12/121202164057.htm : ScienceDaily L.L.C., December 2, 2012 (accessed 11/04/12): — **Journal Source**: Torsten Klengel, Divya Mehta, Christoph Anacker, Monika Rex-Haffner, Jens C Pruessner, Carmine M Pariante, Thaddeus W W Pace, Kristina B Mercer, Helen S Mayberg, Bekh Bradley, Charles B Nemeroff, Florian Holsboer, Christine M Heim, Kerry J Ressler, Theo Rein, Elisabeth B Binder. "Allele-specific FKBP5 DNA demethylation mediates gene–childhood trauma interactions." *Nature Neuroscience*, 2012; DOI:10.1038/nn.3275

87. University of East Anglia. "Family problems experienced in childhood and adolescence affect brain development." *ScienceDaily*. www.sciencedaily.com/releases/2014/02/140219075213.htm (accessed February 19, 2014); — **Journal source:** Nicholas D. Walsh, et al. "General and Specific Effects of Early-Life Psychosocial Adversities on Adolescent Grey Matter Volume." *NeuroImage: Clinical*, 2014; 4: 308 DOI: 10.1016/j.nicl.2014.01.001 <http://dx.doi.org/10.1016/j.nicl.2014.01.001>

88. Robin Lord, "Relax and banish harmful stress," *Cape Cod Times*, http://www.capecodtimes.com/article/20040930/LIFE03/309309 961: Cape Cod Times, September 30, 2004 (accessed 03/13/2007)

89. Tom Valeo, "Forgive and Forget," *WebMD*, http://www.webmd.com/balance/guide/forgive-forget?page=1: WebMD, Inc., September 4, 2007 (accessed 09-04-07)

90. Jenny Hope. "Fasting for One Day a Month 'Cuts the Risk of Heart Attack." *Daily Mail Online*. November 7, 2007. http://www.dailymail.co.uk/news/article-492163/Fasting-day-month-cuts-risk-heart-attack.html. (Accessed 11/04/2007)

91. His findings were published in *Federation of American Societies for Experimental Biology (FASEB) Journal* in 2004 and 2005. Ventura, *"DNA and Cell Reprogramming Via Epigenetic Information Delivered By Magnetic Fields, Sound Vibration and Coherent Water,"* Webinar transcript

92. Nova scienceNOW, transcript of TV program, "Epigenetics," *Nova scienceNOW*, http://www.pbs.org/wgbh/nova/transcripts/3411_sciencen.html: WGBH Educational Foundation, air date July 24, 2007 (accessed 2/25/2008)

93. West, *Theology of the Body Explained*, 6

94. St. Catherine of Siena (2009-06-11). *Dialog of Catherine of Siena* - Enhanced Version (Kindle Locations 1266-1267). Christian Classics Ethereal Library. Kindle Edition

95. Ibid., Kindle Locations 3105-3109

96. John Corbett, "Bethel," The Catholic Encyclopedia. Vol. 2. (New York: Robert Appleton Company, 1907),

http://www.newadvent.org/cathen/02532d.htm, (accessed August 10, 2011)

97. St. Cyril of Jerusalem, "Catechetical Lecture #20; On the Mysteries II. of Baptism," (Third Millennium Media L.L.C., The Faith Database L.L.C., 2008), n.2

98. Catherine of Siena. *Dialog of Catherine of Siena,* Kindle Location 796

99. cf. West, *Theology of the Body Explained.* 314, 411

100. cf. Catherine of Siena, *The Dialogue,* 289

101. Seraphim, *On Acquisition of the Holy Spirit,* Kindle Locations 362-366

102. St. Augustine of Hippo, *On the Holy Trinity,* (Third Millennium Media L.L.C., The Faith Database L.L.C., 2008). Book V, Chapter 15

103. Rev. Pacwa's homily can no longer be streamed or downloaded from EWTN's website. Fortunately, I saved the audio file in both RM (Real Player) and MP3 formats.

104. Hildegard, *Scivias,* 317

105. Aquinas, *Summa Theologiae,* III, q. 1, a. 1

106. Fr. Martin von Cochem, *The Incredible Catholic Mass* (Benziger Brothers, 1896; Tan Books and Publishers, Inc., 1997), 167-168. Used with permission from Tan Books.

107. Giles Emery OP, "The Threeness and Oneness of God in Twelfth-To-Fourteenth Century Scholasticism," *Nova Et Vetera,* English Edition 1, 1 (2003), p. 62-63

108. Ibid.

109. Ibid.

110. Giles Emery OP, "The Threeness and Oneness of God in Twelfth-To-Fourteenth Century Scholasticism," 62-63

111. Joseph Ratzinger (Pope Benedict XVI), *Jesus of Nazareth Part One*, translated by Adrian J. Walker (New York, NY: Doubleday, 2007), Kindle Edition, p. 265-266

112. *Hildegard of Bingen's Book of Divine Works: With Letters and Songs*, All rights reserved. <http://www.Innertraditions.com> Reprinted with permission of publisher. Kindle Locations 533-535

113. Hildegard, *Scivias* , 419

114. Joyce A. Little, "Creation." In *Our Sunday Visitor's Encyclopedia of Catholic Doctrine*, 152-55. Ed. Russell Shaw, Huntington, IN.: Our Sunday Visitor Publishing Division, 1997.

115. Ibid.

116. Ibid

117. *Hildegard of Bingen's Book of Divine Works: With Letters and Songs*. All rights reserved. <http://www.Innertraditions.com> Reprinted with permission of publisher. Kindle Locations 2316-2318

118. Hildegard, *Scivias*, 418

119. St. Hildegard of Bingen, *Scivias* (Mahwah, NJ: Paulist Press, 1990), 419 (© Paulist Press; all rights reserved; all quotations from Hildegard's book, *Scivias*, are used with permission of Paulist Press)

120. John Paul II, *The Theology of the Body: Human Love in the Divine Plan*, (Pauline Books and Media: Boston, MA, 1997), ©Libreria Editrice Vaticana, 46

121. Sarah A. Wagner-Wassen, blog entry, "What Does It Mean to Be in the Image of God? Irenaeus of Lyon Against the Gnostics," Sarah A. Wagner-Wassen, https://swagnerwassen.wordpress.com/research/what-does-it-mean-to-be-in-the-image-of-god-irenaeus-of-lyon-against-the-gnostics/: Sarah A. Wagner-Wassen, accessed 11/12/2013

122. Ibid.

123. Ibid.

124. International Theological Commission, "COMMUNION AND STEWARDSHIP: Human Persons Created in the Image of God", ©Libreria Editrice Vaticana www.vatican.va/roman_curia/congregations/cfaith/cti_documents/rc_con_cfaith_doc_20040723_communion-stewardship_en.html, (accessed 2/19/2014)

125. Ibid., n. 7

126. Ibid., n. 9

127. Ibid., n. 27

128. Ibid., n. 10

129. Ibid., n. 12

130. Ibid., n. 13

131. Ibid., n. 29

132. Francois-Xavier Durrwell, *Holy Spirit of God* (original English translation published by Geoffrey Chapman, a division of Cassell, Ltd., 1986; reprint published by Servant Books, Cinncinati, OH, 2006), 201-203

133. *Hildegard of Bingen's Book of Divine Works: With Letters and Songs.* All rights reserved. <http://www.Innertraditions.com> Reprinted with permission of publisher. Kindle Locations 787-790

134. Hildegard, *Scivias,* 190

135. Durrwell, *Holy Spirit of God*, 81

136. *CCC,* n. 687

137. Leo XIII, *Divinum Illud Munus*, (Third Millennium Media L.L.C., The Faith Database L.L.C., 2008), n. 3

138. *Hildegard of Bingen's Book of Divine Works: With Letters and Song*. All rights reserved. <http://www.Innertraditions.com> Reprinted with permission of publisher. Kindle Locations 2548-2552

139. cf. Hildegard, *Scivias,* 123, 477

140. Durrwell, *Holy Spirit of God*, 31

141. Durrwell, *Holy Spirit of God*, 179-180

142. Catherine of Siena, *The Dialogue*, 289

143. Leen, *The Holy Spirit*, 29-34

144. Durrwell, *Holy Spirit of God*, 14-15

145. Durrwell, *Holy Spirit of God.*, 199

146. Durrwell, *Holy Spirit of God*, 49

147. Durrwell, *Holy Spirit of God*, 30

148. Durrwell, *Holy Spirit of God*, 23

149. *Hildegard of Bingen's Book of Divine Works: With Letters and Song*, Kindle Locations 579-580

150. *CCC*, n. 691

151. Pope Pius XII, *Mystici Corporis Christi* (Mystical Body of Christ, 1943), (Third Millennium Media L.L.C., The Faith Database L.L.C., 2008), n. 4, 23, 33, 68

152. St. Maria Faustina Kowalska, *Diary of Saint Maria Faustina Kowalska*, Congregation of Sisters of Our Lady of Mercy (Poland: Congregation Of Marians, 1987; Marian Press, 2005), 310. Used with permission of the Marian Fathers of the Immaculate Conception of the B.V.M.

153. Durrwell, *Holy Spirit of God*, 25-26

154. Leen, *The Holy Spirit*, 15-16, 18

155. Durrwell, *Holy Spirit of God*, 101-103

156. Leo XIII, *Divinum Illud Munus*, n. 10

157. West, *Theology of the Body Explained*, 193

158. West, *Theology of the Body Explained*, 193

159. Kowalska, *Diary of Saint Maria Faustina Kowalska*, n. 1074. Used with permission of the Marian Fathers of the Immaculate Conception of the B.V.M.

160. Sheen, Fulton J., *The Mystical Body of Christ* (Kindle Locations 215-218), Ave Maria Press, Kindle Edition. This reference is found in the "Introduction of the New Edition" by Brandon Vogt. Excerpted from *The Mystical Body of Christ* by Fulton J. Sheen. Copyright 2015 by The Society for the Propagation of the Faith. Used with permission of the publisher, Ave Maria Press, P.O. Box 428, Notre Dame, IN 46556. www.avemariapress.com

161 Ibid., Kindle Locations 2935-2939. See note #160 above.

162 Ibid., Kindle Location 94. See note #160 above.

163. John Paul II, "Marital Love Reflects God's Love for His People," *The Theology of the Body*, Daughters of St. Paul, General audience of July 28, 1982, ©Libreria Editrice Vaticana, (Boston, MA: Pauline Books & Media, 1997), p. 304-306

164. Aumann O.P., Jordan. "Charisms." In *Our Sunday Visitor's Encyclopedia of Catholic Doctrine*, 88-92. Ed. Russell Shaw, Huntington, IN.: Our Sunday Visitor Publishing Division, 1997. Used with permission.

165. Ibid.

166. Fr. John Hardon, "Gratuitous Grace," *Modern Catholic Dictionary*, http://www.catholicculture.org/culture/library/dictionary/index.cfm?id=33805, (accessed 10/27/14)

167. Hardon, "History and Theology of Grace: Actual Graces," *The Real Presence Association*, http://www.therealpresence.org/archives/Grace/Grace_013.htm: therealpresence.org,

168. Ignatius, *Letters of St. Ignatius of Loyola*, trans. William J. Young (Chicago: Loyola University Press, 1959), 129,

http://www.questia.com/read/1705261/letters-of-st-ignatius-of-loyola.

169. Aquinas, *Summa Theologia*, I-II, q. 111, a. 1

170. Hardon, John (2013-06-25). "Sanctifying Grace," *Catholic Dictionary: An Abridged and Updated Edition of Modern Catholic Dictionary* (p. 456). The Doubleday Religious Publishing Group. Kindle Edition.

171. CCC, n. 460

172. Fr. John A. Hardon S.J., "History and Theology of Grace: Sanctifying Grace," *The Real Presence Association*, http://www.therealpresence.org/archives/Grace/Grace_011.htm: Inter Mirifica, 1998 (accessed 06/23/2014). Used with permission from Inter Mirifica.

173. Hardon, *Catholic Dictionary: An Abridged and Updated Edition of Modern Catholic Dictionary*, p. 456

174. Hardon, John (2013-06-25). "Sacramental Grace." *Catholic Dictionary: An Abridged and Updated Edition of Modern Catholic Dictionary* (p. 442). The Doubleday Religious Publishing Group. Kindle Edition.

175. Hardon. "Sanctifying Grace," *Catholic Dictionary: An Abridged and Updated Edition of Modern Catholic Dictionary*, p. 456

176. Ibid.

177. Ibid.

178. Aquinas, *Summa Theologiae*, I-II, q. 112, a. 1

179. Catherine of Siena, *The Dialogue*, 86

180. F.M. Jelly, O.P., "Mary, Mother Of The Church," *Our Sunday Visitor's Encyclopedia of Catholic Doctrine*, ed. Russell Shaw (Our Sunday Visitor Inc., Huntington, IN, 1997), pg. 423-427. For more information on this topic, some of F.M. Jelly O.P. recommends are the following sources: CCC 964-970; *Lumen Gentium*; *Redemptoris Mater*; *Theotokos: A Theological Encyclopedia of the Blessed Virgin Mary* by Michael O'Carroll. I would also add Tim Staples book, *Behold Your Mother*.

181. Hardon, "History and Theology of Grace: Sanctifying Grace," http://www.therealpresence.org/archives/Grace/Grace_011.htm

182. John A. Hardon S.J., "History and Theology of Grace: Actual Graces," *The Real Presence Association*, http://www.therealpresence.org/archives/Grace/Grace_013.htm: therealpresence.org, 1998 (accessed 05/08/2014)

183. Archbishop Luis M. Martinez, *True Devotion to the Holy Spirit*, translated by Sister M. Aquinas O.S.U. of the 1881 book titled *El Espiritu Sanctu*, (Manchester, New Hampshire: Sophia Institute Press. 2013), p. 12

184. Ibid., 71

185. Ibid., 163

186. John A. Hardon S.J., "History and Theology of Grace: Actual Graces," *The Real Presence Association*, http://www.therealpresence.org/archives/Grace/Grace_013.htm: therealpresence.org, 1998 (accessed 05/08/2014). Used with permission from Inter Mirifica.

187. Ibid.

188. Hardon, "History and Theology of Grace: Actual Graces," *The Real Presence Association*,

http://www.therealpresence.org/archives/Grace/Grace_013.htm: therealpresence.org. Used with permission from Inter Mirifica.

189. Hardon, John (2013-06-25). *Catholic Dictionary: An Abridged and Updated Edition of Modern Catholic Dictionary* (p. 9). The Doubleday Religious Publishing Group. Kindle Edition.

190. Hardon, "History and Theology of Grace: Actual Graces," http://www.therealpresence.org/archives/Grace/Grace_013.htm: therealpresence.org. Used with permission from Inter Mirifica.

191. cf. Ibid.

192. Ibid.

193. Ibid.

194. Ibid. Used with permission from Inter Mirifica.

195. Ibid.

196. Fr. John A. Hardon S.J., "History and Theology of Grace: Grace Considered Exyensively," *The Real Presence Association*, http://www.therealpresence.org/archives/Grace/Grace_002.htm# 05: Inter Mirifica, 1998 (accessed 06/23/2014)

197. Hardon, "History and Theology of Grace: Actual Graces," *The Real Presence Association*, http://www.therealpresence.org/archives/Grace/Grace_013.htm: therealpresence.org,

198. It could potentially lead to theological error to believe that the Holy Spirit is 'sent' in the same manner as the Son is sent. Only the Son is expressed. The Holy Spirit proceeds. Having issued that proviso, the current context is sufficient to understand the meaning of the 'mouth' of God.

199. Durrwell, *Holy Spirit of God*, 36-37

200. cf. Hildegard, *Scivias* 35

201. cf. Leen, *The Holy Spirit*, 32-33

202. Richard Payne and Stephen Payne, "Saint Robert Bellarmine-Part II," *Saints Alive* (Arcadia Films, aired November 16, 2011), Saints Alive is a TV program that airs on EWTN. In this series, an actor portraying a saint is interviewed and his or her response is taken directly from the actual writings of the saint.

203. Hildegard, *Scivias*, 363

204. Aquinas, *Summa Theologiae*, I, q. 45, a. 6

205. cf. CCC, n. 460

206. John Paul II, in his general audience of February 20, 1980, " Man Enters the World as a Subject of Truth and Love," *Theology of the Body*, ©Libreria Editrice Vaticana (Third Millennium Media L.L.C., The Faith Database L.L.C., 2008), n. 4

207. Catherine of Siena, *The Dialogue*, 32, 103-104, 277

208. Aquinas, *Summa Theologiae*, I, q. 76, a. 4

209. Aquinas, *Summa Theologiae*, I, q. 76, a. 1

210. Catherine of Siena, *The Dialogue*, 86

211. Zenit News Service, reprint of Cardinal Georges Cottier's Introduction written for the book, <u>President of the Exorcists — Experiences and Clarifications of Father Gabriel Amorth</u>, "The Church Must Speak About the Devil, translated by Zenit" *Zenit News Service*, https://zenit.org/articles/cardinal-cottier-on-exorcisms/: Zenit., January 22, 2006 (accessed 05/13/2011)

212. Joan Carroll Cruz, *Angels & Devils* (Rockford, IL 61105: Tan Books and Publishers, Inc., 1999), 47

213. Catherine of Siena, *The Dialogue*, 133

214. Ibid., 62 (© Paulist Press; all rights reserved; all quotations from Catherine of Siena's book, *The Dialogue*, are used with permission of Paulist Press)

215. John Paul II, in his general audience of Sept. 5, 1984, "Responsible Parenthood Linked to Moral Maturity," *Theology of the Body,* ©Libreria Editrice Vaticana (Third Millennium Media L.L.C., The Faith Database L.L.C., 2008), n. 1

216. Pope John Paul II, in his general audience of January 12, 1983, "The Language of the Body in the Structure of Marriage," *Theology of the Body,* ©Libreria Editrice Vaticana (Third Millennium Media L.L.C., The Faith Database L.L.C., 2008), n. 7

217. Hildegard, *Scivias*, 345

218. Ibid., 37

219. West, *Theology of the Body Explained,* 94

220. Ibid., 382

221. cf. Catherine of Siena, *The Dialogue*, 141

222. Joseph M. Magee, *Thomistic Philosophy Page,* http://www.aquinasonline.com/Questions/knowgod.html: Joseph M. Magee, Ph.D., 03/21/2015 (accessed 05/02/2017)

223. Hildegard, *Scivias*, 29 (© Paulist Press; all rights reserved; all quotations from Hildegard's book, *Scivias*, are used with permission of Paulist Press)

224. CCC. n. 365

225. West, *Theology of the Body Explained,* 85

226. John Paul II, "The Language of the Body in the Structure of Marriage," n. 7

227. Ibid.

228. Hildegard, *Scivias,* 161

229. Hildegard, *Scivias,* 375 (© Paulist Press; all rights reserved; all quotations from Hildegard's book, *Scivias,* are used with permission of Paulist Press)

230. Pope Benedict XVI, (2011-03-10). *Jesus of Nazareth Part Two, Holy Week: From the Entrance Into Jerusalem To The Resurrection* (pp. 58-59). Ignatius Press. Kindle Edition

231. Catherine of Siena, *The Dialogue,* 41

232. Durrwell, *Holy Spirit of God,* 213

233. Hildegard, *Scivias,* 217 (© Paulist Press; all rights reserved; all quotations from Hildegard's book, *Scivias,* are used with permission of Paulist Press)

234. Catherine of Siena, *The Dialogue,* 141

235. St. Jerome, *Letters* (Third Millennium Media L.L.C., The Faith Database L.L.C., 2008), 54:6

236. Origen, "Commentary on the Gospel of Matthew," Book XIII, 2, translated by John Patrick, from *Ante-Nicene Fathers*, Vol. 9., edited by Allan Menzies, (Buffalo, NY: Christian Literature Publishing Co., 1896.),
http://www.newadvent.org/fathers/101613.htm

237. *Hildegard of Bingen's Book of Divine Works: With Letters and Song*. All rights reserved.
<http://www.Innertraditions.com> Reprinted with permission of publisher. Kindle Locations 657-658

238. Leo XIII, *Divinum Illud Munus*, n. 3

239. Durrwell, *Holy Spirit of God*, 14-15.

240. Ibid., 30

241. Ibid., 12-13

242. Ibid., 14

243. Toner, Patrick. "Relation of God to the Universe." *The Catholic Encyclopedia*. Vol. 6. (New York: Robert Appleton Company, 1909) http://www.newadvent.org/cathen/06614a.htm (accessed 16 Mar. 2016)

244. Aquinas, *Summa Theologiae*, II-II, q. 178, a. 1, answer

245. Aquinas, *Summa Theologiae*, II-II, q. 178, a. 2, answer

246. John Paul II, "Man Enters the World as a Subject of Truth and Love," n. 4

247. Hildegard, *Scivias,* 360

248. Durrwell, *Holy Spirit of God*, 30

249. Josephus, Flavius; Marsh, Ernest; Whiston, William (2010-10-07). *The Complete Works of Flavius Josephus* (Kindle Locations 3599-3600). Unknown. Kindle Edition.

250. Translated by J.G. Cunningham. "Letters of St. Augustine-Letter 55," n. 29, From *Nicene and Post-Nicene Fathers*, First Series, Vol. 1. Edited by Philip Schaff. (Buffalo, NY: Christian

Literature Publishing Co., 1887.) Revised and edited for New Advent by Kevin Knight. http://www.newadvent.org/fathers/1102055.htm, (accessed 04/15, 2012)

251. Josephus, *The Complete Works of Flavius Josephus,* Kindle Locations 3599-3600

252. cf. Hildegard, *Scivias,* 191, 213, 333, 360

253. Seraphim, *On Acquisition of the Holy Spirit,* Kindle Locations 209-210

254. Council of Trent, "Creed,: Article II : And In Jesus Christ, His Only Son, Our Lord," *The Catechism of The Council of Trent,* http://www.catholicapologetics.info/thechurch/catechism/Apostles Creed02.shtml, (accessed 04/16/2012)

255. Translated by Charles Gordon Browne and James Edward Swallow, "Orations (Gregory Nazianzen)," *Nicene and Post-Nicene Fathers*, Schaff, Philip; Wace, Henry, eds., Second Series, Vol. 7, (Buffalo, NY: Christian Literature Publishing Co., 1894), http://www.newadvent.org/fathers/310243.htm, (accessed 10/07/2011), Oration 43, n. 74

256. *Hildegard of Bingen's Book of Divine Works: With Letters and Song,* Kindle Locations 657-658

257. Tertullian (Quintus Septimius Florens Tertullianus), *On The Resurrection of The Flesh* (Third Millennium Media L.L.C., The Faith Database L.L.C., 2008), n. 7-8

258. Hildegard, *Scivias,* 98

259. Koniuchowsky, http://www.hebroots.org/hebrootsarchive/0209/0209b.html

260. Jeffrey, et al., *A Dictionary of Biblical Tradition in English Literature*, 736-737

261. Hildegard, *Scivias*, 400

262. Ibid., 380-381

263. St. Cyprian of Carthage, "Treatise 12," *The Treatises of Cyprian* (Third Millennium Media L.L.C., The Faith Database L.L.C., 2008), n. 16

264. Pope Pius XII, *Mystici Corporis Christi*, n. 7

265. Catherine of Siena, *The Dialogue*, 288-289

266. Hildegard, *Scivias*, 317

267. Ibid., 172 (© Paulist Press; all rights reserved; all quotations from Hildegard's book, *Scivias*, are used with permission of Paulist Press)

268. cf. Ibid., 432

269. CCC, n. 1374-1376

270. John Paul II, *Ecclesia de Eucharistia*, ©Libreria Editrice Vaticana (Third Millennium Media L.L.C., The Faith Database L.L.C., 2008), n. 1

271. Ratzinger *Jesus of Nazareth Part One*, 250

272. Durrwell, *Holy Spirit of God*, 38-39

273. *CCC*, n. 1287

274. Durrwell, *Holy Spirit of God*, 64 and 178-179

275. *CCC*, n. 1085.

276. Durrwell, *Holy Spirit of God*, 143-146

277. *CCC*, n. 691

278. West, *Theology of the Body Explained*, 204

279. Ibid., 206

280. Hildegard, *Scivias*, 254-255

281. Hildegard, *Scivias*, 153 and 395

282. Ibid., 381

283. Cyprian, "Treatise 12," Book 2, n. 20

284. St. Augustine, *City of God*, (Third Millennium Media L.L.C., The Faith Database L.L.C., 2008), Book 11, n. 30

285. Augustine, *On the Trinity*, Book IV, n. 4

286. Methodius, *Banquest of the Ten Virgins*, (Third Millennium Media L.L.C., The Faith Database L.L.C., 2008), Discourse 8, Chapter 10

287. Pope St. Leo the Great, "Sermon 71," (Third Millennium Media L.L.C., The Faith Database L.L.C., 2008)

288. Ibid.

289. Augustine, *On the Trinity*, IV, 5, n. 9

290. Ratzinger, *Jesus of Nazareth Part One*, 253-254

291. Durrwell, *Holy Spirit of God*, 43

292. Ibid., 43

293. West, *Theology of the Body Explained*, 18

294. John Paul II, *Ecclesia de Eucharistia*, n. 54

295. Ibid., n. 57

296. Ibid., n.53

297. Promulgated by His Holiness Pope Paul VI, *Gaudium Et Spes*, Pastoral Constitution on the Church in the Modern World, Second Vatican Council (December 7, 1965), n.22, ©Libreria Editrice Vaticana <http://www.vatican.va/archive/hist_councils/ii_vatican_council/ documents/vat-ii_cons_19651207_gaudium-et-spes_en.html>, (accessed April 5, 2012)

298. Rev. John Hardon, "Synagogue (biblical), " *Modern Catholic Dictionary,* (Doubleday, 1980), retrieved from http://www.catholicculture.org/culture/library/dictionary/index.cf m?id=36751, (accessed 06/04/2011)

299. Barnabas Meistermann, "Temple of Jerusalem," *The Catholic Encyclopedia,* Vol. 14, (New York: Robert Appleton Company, 1912), from http://www.newadvent.org/cathen/14499a.htm (accessed June 3, 2011)

300. Ibid.

301. Ibid.

302. Ibid.

303. Ibid.

304. Ibid.

305. Ratzinger, *Jesus of Nazareth Part Two*, 37

306. Meistermann, "Temple of Jerusalem"

307. Beda Kleinschmidt and Walter Drum, "Temple," *The Catholic Encyclopedia,* Vol. 14, (New York: Robert Appleton Company, 1912), from http://www.newadvent.org/cathen/14495a.htm (accessed June 6, 2011)

308. Hahn, *A Father Who Keeps His Promises: God's Covenant Love in Scripture,* 24

309. Ibid., 29

310. Ibid., 27

311. Koniuchowsky, http://www.hebroots.org/hebrootsarchive/0209/0209b.html

312. Durrwell, *Holy Spirit of God,* 154.

313. CCC, n.1968

314. Hahn, *A Father Who Keeps His Promises: God's Covenant Love in Scripture,* 15

315. Ibid., 27

316. Koniuchowsky, http://www.hebroots.org/hebrootsarchive/0209/0209b.html

317. Ibid.

318. Burge, Gary M. (2012-08-07). *Jesus and the Jewish Festivals* (Ancient Context, Ancient Faith) (Kindle Locations 1184-1187). Zondervan. Kindle Edition.

319. Ratzinger, *Jesus of Nazareth Part Two,* Kindle Locations 3437-3444

320. Cochem, *The Incredible Catholic Mass,* p. 6-7. Used with permission from Tan Books.

321. Ratzinger, *Jesus of Nazareth Part Two,* Kindle Locations, p. 37

322. Ibid., Kindle Location 604-605

323. John Corbett, "Bethel," *The Catholic Encyclopedia.* Vol. 2. (New York: Robert Appleton Company, 1907), from http://www.newadvent.org/cathen/02532d.htm, (accessed August 10, 2011)

324. Hildegard, *Scivias,* 381

325. Cyprian, "Treatise 12," Book 1, n. 15

326. Hildegard, *Scivias,* 380

327. Catherine of Siena, *The Dialogue,* 67

328. Ibid., 109

329. Map can be at: http://bibleatlas.org/full/sodom_and_gomorrah.htm

330. Seraphim, *On Acquisition of the Holy Spirit,* Kindle Locations 84-88

331. Cyprian, "Treatise 12," Book II, Section 20

332. Hildegard, *Scivias,* 153 and 395

333. Pope Pius XII. "Mystici Corporis Christi." n.7, *Libreria Editrice Vaticana,* June 29, 1943. http://www.catholicsociety.com/documents/pius_xii_encyclicals/ Mystici_corporis_christi.pdf.

334. Ibid., n. 26

335. Ibid., n. 9

336. Ibid., n. 14, 64

337. Ibid., n. 62-63

338. Ibid., n. 64

339. Ibid., n. 67

340. Ibid., n. 17

341. Ibid., n. 57

342. Hildegard, *Scivias*, 489

343. *CCC*, n. 751

344. Burge, *Jesus and the Jewish Festivals,* Kindle Locations 1447-1448

345. Ibid.

346. Ibid., Kindle Location 1183-1184

347. Ibid., Kindle Location 1184-1187

348. Ibid., Kindle Location 1189-1190

349. Cochem, *The Incredible Catholic Mass*, 34. Used with permission from Tan Books.

350. Ibid., 7

351. Ibid., 41-42

352. Catherine of Siena, *The Dialogue*, 288-289 (© Paulist Press; all rights reserved; all quotations from Catherine of Siena's book, *The Dialogue*, are used with permission of Paulist Press)

353. Pope Paul VI, *Lumen Gentium*, (©Libreria Editrice Vaticana, 11/21/1964), <http://www.vatican.va/archive/hist_councils/ii_vatican_council/documents/vat-ii_const_19641121_lumen-gentium_en.html> , n. 50

354. Wikipedia, "Swarm Behavior," *Wikipedia*, http://en.wikipedia.org/wiki/Swarm_behaviour#cite _ref-Ballerini_et_al_2-1: Wikimedia Foundation, Inc., April 28, 2012 (accessed 05/04/2012)

355. Ibid.

356. Ibid.

357. Ibid.

358. Durrwell, *Holy Spirit of God;* 22, 95

359. Hildegard, *Scivias*, 414-415

360. Ibid.

361. Tertullian, *On The Resurrection of The Flesh*, n. 8

362. John Paul II, *Ecclesia de Eucharistia*, n. 17

363. John Paul II, "The Language of the Body in the Structure of Marriage," *Theology of the Body*, n.7

364. West, *Theology of the Body Explained*, 85

365. Ratzinger, *Jesus of Nazareth Part One*, 247-248

366. Ibid., 245-246

367. Ibid., 247

368. Ibid., 248

369. Durrwell, *Holy Spirit of God*, 110-111

370. West, *Theology of the Body Explained*, 105

371. John Paul II, in his general audience of Dec. 3, 1980, "Christ Calls Us To Rediscover The Living Forms Of The New Man," *Theology of the Body*, ©Libreria Editrice Vaticana (Third Millennium Media L.L.C., The Faith Database L.L.C., 2008), n. 3

372. Benedict XVI, *Jesus of Nazareth Part Two*, 150

373. Ratzinger, *Jesus of Nazareth Part One*, 68

374. Ibid., 69

375. John Paul II, "Christ Calls Us To Rediscover The Living Forms Of The New Man," n. 1-2, 7

376. Ratzinger, *Jesus of Nazareth Part One*, 92-93

377. Martinez, *True Devotion to the Holy Spirit*, p. 21

378. William Porcher Dubose, *William Porcher Dubose: Selected Writings*, ed. Jon Alexander (New York: Paulist Press, 1988), 127, http://www.questia.com/read/102670695/william-porcher-dubose-selected-writings.

379. Ibid., 102

380. Ratzinger, *Jesus of Nazareth Part One*, 95

381. Pope John Paul II, *Redemptoris Hominis* (©Libreria Editrice Vaticana, 1979), http://www.vatican.va/holy_father/john_paul_ii/encyclicals/documents/hf_jp-ii_enc_04031979_redemptor-hominis_en.html, n. 20

382. Benedict XVI, *Jesus of Nazareth Part Two,* Kindle Locations 3436-3444

383. cf. Hahn, *A Father Who Keeps His Promises: God's Covenant Love in Scripture,* 237-238

384. John Paul II, *Ecclesia de Eucharistia,* n.23

385. Scott Hahn, *A Father Who Keeps His Promises: God's Covenant Love in Scripture,* 15

386. CCC, n. 291

387. Catherine of Siena, *The Dialogue,* 56, 73, 76, 142

388. Ibid., 76

389. Jeremiah Reedy, "Good time to read papal letters on capitalism," TheCatholicSpirit.com, http://thecatholicspirit.com/commentary/good-time-to-read-papal-letters-on-capitalism/, November 7, 2011 (accessed 12-5-2015)

390. Benedict XVI, *Jesus of Nazareth Part Two,* 37

391. John Paul II, *Redemptoris Hominis,* n. 10

392. Catherine of Siena, *The Dialogue,* 205

393. Faustina, *Diary of Saint Maria Faustina Kowalska,* 310. Used with permission of the Marian Fathers of the Immaculate Conception of the B.V.M.

394. Cruz, *The Incorruptibles*, 27

395. Ibid., 33

396. Ibid., 27

397. Ibid., 301

398. Ibid.

399. Ibid., 23

400. Ibid., 301

401. Ibid., 27, 35, 37-38

402. St. Cyril of Jerusalem, "On the Words, and in One Holy Catholic Church, and in the Resurrection of the Flesh, and the Life Everlasting," *Catechetical Lectures* (Third Millennium Media L.L.C., The Faith Database L.L.C., 2008), Lecture 18, n. 16

403. De Munnynck, "Substance," *The Catholic Encyclopedia*

404. Ibid.

405. Dr. Joseph M. Magee, "Natural Philosophy - Substance and Accident," *Thomistic Philosophy Page*, http://www.aquinasonline.com/Topics/index.html: Joseph M. Magee, Ph.D., 08/27/1999 (accessed 05/02/2013)

406. Francis Aveling, "Man," (2011-10-25). *The Catholic Encyclopedia: Complete Vol. 1-15,* ed. Charles George Herbermann, (Kindle Locations 426413-426415). Kindle Edition.

407. Ibid., Kindle Locations 426402-426404

408. Ibid., Kindle Locations 426398-426399

409. Joseph Pohle, "St. Paschasius Radbertus." *The Catholic Encyclopedia. Vol. 11.* (New York: Robert Appleton Company, 1911) http://www.newadvent.org/cathen/11518a.htm (accessed June26, 2013)

410. Ibid.

411. Ibid.

412. Mark Armitage, "St Paschasius Radbertus," *Saints and Blesseds Page; Saints and Beati of Late Antiquity and the Middle Ages,* http://saintsandblesseds.wordpress.com/2009/05/11/st-paschasius-radbertus/: Blog at Wordpress.com, May 11, 2009 (accessed 06/26/2013)

413. Butler, Alban, Rev. *The Lives of the Fathers, Martyrs, and Other Principal Saints,*Vol. 4: April (Dublin: James Duffy, 1866); Bartleby.com, 2010. http://www.bartleby.com/210/4/263.html, (accessed 08/21/2013)

414. Keating, Karl, *Catholicism and Fundamentalism: The Attack on Romanism by Bible Christians* (San Francisco: Ignatius Press, 1988). 238-240

415. Pohle, "St. Paschasius Radbertus." *The Catholic Encyclopedia. Vol. 11*

416. Armitage, "St Paschasius Radbertus," *Saints and Blesseds Page; Saints and Beati of Late Antiquity and the Middle Ages*

417. Michael Ott, "Ratramnus," *The Catholic Encyclopedia. Vol. 12.* (New York: Robert Appleton Company, 1911), http://www.newadvent.org/cathen/12659c.htm, (accessed Aug.18, 2013)

418. Elizabeth Frances Rogers M.A., *Peter Lombard and the Sacramental System* (New York, NY: Elizabeth Frances Rogers, 1917), 30

419. John A. Hardon S.J., "Doctrine of the Real Presence in the Encyclical *Mediator Dei*," chap. in *Homiletic and Pastoral Review*, Vol. 51, _10 (Inter Mirifica, July 1951; www.therealpresence.org, 2000)

420. Aumann O.P., Jordan. "Real Presence." In *Our Sunday Visitor's Encyclopedia of Catholic Doctrine*, 562. Ed. Russell Shaw, Huntington, IN.: Our Sunday Visitor Publishing Division, 1997.

421. Ott, Ludwig (1954-10-07). *Fundamentals of Catholic Dogma* (Kindle Locations 10118-10140). The Mercier Press. Kindle Edition.

422. Pohle, "St. Paschasius Radbertus." *The Catholic Encyclopedia. Vol. 11*

423. Thomas Aquinas, *Commentary on the Four Gospels, Vol. IV,* (Oxford, John Henry Parker; J. G. F. and J. Rivington, London. MDCCCXLI.,1841). Pg. 240.

424. Hildegard, *Scivias,* 248 (© Paulist Press; all rights reserved; all quotations from Hildegard's book, *Scivias,* are used with permission of Paulist Press)

425. Joseph Pohle, "Eucharist," (2011-10-25). *The Catholic Encyclopedia: Complete Vol. 1-15,* ed. Charles George Herbermann, (Kindle Locations 233828-233829). Kindle Edition.

426. Aquinas, *Summa Theologiae,* III, Q. 76, Art. 8

427. Arthur Herlin, "Between Flesh and Bread: The Autopsy of a Eucharistic Miracle," *Aleteia SAS,* http://aleteia.org/2017/01/05/between-flesh-and-bread-the-

autopsy-of-a-eucharistic-miracle/, January 5, 2017 (accessed 1/18/2017)

428. Carlo Acutis, "The Eucharistic Miracles of the World: Argentina, Buenos Aries, 1992-1994-1996," *Associazione Amici di Carlo Acutis*, http://www.miracolieucaristici.org/en/Liste/scheda_c.html?nat=ar gentina&wh=buenosaires&ct=Buenos%20Aires,%201992-1994-1996, accessed 11/18/2016

429. Ventura, "*DNA and Cell Reprogramming Via Epigenetic Information Delivered By Magnetic Fields, Sound Vibration and Coherent Water*," Webinar transcript

430. Pohle, "Eucharist," Kindle Locations 233583-233584

431. Cochem, *The Incredible Catholic Mass*, 143-145. Used with permission from Tan Books.

432. Ibid., 145

433. Ibid., 75-76

434. Pope Pius XII, *Mystici Corporis Christi*, n.6, ©Libreria Editrice Vaticana http://www.vatican.va/holy_father/pius_xii/encyclicals/document s/hf_p-xii_enc_29061943_mystici-corporis-christi_en.html#top, 6/29/1943 (accessed 08/21/2013)

435. John A. Hardon S.J., "Doctrine of the Real Presence in the Encyclical *Mediator Dei*," chap. in *Homiletic and Pastoral Review*, Vol. 51, _10 (Inter Mirifica, July 1951; www.therealpresence.org, 2000)

436. Joseph Pohle, "The Real Presence of Christ in the Eucharist." *The Catholic Encyclopedia*. Vol. 5. (New York: Robert Appleton

Company, 1909). http://www.newadvent.org/cathen/05573a.htm, (accessed Nov. 19, 2013)

437. *Hildegard of Bingen's Book of Divine Works: With Letters and Song*. All rights reserved. http://www.Innertraditions.com. Reprinted with permission of publisher. Kindle Locations 2425-2433

438. Matthew Fox is the editor of this book. I do not agree with many of his beliefs. However, I am using this book because it contains reliable English translations of Hildegard's *De Operatione Dei* (*The Book of Divine Works*) and also some of her letters written to others. I have not been able to locate any other English translations that would be easily obtainable. Only direct translations of Hildegard's writings have been quoted.

439. Aquinas, *Summa Theologiae*, III, Q. 77, Art. 5

440. Ibid., III, Q. 2, Art. 6

441. Ibid., III, Q. 76, Art. 4

442. Ibid., III, Q. 76, A. 1

443. Ibid., III, Q. 76, A. 6

444. John A. Hardon S.J., "Doctrine of the Real Presence in the Encyclical *Mediator Dei*," chap. in *Homiletic and Pastoral Review*, Vol. 51, _10 (Inter Mirifica, July 1951; www.therealpresence.org, 2000). Used with permission from Inter Mirifica.

445. Aquinas, *Summa Theologiae*, III, Q. 76, Art. 3

446. Real Presence Eucharistic Education and Adoration Association, "Eucharistic Miracle," *Real Presence Eucharistic Education and Adoration Association,*

http://www.therealpresence.org/eucharst/mir/lanciano.html,
2000 (accessed 03/23/2009)

447. Elizabeth Mitchell, "Father John A. Hardon, S.J.: Biography,"
Father John A. Hardon Archive and Guild, S.J.,
http://www.hardonsj.org/biography: Father John A. Hardon, SJ,
Archive and Guild, 2013 (accessed 07/31/2013)

448. Ibid.

449. Ibid.

450. James Maldonado Berry, "A Preacher "In and Out of Season":
Fr. Hardon's Cause for Sainthood," *Catholic Exchange*,
http://catholicexchange.com/preaching-the-gospel-%e2%80%9cin-
and-out-of-season%e2%80%9d-fr-hardon%e2%80%99s-relevance-
for-today/, June 22, 2010 (accessed 10/31/2013)

451. James Maldonado Berry, "Father John A. Hardon, S.J.: More
on the Archive and Guild," *Father John A. Hardon, S.J.*,
http://www.hardonsj.org/more: Father John A. Hardon, SJ,
Archive and Guild, 2013 (accessed 07/31/2013)

452. John A. Hardon S.J., "Doctrine of the Real Presence in the
Encyclical *Mediator Dei*," chap. in *Homiletic and Pastoral Review*,
Vol. 51, #10 (Inter Mirifica, July 1951;
http://www.therealpresence.org/archives/Eucharist/Eucharist_03
5.htm). Used with permission from Inter Mirifica.

453. Ibid.

454. John A. Hardon S.J., "The Holy Eucharist is the Whole Christ,"
The Real Presence Association,
http://www.therealpresence.org/archives/Eucharist/Eucharist_00
5.htm: therealpresence.org, 2003 (accessed 07/24/2013). Used with
permission from Inter Mirifica.

455. Fr. John A. Hardon S.J., "The Eucharist and Christ's Real Presence," *www.therealpresence.org,* (Real Presence Eucharistic Education and Adoration Association: Lombard, IL, 2000-2013), http://www.therealpresence.org/eucharst/realpres/a12.html (accessed 08/18/2013). Used with permission from Inter Mirifica.

456. Carol Breslin, "The Real Presence: Christ's Body," *therealpresence.org,* http://www.therealpresence.org/eucharst/intro/christs_body.htm __edn30: Real Presence Eucharistic Education and Adoration Association, 2005 (accessed 07/01/2013). Used with permission from Inter Mirifica.

457. Pope Pius XII, *Mediator Dei,* n. 162-163

458. Dom Jerome Gassner O.S.B., [Excerpt from: *The Eucharist - Witness of the Fathers,* (The Liturgical Press, June 15, 1947), p. 343-355], "The Eucharist a Reenactment of the Entire Opus Redemptionis: Witness of the Fathers," *CatholicCulture.org,* http://www.catholicculture.org/culture/library/view.cfm?recnum= 338: Trinity Communications, 2013 (accessed 7/20/2013)

459. Ibid

460. *Hildegard of Bingen's Book of Divine Works: With Letters and Songs.* All rights reserved. <http://www.Innertraditions.com> Reprinted with permission of publisher. Kindle Location 605-607

461.Ibid, 4786

462. Ibid, 2423-2425

463. Eleonore Stump, "Non-Cartesian Substance Dualism and Materialism without Reductionism," *Faith and Philosophy* Vol. 12, Issue 4 (October 1995), DOI: 10.5840/faithphil199512430, 514

464. Ibid, 657

465. *Hildegard of Bingen's Book of Divine Works: With Letters and Songs,* All rights reserved.
<http://www.Innertraditions.com> Reprinted with permission of publisher. 1047

466. Ibid, 1059

467. Ventura, *"DNA and Cell Reprogramming Via Epigenetic Information Delivered By Magnetic Fields, Sound Vibration and Coherent Water,"* Webinar transcript

468. L Montagnier *et al.,* 2011 *J. Phys.: Conf. Ser.* **306** 012007 doi:10.1088/1742-6596/306/1/012007

469. Yolène Thomas, Larbi Kahhak, Jamal Aissa. "The Physical Nature of the Biological Signal, a Puzzling Phenomenon: The Critical Contribution of Jacques Benveniste," in *Water and the Cell,* ed. Gerald H. Pollack, Ivan L. Cameron, Denys N. Wheatly (The Netherlands: Springer, 2006), Chapter 17

470. *Hildegard of Bingen's Book of Divine Works: With Letters and Songs.* All rights reserved.
<http://www.Innertraditions.com> Reprinted with permission of publisher. 2416-2417

www.ingramcontent.com/pod-product-compliance
Lightning Source LLC
Chambersburg PA
CBHW031828090426
42741CB00005B/173